Hearing the Children

Hearing the Children

Being

Papers given to the President's Interdisciplinary Conference for judges, directors of social services, mental health professionals, academics, guardians ad litem, panel managers and other professionals, held at the Dartington Hall Conference Centre, Dartington Hall, Totnes, Devon, between 12–14 September 2003, together with a record of the discussions which took place in the plenary sessions of the conference.

Edited by
The Rt Hon Lord Justice Thorpe
and
Justine Cadbury
Barrister, Queen Elizabeth Building, Temple

with a Foreword by
The Rt Hon Dame Elizabeth Butler-Sloss
President of the Family Division

Family Law
2004

Published by
Jordan Publishing Limited
21 St Thomas Street
Bristol BS1 6JS

© Jordan Publishing Limited 2004

British Library Cataloguing-in-Publication Data
A catalogue record for this book is available from the British Library.

ISBN 0 85308 925 6

Typeset in house
Printed and bound in Great Britain by The Cromwell Press

CONTRIBUTORS

Dr Jan Aldridge
Clinical Child Psychologist, University of Leeds

Professor Al Aynsley-Green
National Clinical Director for Children, Department for Health

Ashok Chand
Centre for Social Work, School of Sociology and Social Policy,
University of Nottingham

Peter Clarke
The Children's Commissioner for Wales

Andrew Cozens
Director of Social Services, Leicester
Senior Vice President, ADSS

Dr Jonathan Green
Senior Lecturer in Child and Adolescent Psychiatry, University of Manchester
Psychiatrist, Booth Hall Children's Hospital

Jane Held
Director of Social Services, Camden
ADSS Children and Families Committee

Dr David Jones
Consultant Child Psychiatrist, Park Hospital for Children

Y Penny Lancaster
Coram Family's Listening to Young Children project

Andrew Moylan QC
Queen Elizabeth Building

Peter Newell
Former Chair, Children's Rights Alliance for England

Mark Powell
Association of Lawyers for Children

Charles Prest
Director of Legal Services and Special Casework, CAFCASS

Beverley Prevatt-Goldstein
Director, BECON

Dr Gillian Schofield
Co-Director, Centre for Research on the Child and Family, University of East Anglia

Dr Miriam Steele
Psychologist, Anna Freud Centre

Professor June Thoburn
Social Work Academic, University of East Anglia

Dr Guinevere Tufnell
Consultant Child and Adolescent Psychiatrist, Traumatic Stress Clinic

Dr Maureen Winn-Oakley
NSPCC Senior Research Fellow, University of Warwick

Ruth Marchant
Triangle
and
Dr Helen Westcott
Lecturer in Psychology, The Open University
also made a contribution.

FOREWORD

Dartington Hall Conference, 12–14 September 2001

The Interdisciplinary Committee of the President of the Family Division organised its final conference at Dartington in Devon before the advent of the Family Justice Council. True to the record achieved by the organisers in their earlier conferences, it was memorable. It provided a valuable opportunity to look at the increasingly important issue of hearing the child in family proceedings and, with the help of highly respected experts in their fields, to explore the many complexities which hearing children involves.

The conference was particularly well timed since it was held shortly after the publication of the Department for Education and Skills' Green Paper, *Every Child Matters* (previously known as *Children at Risk*). There was a fascinating interchange of ideas between the judiciary at every level and a wide variety of professionals who are deeply involved in child care. At a crucial and possibly defining moment in the history of child legislation the delegates to the conference had an unusually good opportunity to make a valuable contribution to the moulding of future arrangements for children. The papers presented to the conference and the discussions ought to form part of the wider consultation on the DfES initiatives.

I am delighted that the conference rapporteur Justine Cadbury has collated the conference material and that this publication can inform a wider audience as a new Children Bill comes before Parliament.

Elizabeth Butler-Sloss

Dame Elizabeth Butler-Sloss
President of the Family Division

CONTENTS

EDITORIAL INTRODUCTION

The Rt Hon Lord Justice Thorpe

I write this short introduction with mixed emotions. First, gratitude that the 2003 Conference proved such a success; allied with that, thanks to those within the Lord Chancellor's Department and the Department of Health, who have relieved me of anxiety over funding.

Secondly, wonder at the commitment and enthusiasm of a number of vital contributors who have borne the standard of interdisciplinarity high when working both in court and out of court in the Family Justice System; allied to that, some sense of pride, sinful no doubt, at what has been achieved.

Thirdly, sadness that this will be the last in a series of extraordinary conferences. We may not have rescued the Family Law Act 1996 or reformed the Children Act 1989, but we have unquestionably influenced the debate. Perhaps our greatest achievement has been to prepare the way for the Family Justice Council, which will arise from our ashes. As we survey our demise, it is important to remember our beginnings. More than a decade ago, the Portman Clinic initiated training in forensic psychotherapy. Lord Lloyd of Berwick and I both served on an advisory group to oversee the venture. Lord Lloyd saw how much the clinicians and thinkers in the world of psychotherapy had to offer judges in the Criminal Justice System. He persuaded the Home Office to fund a residential conference that brought together leading members of both worlds. His conference was the model for our first interdisciplinary Family Justice Dartington Conference. Given those origins, our first conference considered the impact of psychoanalytical theory and practice on the work of all disciplines within the Family Justice System. The product was our first publication, *Rooted Sorrows*, which has out-sold all our other conference publications and which continues to sell (indeed we are now working on a second edition). This heritage also ensured for us the rich and sustained contribution that the mental health professions have made not only to these conferences but also to the routine work of the President's Interdisciplinary Committee.

Fourthly, hope and perhaps faith, that the achievements of the President's Interdisciplinary Committee over the last 10 years will be dwarfed by the achievements of the Family Justice Council over the decade ahead. Of course there will be losses, such as the easy informality and the freedom that accompanies a low level of accountability. But these losses will be far out-weighed by the gains, such as budget and a secretariat that will permit innovative work.

It would be impossible to single out without unfairness or oversight, the individuals who have made outstanding contribution to the President's Interdisciplinary Committee and its conferences. Indeed, even confining myself to this, our last conference, I will be selective in thanking only Ananda Hall, the President's Legal Assistant, who has acted as secretary to the conference, Malcolm Welsh, our Conference Administrator, and Justine Cadbury, our rapporteur. Their contributions have been of the highest standard and crucial to the success of the conference.

INTRODUCTORY REMARKS

The Rt Hon Lord Justice Thorpe

The Rt Hon Lord Justice Thorpe commenced his introductory remarks by looking back to previous interdisciplinary conferences. This was the fifth interdisciplinary residential conference and, since the conference only takes place every alternative year, it represents a decade of work. He said that it had been a decade of considerable achievement, the greatest of which had been to persuade the Department of Health and Lord Chancellors' Department that the conference was good value for money. Ever since that persuasion the conference has had the security of financial support. There has always been a most harmonious collaboration with the departments in agreeing subjects for conferences, themes within those subjects, and the distribution of the publications which always follow. He emphasised that one of the most important aspects of these conferences is that the papers which are delivered, and the discussion which the papers provoke, is published and distributed. This provides the opportunity to make a far-reaching impact.

Lord Justice Thorpe spoke in particular about the first conference which was aptly entitled *Rooted Sorrows*. He said that of all the publications, that has been the number one seller. In his view the success of that publication was due to the fact that it tackled the question of the importance of psycho-dynamic thinking on the work of all those in the family justice system, a crucial topic. Lawyers in general are taught to think in a disciplined way and to operate intellectually: only family lawyers have to learn to work in a different way and look beneath appearances and surfaces. The training that lawyers receive to do that is haphazard. Those who acquire those skills do so through their experience as practitioners and then from judicial work. He pointed out that lawyers, in particular, need the influence of the mental health professions, if they are to do their work in a way that is likely to achieve good results for the families who are dependent on their judgments.

Turning to the present, Lord Justice Thorpe said that the themes for the conferences have to be chosen 18 months in advance. It is therefore something of a gamble as to whether or not the theme will still be relevant by the time the conference takes place. He said that the choice made for this conference has proved to be very good, and commented that a folder of first class papers of high topicality had been assembled.

Looking towards the future, he said that this conference would be the last of its kind, as even the most extreme pessimist would expect to see the creation of the Family Justice Council before September 2005. Lord Justice Thorpe was confident that the Family Justice Council would be meeting to decide the way ahead, and in particular the form of regional Family Justice Councils, within the next 6 months. One consequence of the birth of the Family Justice Council will be the demise of the President's Interdisciplinary Committee. He stated that it was his conviction that the conference planned for September 2005 would be the first one organised by the Family Justice Council

PLENARY ONE

CONCEPTS OF CHILD ATTACHMENT

Dr Jonathan Green
Senior Lecturer in Child and Adolescent Psychiatry, University of Manchester
Hon Consultant in Child and Adolescent Psychiatry, Central Manchester and Manchester Children's Hospitals Trust

Summary of paper

Dr Jonathan Green said that it was his intention to give an overview of his paper, and he went on to highlight three main issues:

- *The language used in discussing attachment concepts*
- *The origin and consequences of attachment relationships*
- *Issues of assessment and measurement*

The language of attachment

Dr Green said that he first wanted to address the language used in describing attachment concepts, because these had often caused confusion. He made it clear that attachment is not 'bonding' and it is not unalterably fixed, nor is it strictly a descriptor of parents' feelings towards their children. Attachment is not synonymous with the whole parent-child relationship, nor is it the only factor predicting risk or poor outcome generally, or in the adoption process it is not the only theory that explains the development of children.

The concept of attachment refers to a child's experience of certain aspects of the parent-child relationship. Sometimes it is used 'narrowly' in the sense of the aspects of the relationship related to the assuagement of distress, sometimes it is used 'broadly' as synonymous with wider features of the relationship. The narrow use of the term is its most scientific and technical use and it is the most ethologically valid. Used technically in this sense the term is scientifically meaningful and predictive. Dr Green said that he prefers to use the term in a narrow sense. He made clear that the use of the term should not substitute for specific descriptions of behaviour and mental state. To describe a 'good attachment' between child and parent is a statement that needs to be backed up by specific behavioural evidence.

Origins and consequences of attachment relationships

Attachments that put children at later vulnerability seem often to be with parents who themselves have suffered unresolved traumas or loss. Such parents tend to display types of parenting behaviour which are atypical, such as bizarre forms of communication, intrusiveness, frightening behaviours, and the more subtle notion that the parent is preoccupied and frightened themselves for no apparent reason. It is thought that these forms of parental communication can confuse the child in relation to their attachment.

Dr Green went on to address the question of the relevance of individual differences in children to attachment relationships. Since the sensitivity and appropriateness of parental response is the key parenting variable promoting secure attachment in children, it may be that this can act to 'buffer' individual differences in children. In so far as parents can adjust their responses in relation to these differences, the quality of the relationship comes to depend more on this sensitivity than on the individual characteristics of the children. But it is the case that some child characteristics can make this buffering process more difficult and demand more from parental adaptation.

As far as the consequences of attachment are concerned, we know that insecure attachments have significant effects on later social functioning and psychopathology in childhood. In particular, children with disorganised attachments lack coherent strategies for managing stress. The absence of any attachment at all is very rare; more commonly there is attachment but it is sub-optimal or problematic.

Assessment

A significant part of the expert's function before court is to present an assessment of parent-child relationships. In relation to these assessments, Dr Green reiterated the following:

- *The need for multiple and independent sources of evidence. Evidence must be gathered over different contexts. If there is convergence between independent evidence from a number of different situations then stronger inferences can be drawn.*
- *Descriptions of attachment quality must be qualified by specific behavioural examples.*
- *Other kinds of developmental or psychiatric disorder can mimic the effects of disturbed attachment as well as being their consequence. It is a cardinal error to assume that a particular kind of behaviour is due to a specific cause without appropriate enquiry.*

Dr Green explained that the assessment process would generally involve looking at least three elements: the parent, the child, and the interaction between them. The assessment of the parent is made up of four factors, parental attachment status, personality development, current mental state, and current level of social stress and support. In relation to the child there are lots of different factors that have a bearing on attachment; these include developmental status, mental state, attachment representation and wider functioning in home and school. Parent-child interaction is assessed over time in different contexts, and on the basis of information gathered from other professionals as well. Dr Green argued that if the assessments are carried out along the lines of those general principles they are more likely to be predictive, accurate and just.

Outline

My aim is to provide an introduction to the current concepts and research into attachment theory with particular reference to issues likely to be relevant to judicial work.

(1) What is the 'attachment' component of the parent-child relationship?
- Attachment describes a crucial part of the parent-child relationship but is not synonymous with the whole. I argue against the ill-defined general use of the term to describe every general aspect of parenting.

(2) Patterns of attachment and what determines them.
- The key evidence (psychosocial/genetically informed) is for parenting determinants of attachment patterns.

(3) Consequences of attachment failure
- Attachment distortion/failure often has serious and specifically definable consequences for general sociability and psychopathology;
- Specific 'attachment disorder' syndromes exist but on a spectrum of other attachment failures/distortions; and
- Attachment disorders can usefully be considered as general social impairment syndromes.

(4) Can attachment be measured?
- Yes, but that there is no 'magical' reductive method here in the court context;
- Any assessment of attachment must be taken in context of a broader overall assessment.

(1) The concept of attachment: What is the attachment component of the parent-child relationship?

John Bowlby's (1982/88) theory of infant attachment developed a core idea that the human infant was born with a tendency to certain 'behavioural action patterns' (derived from observations of goal-directed behavioural patterns in animals in response to specific triggers or contexts). One of these was a behavioural response to a sense of internal distress and threat – the infant would seek proximity with a familiar figure in their environment and this would assuage their distress. Bowlby hypothesised that this threat-related behaviour existed alongside a complimentary 'exploratory behavioural system' related to the child's curiosity and drive to learn and explore. The core hypothesis of the theory relates to this sequence of internal arousal; proximity seeking behaviour; assuagement of arousal; and return to exploration.

Bowlby described the development of 'internalised' patterns of thinking and feeling derived from these behavioural interactions in early childhood. An 'internal working model' of attachment would be elicited by similar experiences of anxiety, distress and threat to the self. These patterns of thinking would be likely to also influence the child's response to *new* social situations because they would embody acquired sensitivities, learned reactions and so called state dependent learning. In this theory of inner working models Bowlby anticipated many more recent developments in cognitive psychology that have identified similar patterns of thinking related to different 'domains' of experience.

Key implications of this theory are that:

- I – as a child – learn early on that relating with another helps me contain and modulate frightening internal states – so social life is valuable to me. Attachment relationships are in this sense a *primary social experience* – confirming the value of others to my own life.
- I – as a child – also learn that the circle of familiar others is generally helpful and trustworthy, and to differentiate this from a healthy wariness of strangers.
- I – as a child – am generally trusting and *motivated* to be social because it is in my interest to be so. I want to invest in others and maintain my social relationships. This 'motivational' view of how prosocial behaviour develops and is maintained is different in many ways from a view that prosocial behaviour is learned by example or fear or discipline. It asserts that humans are primarily social – rather than the opposite.
- The theory links phenomena of internal emotion and arousal, goal-directed behaviour with others and cognitive assumptions about relationships in ways that are theoretically and practically useful.
- Attachment 'representations' continue as a latent aspect of thinking in later childhood and into adulthood – ready to be mobilised under conditions of basic threat to self. Imagine yourself just having survived a car crash – what would your first thought/action be?

Attachment aspects of relationship are not synonymous with the whole relationship

This concept of attachment applies to a specific aspect of parent-child relationship and the child's representation of it. There are other conceptually different aspects of the relationship such as:

- Provision of basic care;
- Organisation of time and space;
- Education; and
- Friendship etc.

These other aspects are conceptually different although of course may covary with each other in quality.

The attachment relationship as a child construct

Children's representations of attachment are *constructed by the child* from the materials of their experience (or some would say *co-constructed* by the child along with a significant adult). This 'constructedness' idea of attachment makes the child an active participant in understanding and interpreting their world. The way that a child constructs their representation has prognostic value (Grossman and Grossman, 2003). It is the 'way' that adults talk about their memories of early relationships rather than the 'content' of those relationships themselves that turns out to be prognostic. This cognitive re-working of experience can be seen from the earliest stages in development and will be influenced by factors within the child as well as other extraneous experience such as presence of other positive factors or people in their lives or later experience following early disrupted care. This capacity to change the representation based on new experiences offers significant opportunity for hopefulness for many children if their environment can be improved. Furthermore, the child's representation of attachment relationships should not be considered static – if a child is seen in the early school years and then again in the beginning of adolescence it should not be assumed that they have the same 'attachment status'.

(2) Patterns of attachment and their origins

Convergent evidence suggests that child attachment relationships are strongly related to parenting style.

- In Israeli kibbutzim children's homes where babies who are non-birth related are brought up with the same psychological parent (metapelet) there is a similar 70% concordance in attachment pattern between them (Sagi et al, 1995); similar to biological sibling concordance (62%, IJzendoorn et al, 1995).
- *Twin studies* compare identical twins (sharing all their genetic material) and non-identical twins (sharing half their genetic material) to provide a test of the genetic influence on the trait. When attachment relationships have been looked at in this way it is an aspect of the common environment of the children (likely to be the parenting) that is mainly responsible for the pattern of attachment and there is a negligible genetic effect.
- *Adoptee studies*, where children are adopted from birth families at high risk and then later followed up at their adoptee families, suggest similar conclusions. In Dozier et al, 2001, 50 very high-risk children were placed in adoption at a mean age of 7.7 months and assessed after a mean of nine months in care. These adopted children did not show the attachment patterns that would be predicted from their very high risk birth backgrounds,

rather they showed attachment patterns similar to the normal population: the expected level of high risk attachment disorganisation was reduced. Moreover, where children had remained 'disorganised' in attachment this tended to be with mothers who themselves were assessed as having non-secure attachments. In Stams et al, 2002, 146 children internationally adopted after early placement were followed at seven years. Generally, the outcome was found to be similar to that as would be expected in birth children in similar families. Children who showed attachment 'security' had better social cognitive development. Children who were shown to have disorganised attachment as well as temperamental difficulties showed a poorer adjustment and lower cognitive development.

Patterns of attachment

Different patterns of attachment relationship have been described which broadly relate to styles of caregiving.

Secure attachments patterns

Parental responsiveness and sensitivity to the child's distress tends to result in the kind of 'secure' base pattern of attachment behaviours described above – where the child can successfully use interpersonal contact to assuage distress.

Avoidant attachments patterns

When parents are hostile, intrusive and insensitive and lacking in warmth the child tends to show 'avoidant' patterns of attachment. The child will tend to avoid using interpersonal solutions to distress, instead either minimising the distress itself or finding other forms of behaviour or patterns of self-care to assuage the distress. Children who have developed effective patterns of self-care in this way may be self-sufficient and perhaps restricted socially but by and large can often function well.

Ambivalent attachment patterns

Parents who are behaviourally and emotionally inconsistent tend to result in child behaviours that are themselves inconsistent and 'ambivalent'.

Disorganised attachments

More recent research in high-risk populations has emphasised patterns of attachment 'disorganisation'. This notion of disorganisation of attachment has become a key concept in clinical and psychopathological research (Greenberg, 1999). Here the child seems not to have a behavioural strategy for assuaging distress at all – or shows a number of simultaneous incompatible strategies or a strategy is complicated by sudden paradoxical behaviours. Atypical and extreme forms of parenting abnormality have been associated with the development of disorganised attachment patterns (Lyons Ruth et al, 1999). These include direct frightening of the child, unpredictable withdrawal or dissociation from the present by the parent, complex contradictory emotional communication assumptions about the 'reversal of care' (ie it is the infant who should be looking after the parent not vice versa).

Attachment and later social development

Insecure and particularly disorganised attachments have significant effects on later social functioning and psychopathology in childhood (Greenberg, 1999). The study illustrated below indicates how pre-school attachment to mother and father separately affect the way that children are found to adjust socially in middle childhood. Children showing 'bizarre' (disorganised) attachment representation with their fathers preschool have significantly worse social functioning in middle childhood rated by teachers. Children showing 'bizarre' (disorganised) attachment with mothers are rejected by peers at 9 years. This is a theme I return to below in relation to attachment disorder.

Attachment to father at age 5 and teacher ratings socioemotional competence at age 9 (Verschueren et al, 2001 with permisison)

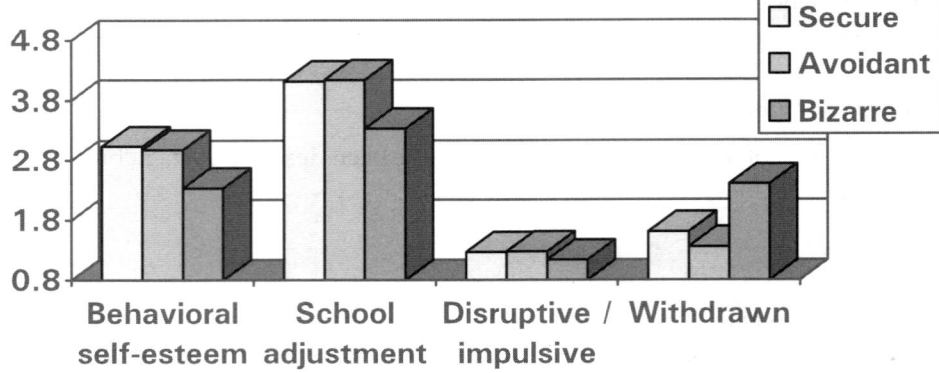

Attachment to mother at age 5 and acceptance among same-sex peers at age 9 (Verschueren et al, 2001)

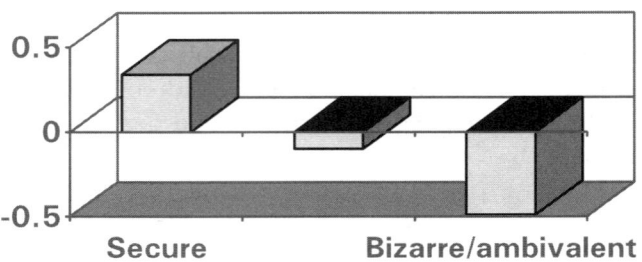

What about intrinsic differences between children?

These results at first sight seem inconsistent with the increasing amount we know about individual difference in children, and temperamental and genetic influence on child outcomes in sociability and aspects of psychopathology. This paradox in the evidence is real and may to some extent be explained by different research approaches leading to different conclusions – but such methodological explanations cannot be the whole story. One way of resolving the different findings is to suggest that *parental sensitivity 'buffers' the individual differences in children.* The essence of parental sensitivity is flexibly to adjust to child individual difference: if this is successful, then arguably individual differences within the child will not determine the final attachment *relationship.* In other words a good relationship is possible with many different kinds and types of children if the parent is able to adapt to the child's specific needs. This 'buffering' may fail in situations of extreme child difference or loss of parental flexibility – for instance in parental preoccupation, distress or insensitivity.

(3) Severe failures of attachment – Attachment disorders

Two attachment 'disorders' are currently described – resulting from severely distorted or absent attachment experience (see appendix, p 11).

Disinhibited attachment disorder

This seems to relate primarily to the absence of opportunities to make any selective early attachment – classically in institutionalised settings. There have been many reports of these children's common later difficulties in making ordinary social contact or intimate relationships. Systematic studies of this kind of disorder have been sparse until recently in the UK because of the effective abolition of institutional care in this country. However, in recent years the opening up of transnational adoption gave an opportunity for researchers to re-visit this area of work. The England Romania Adoptees (ERA, O'Connor et al, 1999) study has come up with some suggestive findings. Follow-up in the early school years has provided substantial support for the concept of disinhibited attachment disorder. 44% of the UK adoptees had an attachment disorder of this kind at 6 years with a combination of indiscriminate superficial social approach, poor attention style and lack of general social relatedness. Many children had problems with inattention, in 50% related to the attachment disturbance. (Of course it is necessary to note that this means that about a half were on the contrary doing well.) Later adoption generally increased the risk.

An even more striking finding (Rutter et al, 1999) was that 12% of the sample showed a social impairment of a quality and degree that could be classifiable as autistic or quasi autistic. 6% of the sample had an apparently full autistic syndrome and a further 6% a syndrome with more isolated or atypical features. This profound social cognition impairment showed some substantial differences from classical autism (which is known to be substantially constitutional in origin) – eg it showed an equal sex ratio (classical autism has a significant predominance of males) and the quasi autistic syndrome also tended to improve with time in ways that the classical syndrome does not.

This finding suggests that the absence of adequate early social relationships can have profound consequences for later socialization and social understanding. The results could not be explained on the basis of genetic abnormality, poor nutrition, general maltreatment or other aspects of the environment. These cases are an extreme group and are not representative of most children who suffer early disrupted or distorted attachment relationships. However, their presence does raise questions about possibly homologous social impairments following other degrees of attachment difficulty and there are some suggestions of this in the literature (Zeanah, 1996; Howe, 1995).

Reactive attachment disorder of childhood (RAD)

This kind of attachment disorder is more commonly seen in the UK. Its definition is shown in the appendix. Reactive attachment disorder is strongly associated with abnormal early parenting and indeed some argue that this aetiological factor should be an intrinsic part of the definition (others disagree). The phenomenology of reactive attachment disorder is marked by contradictory and ambivalent social response, mood disturbance, hypervigilance, excessive arousal and disturbed or aggressive behaviour. This has been a problematic concept largely because it seems to contain such a bewildering collection of different symptoms and shares so many characteristics with other disorders (Hanson et al, 2000; Richters et al, 1994). It is true that this is how many children who have experienced early maltreatment present in later childhood but it is a difficult and complex presentation to evaluate properly, to break down into its constituent parts and to approach in terms of treatment. I have proposed that one way of doing this would be to separate out a core social impairment syndrome (which might have similarities to social impairments in other kinds of attachment disturbance), from other ('co-morbid') psychological difficulties related to different specific aspects of the aetiology, eg post-traumatic stress disorder (Green, 2003). These may exist in different combinations and degrees in different children and may need differentiated treatments. By breaking down the overall syndrome in this way it may be that the component elements can be identified and understood. As in disinhibited and disorganised attachment disorders above, these children often find intimacy and the regulation of ordinary social relationships near impossible. This may be explained by the effects of a trauma related avoidance of social contact or possible additional impairments in social understanding.

Attachment and a spectrum of social impairment

The core features of 'attachment disorders' are set out in the table below alongside core features of 'disorganised' attachment. It will be seen that RAD and disorganised attachment share many features in common. Running like a thread through all of the disorders are difficulties in the general ability to form reciprocal social relationships and often also to regulate mood and attention.

One can identify a notional spectrum in this attachment failure and social disturbance. At the most severe (and rarest) end the impairment related to disinhibited attachment disorder can be so profound as to shade into phenomena that are similar to those in the autistic spectrum. In this group typically there is lack of early selective attachment but an absence of frightening trauma, maltreatment, or neglect. By contrast in reactive attachment disorder there will often be specific, if deviant, attachments to carers but in addition the child will usually have experienced fear, unpredictable trauma, neglect and uncertainty. These features may result in emotional disturbances characteristic of RAD, which may be additional to core difficulties in social understanding in some cases. At the other end of the spectrum, disorganised attachments are more prevalent (15% base rate in low risk and up to 80% in high social risk groups, compared with an estimated prevalence in RAD of about 1%) but share many features in common with RAD and a similar aetiology (eg severely atypical parenting and the exposure to traumatising experiences). They also as we have seen, result in more subtle but still specific difficulties in later social adaptation and later psychopathology.

Comparison of described behaviours in attachment disorders and attachment disorganization (adapted from Green and Goldwyn 2002)

	Disinhibited attachment disorder	Reactive attachment disorder	Sequelae of disorganised attachment
Mental state/ cognition	Attentional difficulties *	Cognitive and communication delays+ Poor social perception+	Bizarre fantasy Poor self esteem Disorganised cognitions Poor social perception
Behaviour	Non selective attachments** Superficially and indiscriminantly friendly** Poor peer interactions** Quasi autistic social impairment*	Contradictory ambivalent responses** Emotional disturbance** Hypervigilance and arousal** Aggressiveness** Social impairments**	Contradictory ambivalent responses Emotional disturbance Hypervigilance and arousal Aggressiveness Controlling interactions with others

* *O'Connor et al. (1999), Richters & Volkmar (1994), **Features from ICD10*

There is little research as yet into the details of notional social cognition difficulties in different forms of attachment disorder and some of the following paragraph is hypothetical. However, the implications are potentially important. For some of the most difficult children following disrupted early relationships, adjustment into adoptive care is extremely difficult. Despite the best efforts of foster or adoptive parents they seem unable to cope with the demands of family life or be able to develop reasonable intimacy with others in the home. These children are usually thought to be avoiding new relationships in the present because of unresolved conflicts in relation to previous traumas or attachments. However, the possibility exists that they may also in some instances have impairments in the basic understanding of social relationships or social communication in a way subtly homologous to the ERA findings. The implications here for the management and treatment of the child would be rather different. Communication may have to be modified and expectation adjusted. Treatment is more likely to be focused on the acquisition of social and independence skills through a more didactic approach or group social skills training. My own clinical experience is that complex mixtures of social cognition deficits and intrapsychic conflicts exist in many clinical cases of this kind and need careful elucidation; just because the management implications are rather different.

Attachment and social deficit? – a case history

James was seven when he was first referred with a question as to whether he had Asperger's syndrome (an autistic spectrum disorder). He had had a severely disrupted and traumatic early history marked by early parental maltreatment and neglect, unpredictable fear, violence and possibly sexual abuse. He was taken into care in his third year and had been with a number of different foster parents before the adoption at five years by wealthy parents desperate for a child after many conception failures.

At assessment, James did not have Asperger's syndrome but he was showing signs of great difficulty in adapting to his private prep school. On the one hand this could be put down to cultural difference – certainly the social workers involved in the case were concerned about this. However, at interview the child was seriously vacant and difficult to engage. He seemed to have enormous difficulty accessing emotions or being clear about life or what his difficulties at school were. This again could be put down to 'dissociation' or 'resistance'.

James had been referred for psychotherapy and was seen over many years by an extremely experienced therapist from the NSPCC. I was in very close contact with the therapist as well as the family over a number of years. The therapy did not progress. There was no real sign that James could use the therapeutic techniques skillfully provided in a productive way. Although the therapy was felt to be enormously helpful as a support and ongoing evaluation he showed no real evidence of developmental progression or emotional evolution in the treatment.

As James moved through middle childhood he became more and more disconnected and alienated from his family. His mother would describe how she could not get close to him that he was 'cold' to her touch, that he seemed unresponsive and unable to make sense of what his parents were trying to give him. His behaviour became more seriously abnormal and he became troubled in school. He had no real peer friendships and drifted into law breaking. By his early teens he was known to the police. The situation at home was becoming critical and his parents were in despair as to how to manage him. The social workers involved in the case tended to feel that the parents were contributing to the child's difficulties by their (latent) hostility, probably based on class-related expectations that he could not fulfil. They were felt to be undertaking a subtle rejection and disabled of the placement. James was admitted into a children's home to try and avoid complete breakdown of his adoptive placement.

It was at this point in the evolution of the problem that I tested the possibility with the parents of a different formulation for James' problems, one based on social impairment rather than traumatic or social deviancy. Taking as a model from an autistic disorder and explaining an impairment view of his behaviour relationships the parents felt suddenly understood. His behaviour 'clicked' into place in many aspects. Framing his difficulties as an impairment took a huge amount of pressure off his parents. It allowed them not to feel so much a failure and also to generate strategies based around his significant difficulties.

James never returned home although the family kept up contact and material and moral support of him. He was placed in a residential school and then moved to a transitional hostel environment. He remained friendless and socially isolated finding it difficult to engage in work. His syndrome and prognosis seemed extremely poor.

How common is this kind of picture in which the problem is best understood as impairment rather than a deviation? Earlier recognition of this could have perhaps set in train different models of prevention. As it was James had many years of conventional psycho-therapeutic treatment with no benefit although the treatment was done with the greatest commitment and respect to him.

(4) Can attachment be measured?

Validated ascertainment measurement methods do exist. However, it is a mistake to think there is a simple reductive 'test' for attachment relationships outwith the context of overall assessment.

In early childhood and infancy the so called 'strange situation procedure' developed by Ainsworth (1978) is one such measure. It is based on the idea that the attachment system is mobilised under conditions of distress – thus Mary Ainsworth set up a 'strange' situation in which the child would become distressed and experience this in the context of (a) being alone (b) with a stranger and (c) with their parent. The distressed child's behaviour at reunion with a stranger or particular parent was shown to be a crucial indicator of their experience and assumptions around attachment. Later in the pre-school years modified versions of this reunion procedure have been developed along with measures aiming to capture cognitive representations of attachment.

These 'representational measures' use various forms of prompt or stimulus to gain access to the child's characteristic pattern of thoughts and associations regarding attachment relationships. One such assessment used early on was the Separation Anxiety Test in which the child is asked to imagine scenarios in which a child is left alone after parents have left home for a number of days or weeks. A different methodology uses so called 'vignette completion' procedures, a method that equates with a semi-structured verbal interview. A structured story stem around attachment themes is set out by the examiner to focus the child, and then the child is asked to complete it. There is persuasive evidence that the way that such narratives are completed reflects vividly on the child's 'inner working model' or cognitive representation around a specific topic. There are a number of instruments of this kind that have received empirical support. One such has been developed in my department (the Manchester Child Attachment Story Task, MCAST), with a particular orientation towards eliciting attachment disorganisation and work in clinical practice (Green et al, 2000; Goldwyn et al, 2000) and I will be giving some examples of what this method can reveal. One of my colleagues on the panel has used similar methods with adopted and fostered children (Steele et al, 2001).

Both representational and behavioural methods of assessing attachment have been used in the early school years and appear to have validity in accessing and coding different forms of attachment. There is some evidence that representational methods may have better predictive validity in terms of long-term outcome. They are also more likely to be able to allow parallel assessments of child development and mental state. In the kinds of groups that are likely to be relevant to court processes and for reasons outlined above, disorganised attachment patterns and attachment disorders are likely to be the kinds of attachment most of interest during measurement. Hence it is important to use assessment methods that are able to code such phenomena reliably.

The context of overall assessment

Assessments using attachment procedures of this kind need to be embedded in a range of other relevant assessments including parenting.

It is important not to consider the presentation or origin of parenting behaviour as an undifferentiated whole. In a method of analysing attachment aspects of parent-child relationships developed in our department (Green, 1996) – other similar methods have been described – I take a 'medical model' or differential diagnostic approach to assessment; suggesting that child, parent and interactional variables need to be considered independently and that each may have a number of causes. We can then look for convergence between these different forms of assessment into a more robust formulation about the attachment dynamic within the parent relationship.

In this model, the assessment of the parents distinguishes four factors, which may impact on parenting:

- Parental attachment status;
- Parental personality structure;
- Parental current mood state; and
- Current social circumstances including social stress and support.

There is independent evidence that each of these factors may impact on parenting. Although they often act in synergy, for the purposes of the assessment they are assumed to act and are assessed independently. This allows a more differentiated assessment of the cause (and thus management) of parenting failure. For instance, concurrent depression related to some current event (say a loss or a trauma) may severely disrupt parenting in a parent whose basic parenting ability may be reasonably intact.

Case example – diagnosing parental failure

A parent whose three children were taken into care because of progressive neglect was found to have a relatively positive attachment history herself although currently estranged from her own mother. The cause of her acutely dysfunctional parenting was found due primarily to her depressed mood state. This in itself was related to the presence of an abusive and sociopathic partner. This impression was reinforced by the positive attachment representation that the eldest child had about her mother. My recommendation to the court was that if the influence of the father on the family be reduced (he had spontaneously left the family by this time) and should the mother get increased support from her own family, then her parenting would be likely to improve. The court accepted this view and the children were placed back with mother and they went to live with maternal grandmother. An injunction was taken out against the father. At follow-up the placement was intact and the children thriving.

Similar considerations apply to the *assessment of the child*. Although the child's attachment representation may be an important consideration in judging the success of the family placement, it will not be the only consideration nor the only influence on child outcome.

The child's attachment representation must thus be assessed alongside the child's mental state and developmental progress. We have evidence that a child's general *cognitive* and *language* abilities can represent important confounding variables in assessing representational methods. These must be assessed and taken into account. A child's *current mental state* can also affect the way they represent attachment relationships. All this can be a difficult clinical task to unravel. For instance, a child who may have been recently forcibly separated from parents is likely to have a state of mind that will affect their description of the attachment relationships with the same parents. Similarly concurrent depression may be a confounding variable.

Children with covert *developmental impairments* in the autistic spectrum provide an additional interesting and topical example. Although the diagnosis of classical or severe autism is usually quite obvious, there can be more subtle forms of social impairment due to autistic spectrum disorder, which are still essentially constitutional in origin. However, these impairments can be difficult to disentangle from social impairments related to the consequences of the parenting failure and the parenting failure itself can at times be the consequence of stress resulting from intrinsic child development difficulties. Thus it becomes crucial to consider a child's attachment status in the context of other wider aspects of development and careful assessment needs to unpick the relative balance of nature versus nurture in a particular child's developmental presentation. As we know more about the genetic origins of child social adaptation we see that errors can be made by ascribing every problem of social functioning in children to problems in child rearing or parenting. It can be particularly important to be alert to this in situations of high risk of parenting failure coming to the judicial system; since it is just here that uncritical assumptions may be made about the origin of difficulties based on probability or overgeneralisation rather than from careful assessment and consideration of the individual child in their context.

APPENDIX – Definitions of Attachment disorder (International Classification of Diseases, ICD10, WHO 1992)

Disinhibited attachment disorder of childhood

(a)   Diffuse attachments are a persistent feature during the first 5 years of life (but do not necessarily persist into middle childhood). Diagnosis requires a relative failure to show selective social attachments manifested by:

      (1)   a normal tendency to seek comfort from others when distressed; and

      (2)   an abnormal (relative) lack of selectivity in the people from whom comfort is sought.

(b)   Social interactions with unfamiliar people are poorly modulated.

(c)   At least one of the following must be present:

      (1)   generally clinging behaviour in infancy;

      (2)   attention-seeking and indiscriminately friendly behaviour in early or middle childhood.

(d)   The general lack of situation-specificity in the above features must be clear. Diagnosis requires that the symptoms in criteria A and B above are manifest across the range of social contacts experienced by the child.

Reactive attachment disorder of childhood

(a)   Onset is before the age of 5 years.

(b)   The child exhibits strongly contradictory or ambivalent social responses that extend across social situations (but that may show variability from relationship to relationship).

(c)   Emotional disturbance is shown by lack of emotional responsiveness, withdrawal reactions, aggressive responses to the child's own or other's distress, and/or fearful hypervigilance.

(d)   Some capacity for social reciprocity and responsiveness is evident in interactions with normal adults.

(e)   The criteria for pervasive developmental disorders are not met.

References

Ainsworth, MDS, Blehar, M, Waters, E, & Wall, S. 1978. *Patterns of Attachment*, Hillsdale, NJ: Erlbaum.

Boris, NW, Fueyo, M, & Zeanah, CH. 1997. The clinical assessment of attachment in children under five. *Journal of the American Academy of Child Adolescent Psychiatry*, **36 (2)**: 291–3.

Bowlby, J. 1982. *Attachment and Loss:* Vol. 1. *Attachment*. New York: Basic Books.

Bowlby, J. 1988. *A Secure Base*, New York: Basic Books.

Goldwyn R, Green JM, Stanley C, Smith V. 2000. The Manchester Child Attachment Story Task: Relationship with Parental AAI, SAT and Child Behaviour. *Attachment and Human Development*, **2 (1)**: 65–78.

Green, J (in press). Commentary: Are Attachment disorders best seen as social impairment syndromes? *Attachment and Human Development*.

Green, JM & Goldwyn, R. 2002. Annotation: Attachment disorganisation and psychopathology: new findings in attachment research and their potential implications for developmental psychopathology in childhood. *Journal of Child Psychology and Psychiatry*, **43 (7)**: 835–846.

Green JM, Stanley C, Smith, V, Goldwyn, R. 2000. A new method of evaluating attachment representations on young school age children – the Manchester Child Attachment Story Task. *Attachment and Human Development*, **2 (1)**: 42–64.

Green, JM. 1996. A structured assessment of parenting based on attachment theory: Theoretical background, description and initial clinical experience. *European Journal of Child and Adolescent Psychiatry*, **5 (1)**: 33–138

Greenberg, MT. 1999. Attachment and Psychopathology in Childhood. In *Handbook of Attachment, Theory, Research, and Clinical Applications*, J Cassidy & PR Shaver (eds), pp 469–496. New York: London. Guildford Press.

Hanson, RF & Spratt, EG. 2000. Reactive Attachment Disorder: what we know about the disorder and implications for treatment. *Child Maltreatment*, **5 (2)**: 137–45.

Howe, D. 1995. Adoption and attachment. *Adoption and Fostering*, **19**, 7–15.

Lyons-Ruth, K, Bronfman, E & Parsons, E. 1999. Maternal disrupted affective communication, maternal frightened or frightening behaviour, and disorganised infant attachment strategies. In JI Vondra & D Barnett (eds), *Atypical attachment in infancy and early childhood among children at developmental risk*, pp. 172–192. Monographs of the Society for Research in Child Development, **64, 3** (serial no. 258).

O'Connor, T, Bredenkamp, D & Rutter, M & the ERA study team. 1999. Attachment disturbances and disorders in children exposed to early severe deprivation. *Infant Mental Health Journal*. **20 (1)**: 10–29.

Richters, MM & Volkmar, FR. 1994. Reactive Attachment disorder of infancy or early childhood. *Journal of the American Academy of Child and Adolescent Psychiatry*, **33 (3)**: 328–332.

Rutter, M, Anderson-Wood, L, Beckett, C, Bredenkamp, D, Castle, J, Groothues, C, Kreppner, J, Keaveney, L, Lord, C & O'Connor, T. 1999. Quasi-autistic patterns following severe early global privation. *Journal of Child Psychology and Psychiatry*, **40 (4)**: 537–549.

Sagi, A, van IJzendoorn, M, H, Aviezer, O, & Donnell, F. 1994. Sleeping out of home in a kibbutz communal arrangement: it makes a difference for infant-mother attachment. *Child Development*, **65**, 992–1004.

Steele, M, Hodges, J, Kaniuk, J, Henderson, K, Hillman, S, & Bennett, P. 1999. The use of story stem narratives in assessing the inner world of the child: Implications for adoptive placements. In *Assessment, preparation and support: Implications from research*, pp 19–29. London: BAAF Publications.

van IJzendoorn, MH, Schuengel, C & Bakermans-Kranenburg, MJ. 1999. Disorganised attachment in early childhood: Meta-analysis of precursors, concomitants and sequelae. *Development and Psychopathology*, **11**, 225–249.

Verschueren, K, & Marcoen, A. 1999. Representation of self and socioemotional competence in kindergartners: differential and combined effects of attachment to mother and to father. *Child Development*, **70 (1)**: 183–201

Verschueren, K. 2001. Narratives in attachment research. *Biennial meeting of the European Society of Developmental Psychology*, Uppsala.

World Health Organisation. 1992. *The ICD-10 classification of mental and behavioural disorders: clinical descriptions and diagnostic guidelines*. Switzerland: WHO.

Zeanah, CH. 1996. Beyond insecurity: a reconceptualization of attachment disorders of infancy. *Journal of Consulting and Clinical Psychology*, **64 (1)**: 42–52.

ATTACHMENT THEORY AND RESEARCH: RECENT ADVANCES AND IMPLICATIONS FOR ADOPTION AND FOSTER CARE

Dr Miriam Steele
Psychologist, Anna Freud Centre

Summary

Dr Miriam Steele began by posing the following question: what can attachment theory bring to clinical practice and research? She identified a number of different factors:

- *A model of affect regulation: what we do with our feelings, and how we manage our emotions;*
- *A broad evidence-based knowledge of parents, infants, children and adolescents;*
- *A window upon the inner world ('a move to the inner level of representation' via 'surprising the unconscious');*
- *A focus on resolution of trauma and loss;*
- *A high regard and respect for parents and infants.*

She went on to outline the way in which an adult attachment interview (AAI) is conducted, and explained that the aim is to go beyond a check-list type assessment and to get people to describe their childhood in their own words, and explain how they view their relationship with their parents; and how their childhood has influenced the kind of person they are today, providing examples and evidence.

Dr Steele also explained the intergenerational patterns of attachment, for example if a baby is avoidant there is a very high probability that their parent will be given an avoidant rating after their interview; and 75% of infants who are secure have parents who are also secure. There is also a very strong link between babies who are disorganised and parents who have unresolved trauma.

The Adoption and Attachment study examined attachment status and tracked the following:

- *changes in adopters' responses to the task of parenting;*
- *the level of parenting stress;*
- *perceptions of a child's strengths and difficulties.*

The study found that those children with more caregivers prior to their adoption were reported by their mothers to have higher levels of aggression, more controlling behaviour, were less affectionate and more rejecting. Their mothers reported higher levels of anger, greater needs for emotional support and had lower confidence and lower degrees of warmth. However, after two years, the children with more caregivers did not show differences, so it is clear that this is an issue which can be ameliorated over time.

The study also looked at the correlations between a child's age and the Experience of Parenthood Interview (EPI) at placement. The results tended to show that if the child was older at placement, the mother was more disappointed, and the child was less happy and less affectionate. For 'insecure' mothers, if the child was older the mother was more angry and less warm, and the child was thought to be less affectionate. For 'secure' mothers, the child's age at placement was unrelated to the mother's experience of parenting.

At one year follow-up, for mothers rated as autonomous-secure, there was less depression, social isolation and parent-related stress, and more competence. For mothers rated as unresolved with regard to loss or trauma at placement, there was a greater need for emotional support, and more disappointment and hostility, and less joy, competence, and confidence; one year on the child was more demanding and distractible and there was more parent depression, social isolation and total stress.

The study concluded the following:

- *The earlier the adoption, the better;*
- *The more caregivers in a child's background, the greater the strain on the adoptive parent;*
- *The burden of parenting a late-adopted child is greatly influenced by the context of parenting created by (1) child characteristics; (2) the mother's attachment status; (3) the mother's representation of the child and her parenting experience;*
- *Children's difficulties may be exacerbated by being placed with a parent who carries into the placement attachment insecurities and, particularly, unresolved grief.*

Introduction

'…The inheritance of mental health and mental ill health through the medium of family micro-culture may well be far more important, than is their inheritance through the medium of genes.'(John Bowlby, 1973, p 322)

Why attachment theory?

This contribution will endeavour to answer this question as to why the construct of attachment theory and the concomitant research literature using this theory has become such a vital perspective in helping to understand the development of mental health and psychological well-being in children and their families. This contribution will outline the main tenets of attachment theory as delineated by John Bowlby and his colleagues; will describe recent advances in the assessment of the attachment construct in both children and adults; and finally will present some recent findings from a study devoted to studying the development of new attachment relationships between adoptive parents and the previously maltreated children they have permanently placed with them.

Attachment theory based on the original and enduring ideas of John Bowlby defines attachment relationships as those 'intimate bonds between specific individuals that endure over time.' (Bowlby, 1973, p 62). Bowlby theorised that humans are biopsychologically motivated by the need for attachment to others and that our survival is inextricably linked to, and dependent upon, the capacity to establish and maintain emotional ties to others. Attachment theory is unlike other theories positing that parents greatly bond with their children. This is because of the powerful range of attachment research methods which have validated the theory. Thus those interested in assessing parents and children in order to better understand and promote family well-being are drawn to attachment research. In child psychotherapy, child psychiatry, clinical psychology and social work, attachment theory has now assumed a position of central importance.

The following four basic assumptions of attachment theory have been robustly supported by observational and empirical research which helps us understand the fundamental and enduring influence parents in one generation have upon the next (and later) generations. These four assumptions which convey the essence of Bowlby's attachment theory are as follows:

(1)   intimate emotional bonds between individuals have a primary status and biological function;

(2) the way a child is treated has a powerful influence on a child's development and later personality functioning;

(3) attachment behaviour is to be viewed as part of an organisational system which utilises the notion of an 'internal working model' of self and other to guide expectation and the planning of behaviour; and

(4) attachment behaviour is resistant to change, but there is a continuing potential for change so that at no time in a person's life are they impermeable to adversity or to favourable influence.

(1) The primary status and biological function of intimate emotional ties

The essence of attachment theory is that our survival as individuals and as the human species depends upon the ability to establish and maintain emotional ties to others. Operational from birth and evident across the lifespan (especially at times of crisis), the 'instincts' of crying, reaching out, and holding on, are the functional expressions of a biological imperative with evolutionary origins. Bowlby's ideas about the importance of relationships in human motivation, have strong links with the latest advances in neuro-chemical, cognitive, ethological and evolutionary theory (see Cassidy & Shaver, 1999; Schore, 1994; Suomi, 1999).

Mary Ainsworth (a close colleague of Bowlby's) and her colleagues (1978) built on Bowlby's premises about the biological basis of attachment, and the importance of actual experiences with caregivers, highlighting the need to 'stress' or activate the attachment system in order to study and measure it. By introducing the one year old, and his/her mother, into a brightly decorated toy-laden playroom, she aimed to activate the child's exploratory (or play/work) system. By minutes later engineering the separation of mother from child, she aimed to activate the attachment system. With one system called into action, she anticipated, the other would (normally) recede. And so it was, for the normal or securely attached child who played joyfully in the presence of the mother, showed a diminishment of play and joy upon separation, and then bounced back upon reunion. For such children, home observations confirmed a history of sensitive-responsiveness from the mother. But for other children, less than joyful and often ineffective exploratory play behaviours predominated, and appeared to be used defensively to mask inner distress upon reunion. For these children, home observations confirmed a history of insensitive (interfering) and/or unresponsive (rejecting) maternal behaviour. For still other children, exploration was ineffective, and distress prevailing across the lab-observation and home observations confirmed an ineffective style of maternal behaviour, despite (as is always the case) good intentions.

One of the key features of the Strange Situation assessment paradigm that needs to be conveyed to those wishing to assess the nature of a child's attachment relationship with a specific parent or carer, is that the focus must be on the child's reaction to the caregiver upon reunion, not their behaviour during separation. This is an example of the need to be informed by robust research lest we be misled to judge a child as securely attached with a carer because they showed signs of upset when they left the room. Far more informative, is the child's reaction to the carer's return after being separated, even for a brief time if the child is left in an unfamiliar room alone or with an unfamiliar adult.

There is much research exploring the developmental sequelae of attachment with longitudinal studies across the globe which have data on individuals who as one year olds were observed in the Strange Situation with mother. Some of these findings include: children who develop secure attachments to caregivers show more competent problem-solving skills as toddlers (Matas, Arend, & Sroufe, 1978) more independent and confident behaviours with teachers as preschoolers (Sroufe, 1983), and more competent interactive behaviours with peers at school age (Elicker, Englund & Sroufe, 1992).

(2) *The way an infant is treated by caregivers has a profound influence on their development*

Mary Main and colleagues observed that some of the infants appeared not to have an organised strategy for dealing with the stresses presented by the strange situation. These children, paradoxically, showed fear in the presence of the caregiver and were observed to lack a strategy for dealing with the stressful situation. These infants' attachment was said to be disorganised. Main & Hesse (1990) suggest that the infant is expressing his/her uncertainty of which behaviour would be appropriate in the presence of the parent, sometimes showing avoidance of his/her caregiver, other times ambivalence, perhaps attending more closely to the stranger than the parent upon reunion, and/or demonstrating extreme self-protective gestures such as covering the face, lying prostrate or maintaining a frozen posture. This bemused stance runs counter to the child's inner striving for integration and security and cannot long be maintained by the infant. As Main and Hesse describe, the attachment figure 'is at once the source of and the solution to its alarm,' (Main and Hesse, 1990, p 163). The incidence of disorganisation in non-clinical or low risk populations ranges from 10 to 15%. By contrast, in populations where levels of risk to the parent-child relationship, ie child maltreatment, parental psychopathology, levels of disorganisation soar to 90% (Lyons-Ruth & Jacobvitz, 1999). Careful home observations of mothers and their infant found that maternal frightening behaviour; extreme parental mis-attunement to the specific content of an infant's attachment-related communication; and the display of competing caregiving strategies that both elicited and rejected infant attachment affects and behaviours contributed to disorganised attachment (see Lyons-Ruth & Jacobvitz, 1999).

Disorganised infant-mother attachment is associated with more behavioural problems during the preschool and early school years (Lyons-Ruth, Alpern, & Repacholi, 1993; Shaw, Owens, Vondra, Keenan & Wislow, 1996) and dissociative symptomology evidenced throughout childhood (Carlson, 1998).

While the separation and reunion behaviour assessed in the Strange Situation comprises the gold standard of measuring parent-infant attachment relationships in the one to two year old, the older child needs to be assessed in ways that take into account their developmental competencies. For children between the ages of four and eight years, a technique known as story stem completions has been usefully employed to tap into the inner world of the child as a way of assessing their attachment representations. Several researchers and clinicians have embarked on using this task as a way of gaining access to the child's inner world of thoughts and feelings concerning their attachment figures (Green et al, 2001; Oppenheim et al, 1997; Robinson et al, 2000). Findings from studies utilising this approach have found that when story stem narratives are collected from maltreated children there is a preponderance of negative themes, which depict scenarios full of sadness, anger, confusion and aggression which differentiates them from non-maltreated children (Robinson et al, 2000; Toth et al, 1997).

One approach that has a particularly strong link with assessing the inner world of maltreated children was developed by Jill Hodges and colleagues (see Hodges & Steele, 2000; Hodges et al, 2000; Steele et al, 2003, Steele et al, 2003). Children are asked to respond to a set of story stems where they are given the beginning of a 'story' highlighting every day family scenarios each of which contains an inherent dilemma. Children are then asked to 'show me and tell me what happens next?' This allows an assessment of the child's expectations and perceptions of family roles, attachments and relationships, without asking the child direct questions about their own family, adoptive or biological, which might cause them undue anxiety. It also has the advantage for younger children of allowing both verbal and non-verbal means of communication. The latter is important as it allows children to display memories and expectations which are not part of verbally based memory, and which they may be anxious about putting into words. The stems are designed so as to elicit themes concerned with the child's expectations of relationships between parents and children. These included such areas as giving affection, and setting boundaries, as well as those most central to the construct of security of attachment, namely whether the child displays expectations that parents will be aware of when children need protection or comfort and will respond appropriately to this need. The scoring of the story stems covers a range of themes from the quality of the aggression, either coherent of extreme, representations of the child and adult as endangered or endangering, realistic mastery of the conflict and the process of responding to the narrative stem, ie disengagement or changing the stories constraints. Coding the children's responses has been manualised and a training package is available for mental health professionals (Hodges, Steele et al, 2003).

(3) Internal working models

The idea of an internal working model of self and attachment figure(s) which organises thoughts and feelings regarding relationships and guides expectations arose out of a synthesis between classical psychoanalytic thinking and cognitive psychology. Bowlby points directly to the notion that we each carry within ourselves a representation of the self and other, and the self in metaphorical conversation with the other. The issue as to how to assess an adult's internal working model of attachment relationships remained an elusive enterprise until the advent of a unique interview that yielded a valid measure of parenting, from an attachment perspective. The Adult Attachment Interview ('AAI') developed by Mary Main and her colleagues (1985) elicits the adult's representations of self, attachment figure(s), and implicit strategies for regulating emotional arousal. The AAI depends crucially upon listening to the adult tell a story, in his or her own words, of their family history, which affords a narrative transcript which is rated according to a validated and reliable coding system. In this way the AAI researcher is able to collect information from relatively large groups of individuals and to apply a rigorous and detailed method of analysis, with a lengthy written set of guidelines (Main & Goldwyn, 1998). In the hands of a trained rater, this leads to a highly reliable measurement of the interviewee's probable childhood experiences, and their current state of mind regarding attachment, as well as to classification of the adult's overall pattern of attachment. The now well-known patterns of attachment, expressions of the adult's internal working model of attachment and caregiving, are as follows:

- **Secure** – adults who receive this rating provide narratives that are coherent, giving evidence for what they say by way of illustrative memories of their childhood experiences. They indicate a willingness to contemplate negative elements in their childhood, show a valuing of attachment which arises either from a supportive background or when deleterious experiences prevailed, they provide a convincing degree of having worked through their difficulties. These adults are most likely to have children who are securely attached, which is linked to their sensitive and attuned caregiving.

- **Insecure/avoidant** – this rating is given to the narratives of adults who provide economical narratives which are often characterised by an inability to recall much of their childhoods or show high levels of idealisation of their childhood experiences however, often unable to provide convincing evidence for the glowing reports. These parents are associated with infants who behave in an avoidant manner as a response to their parents' demands for independence and reluctance to engage with negative feeling states.

- **Insecure/enmeshed** – this rating is given to the narratives provided by adults who provide interviews which convey an inability to move beyond their attachment relationships and convey current anger or a passive helpless stance with regard to their parents. These narratives are often long, and lacking in coherence as the individual struggles to deal with the flood of negative feelings. These parents who have been observed to show inconsistent caregiving patterns are most often associated with infants who show ambivalence with clingy and demanding behaviour toward their attachment figures, seeking out their caregivers but unable to be truly comforted by them.

- **Unresolved** – this rating is applied to narratives in which the individual suffered a loss or abusive experience which they speak about in terms that convey a continued absorption, or lapses in their monitoring of their discourse. As parents these individuals have been observed to be either frightening towards their children or to appear frightened of them or that there is a misattunement especially with regard to feeling states between parent and child.

In diverse cultural and linguistic settings, these adult patterns of conversation regarding attachment have been observed to be associated with infant-parent patterns of attachment (secure, avoidant, resistant, disorganised respectively), and thus intergenerational consistency has been widely reported (see Hesse, 1999; van IJzendoorn, 1995; Steele et al, 1996). A closer look at the AAI may reveal why this interview, comprising of 15 questions of which only two or three specifically address beliefs about parenting, is nonetheless such a powerful predictor of parenting capacities.

The Adult Attachment Interview is structured entirely around the topic of attachment, principally the individual's relationship to mother and to father (and/or to alternative caregivers) during childhood. Subjects are asked to describe their relationship with their parents during childhood and to provide specific memories to support global evaluations. The interview's power rests in the systematic method of eliciting this attachment story. Importantly, the rater is not looking for whether the individual's childhood experience was positive or negative, but rather the degree to which the individual is able to make sense of their experiences and where there were negative experiences that there is a sense in which the speaker is emotionally present and balanced, and that s/he has come to terms with their past adversity.

Notably, the Adult Attachment Interview questions may be seen to comprise three distinct challenging modes of inquiry into memories for, and current evaluations of, past experiences of attachment-related distress. First, there are questions that ask about negative experiences and related emotions which are part of *everyone's* childhood experiences, including emotional upset, physical hurt, illness and separations from parents. Second, there are questions about negative experiences and related emotions that are part of *some people's* childhood experiences, including loss and abuse. And, third, there are questions which demand that the speaker think about the possible meaning and influence upon adult personality of childhood attachment experiences, including requests that the speaker provide an account of why parents behaved as they did during childhood.

Especially important for its clinical relevance, we have found that looking at the extent to which the individual is able to show an awareness of mental states as motivators of behaviour in oneself *and others*, that is to put themselves in the hearts and minds of their caregivers, the more likely they are to form a secure attachment relationship with their children (Fonagy, Steele, Steele, Moran & Higgitt, 1991). Specifically we found that if we look at individuals who suffered from deprivation in their childhoods and yet showed a capacity to reflect upon these experiences there was a strong likelihood that despite the adversity they would develop a secure parent-child attachment relationship with their own child. These individuals contrasted with those who suffered equally deleterious childhoods but if they were unable to reflect upon these experiences, the likelihood was that their children were insecurely attached to them. Here then, we have some sense of one of the keys to breaking the cycle of abuse, that is, if the individual possesses a capacity to provide a coherent narrative about their experiences with minimal defensive strategies to put the painful feelings at bay, they can then in turn, provide for their children a nurturing and sensitive environment which facilitates the development of optimal mental health.

A further important consideration when rating and classifying attachment interviews concerns past loss and trauma. In sum, this comes down to determining the extent to which the overwhelmingly negative experiences are (a) identified as such and (b) spoken about in such a way as to indicate that they have acquired the characteristics of belonging to the past and so are considered resolved. Unresolved mourning is most notable when the speaker shows a lapse in the monitoring of what they are saying and so make errors in their discourse which they seem oblivious to, ie 'I died, when I was 14 years old' or speaking of the dead parent as if they were alive for the entire interview until asked specifically towards the end about the loss (after Main & Goldwyn, 1998). Where loss has occurred, it is important for the speaker to demonstrate full awareness of the permanence of this loss. And, where abuse has occurred in speakers' childhood experiences, it is important for speakers to at once acknowledge the abuse, and also show that they understand they are not responsible for the maltreatment they suffered. Important clues as to the extent of resolution in the speaker's mind follow from careful study of the narrative for a logical and temporally sequenced account of the trauma which is neither too brief, suggesting an attempt to minimise the significance of the trauma, nor too detailed, suggesting ongoing absorption.

Unresolved responses of mothers when asked about past loss and/or abuse in the AAI context have been linked, in multiple independent investigations, to disorganised/disoriented attachments in the infant-mother attachment. Main & Hesse (1990) speculated, and subsequent research (Lyons-Ruth & Jacobvitz, 1999; Schuengel, Bakermans-Kranenburg & van IJzendoorn, 1999) has confirmed, that frightening or frightened maternal behaviour is the likely intervening mechanism. Put simply, a woman who is still frequently haunted by ghosts from her past is likely to create, however unwittingly, in her child's experience an ongoing sense of potential terror in the relationship.

(4) Continuity and potential for change in attachment patterns

Just because an internal working model reflecting early attachment experiences has been set up, life's adversities, if severe or cumulative enough, can topple a secure base. But, equally, an early insecure base can become more stable and hardy if a sufficiently positive set of relationship experiences follow early adversity. Bowlby repeatedly pointed out that at no time in life is positive change impossible. From this starting point, we embarked on a collaborative effort between Jeanne Kaniuk of Coram Family Adoption Service, Jill Hodges from Great Ormond Street Hospital and myself in a study funded by the Tedworth and Glasshouse Sainsbury Family Trusts. The aim of the study was to track the development of new attachment relationships as they develop between adults adopting children deemed 'hard to place', both because of the severity of the adversity they suffered and their relatively late age at which a placement was being sought. The decision to concentrate on the 4–8 years age group was made on the basis of the numbers of such children awaiting permanent placement and because they have tended to be under-researched to date due to the paucity of assessment measures applicable to this age group.

Briefly we were interested in collecting data from both the parents and the children involved that would go beneath the surface of the more widely used questionnaire measures most often used. The focus of the study was to collect information that would highlight the attachment representations of both the parents and the children as a way of discerning what each would bring to the new relationship. To this end we conducted Adult Attachment Interviews with adults (both mothers and fathers to be) who had been approved to adopt one and sometimes more of the 'hard to place' children, the speciality of the Coram Family Adoption Service. The 65 children in the study were all between the ages of four and eight years when they were first placed. We recruited a further 48 children as a comparison group who were also now aged between four and eight years, but who were adopted within their first year of life. This allows for a comparison of children who have adoption history but who did not suffer from the same level of extensive adversity as the maltreated late adopted children. Once the late adopted child(ren) were in placement, we asked that the families visit with the research team so that we could assess the child's inner world of feelings and expectations concerning attachment relationships, and interviewed the mothers about their thoughts and feelings about the child with whom they were embarking on developing a new attachment relationship. The assessments were repeated at one year and two years post-placement. Alongside the attachment assessments; a range of other assessments (eg perceived strengths and difficulties in the child, indices of parenting stress, child's IQ.) were administered.

The core of the child assessments was the story stem narrative protocol and coding system (Hodges, Steele et al, 2003) which was administered alongside assessments of the child's IQ. and self esteem. While space considerations prevent a full presentation of the findings from the Adoption and Attachment Representations study, I should like to highlight some of the early results.

- **Children's Story Stem Themes: Changes over Time**

We have some interesting results concerning the themes the children express in response to the story stem assessments conducted at placement, and again one and two years post-placement. Firstly, we found significant differences when we compared those children who were adopted during their first year of life (Early Adopted) and those who were maltreated and adopted between the ages of four and eight years (Late Adopted). The Early Adopted group showed many more positive themes (adults being helpful and showing affection; being aware of the child's distress, more themes of routine family life) and less negative themes (adults portrayed as being unaware of the child's distress; being thrown away, disengaging from the task). However, after two years of being placed in permanent adoptive homes the children showed a decrease in the negative themes, and an increase in many positive themes. However, there still remained significant differences between the two groups of children. Those that were placed as older children still expressed negative themes alongside positive ones. This can be understood in terms of the process of building up new more positive representations which are in part a result of now being in a more benign and attachment promoting environment (Hodges et al, 2003).

- **Maternal Attachment Representations and Children's Story Stem Themes**

Firstly, we would like to point out that the distribution of attachment patterns within the adoptive mothers, more or less mirrors the distribution found in studies of non-clinical populations, with the exception of more mothers providing Adult Attachment Interviews that were rated as Secure in the Adoption Study, a slight increase in those rated as Dismissing and Unresolved, and a smaller number rated as Pre-Occupied.

	General Population	**Adoptive Parents**
Secure	55%	71%
Dismissing	16%	23%
Pre-Occupied	9%	5%
Unresolved	19%	21%

It is interesting to note that the increase in the number of adoptive mothers who were rated as Secure is testament to the quality of the social workers' extensive assessment of these parents.

If we look at the associations between the Adult Attachment Interview ratings of these mothers and the story stem themes that were produced by the children who were placed with them, we have some fascinating findings. First, if we look at the first assessment that was conducted within 3 months of the children being placed we see that in comparison with children placed with mothers who were rated as Secure, those who were placed with mothers who were rated as Dismissing showed significantly elevated levels of negative themes, such as catastrophic fantasies, child and adult aggression, bizarre or atypical responses, adults and child portrayed as injured or dead. More specifically, we found that if mothers were able to provide a coherent and thoughtful account of their childhood experiences, the children they had placed with them tended not to use aggression as a theme to resolve conflict inherent in the story completion task.

Even more striking is our finding about mothers whose Adult Attachment Interview was classified as Unresolved with respect to loss or trauma. When children were placed with mothers with this rating, there was a significant likelihood that their story stem themes showed parents appearing child-like; elevated levels of adult aggression; themes depicting characters being rubbished or thrown away. As compared to children who were placed with mothers who were not rated as Unresolved, these children also tended to show less themes of being able to realistically master the conflict presented in the story and had fewer stories where peers or siblings were shown to be helpful in the conflict scenarios.

We have come to understand how it could be that the state of mind concerning attachment of a mother who so recently was matched with a maltreated child to impact the child's state of mind within such a relatively short period of time. We know from the studies of disorganised attachment patterns cited above, that there is a propensity for the mother-child relationship to include elements of fear or for the mother to be overwhelmed by intense feeling states. These children, by virtue of their histories, present as vulnerable in varying degrees. This vulnerability, when met with by the vulnerability inherent in the unresolved parent, heightens the vulnerability in both partners. These children also seem especially well able, perhaps through their own hypersensitivity, to be aware of the affective states of others. Indeed, their caregivers often report the child's great skill in 'pushing the right buttons' of their caregivers.

We have also learned from the Adoption and Attachment representations study that these unresolved mothers report more difficulties in their children from when they are first placed with them, one and two years later. When interviewed about their thoughts and feelings concerning the child they have placed with them they report a greater need for social support, that they are more disappointed and in a state of despair with regard to the child, and convey less joy, less competence, and less confidence in their role as parent. The overall coherence of the narrative they provide when talking about their child is lower than those mothers who provided Adult Attachment Interviews that were rated as secure. The mothers who were rated as unresolved also are rated as having less of a 'child focus' which indicates that in terms of their motivation for engaging in the adoption process, the focus was more on what the child might be able to bring them, rather than a view of themselves in the role of facilitating the child's development.

These mothers who were rated as unresolved on the Adult Attachment Interview also report more stress in the parenting role and that their children suffer from more behavioural difficulties as measured by widely used, reliable and valid questionnaires focussed on childrens' strengths and difficulties (Strengths and Difficulties Questionnaire; Goodman, 1997; Parenting Stress Index; Abidin, 1981).

The study also found interesting age related associations. Firstly, while all the children in the late adopted group were considered to be 'older' with regard to being adopted, age still made a difference. When we divided our sample into younger (4–6 years v 6–8 years), we found that while all the children showed improvement (apart from the nine placed with the mothers who were rated as unresolved) the younger the child, the more rapidly they made positive changes as measured by the story stem assessments. So, even with what might be considered 'older' children, ie beyond the age of four years, the need to find them permanent placements makes a critical difference. However, if we look further at this particular finding we see that this is the case, mainly for the mothers who were rated as insecure with regard to their attachment history. These mothers perceive the older adopted child as more disappointing, more angry, less happy and less affectionate. The mothers who were rated as secure with regard to their attachment history did not show these differences in terms of the age of the child they adopted. This finding has obvious implications for decision making in terms of potential matching of adopters and children.

It is important to note, that even if we take into account the outcome of those children placed with the unresolved mothers, adoption as a solution for these previously maltreated children can be considered a resounding success. That is, there was only one case of disruption in the sample of 65 children. And while the children in the group placed with unresolved mothers did not fare quite as well as those placed with the mothers who were rated as secure, the placements survived and the children continued to benefit from being placed in a permanent home. Overall, the children that we tracked over a two-year period made improvements in their perception of adult caregivers as being able to protect and care for them, in their peer and sibling relationships and in the way they perceived themselves.

These findings have implications for practice in terms of highlighting the advent of incorporating systematic assessment techniques with which to better understand some of the crucial issues facing child clinicians and social workers, and colleagues in the legal professions. While we don't envision that the resources would become available so that every adopter will undergo the in-depth assessment of the Adult Attachment Interview or that every child receive a story stem assessment, these tools can be vital in terms of individual cases that need specialist assessment. As well, by sharing with the clinicians and child care professionals some of the thinking that underpins these assessment techniques, for example the importance of coherence in the narrative of an adult or the defensive manoeuvres a child may display in play, the ongoing work of the professional may be enhanced.

With new government initiatives (Department of Health, June 2002) promising to provide adopters with support, it could be that the assessment techniques highlighted in this paper may be of use in helping to address and target needs in a more strategic way. While we are not yet at the point of understanding which therapeutic input might be of most benefit to an adult adopter who remains unresolved with respect to a previously suffered loss or trauma, we do know that they and the children placed with them will require additional support.

The current applications of his seminal contributions to understanding the complexities of parent-child attachment relationships re-echo a sentiment Bowlby expressed in 1951, and frequently included in his later writings, 'if a society values its children, it must cherish their parents.'

References

Ainsworth, MDS. l967. *Infancy in Uganda: Infant care and the growth of love*, Baltimore, MD: Johns Hopkins University Press.

Ainsworth, MDS, Blehar, MC, Waters, E & Wall, S. 1978. *Patterns of Attachment: A Psychological Study of the Strange Situation*. Hillsdale, NJ: Erlbaum.

Bowlby, J. 1951. *Maternal Care and Mental Health*. Geneva: World Health Organization.

Bowlby, J. 1973. *Attachment and Loss*: Vol 2. 'Separation: Anxiety and anger'. New York: Basic Books.

Bowlby, J. 1988. *A Secure Base: Clinical applications of attachment theory*. London: Routledge.

Carlson, E. 1998. A prospective longitudinal study of disorganized/disoriented attachment. *Child Development*, **69**, 1970–1979.

Cassidy, J & Shaver, P (eds.) 1999. *Handbook of Attachment*, New York: Guilford Press.

Elicker, J, Englund, M & Sroufe, L (1992). Predicting peer competence and peer relationships in childhood from early parent-child relationship. In *Family-peer Relationships: Modes of Linkage*, ed. RD Parke & GW Ladd, pp 77–106. Hillsdale, N.J: Erlbaum.

Fonagy, P, Steele, M, Steele, H, Leigh, T, Kennedy, R, Mattoon, G & Target, M. 1995. Attachment, the reflective self, and borderline states: The predictive specificity of the Adult Attachment Interview and pathological emotional development. In *Attachment theory: Social, Developmental and Clinical Perspectives*, ed. S Goldberg, R Muir & J Kerr, pp 233–278. New York: Analytic Press.

Green, J, Stanley C, Smith, V & Goldwyn, R. 2001. A new method of evaluating attachment representations in young school age children: The Manchester Child Attachment Story Task. *Attachment and Human Development*, **2**, 48–70.

Hodges, J, and Steele, M. 2000. Effects of abuse on attachment representations: narrative assessments of abused children. *Journal of Child Psychotherapy*, **26**, 433–55.

Hodges, J, Steele, M, Hillman, S & Henderson, K. 2003. Mental representations and defences in severely maltreated children: A story stem battery and rating system for clinical assessment and research applications. In *Revealing the Inner World of the Child*, ed. R Emde, D Wolf and D Oppenheim, University of Chicago Press.

Hesse, E. 1999. The Adult Attachment Interview: Historical and current perspectives. In *Handbook of Attachment*, ed. J Cassidy & P Shaver, pp 395–433. New York: Guilford Press.

Lyons-Ruth, K & Jacobvitz, D. 1999. Attachment disorganization: Unresolved loss, relational violence, and lapses in behavioural and attentional strategies. In *Handbook of Attachment*, ed. J Cassidy & P Shaver, pp 520–555. New York: Guilford Press.

Lyons-Ruth, K, Repacholi, B, McLeod, S & Silva, E. 1991. Disorganized attachment behaviour in infancy: Short-term stability, maternal and infant correlates, and risk-related subtypes. *Development and Psychopathology*, **3**, 397-412.

Main, M & Goldwyn, R. 1998. *Adult Attachment Scoring and Classification System*. Unpublished manuscript, University of California at Berkeley.

Main, M & Hesse, E. 1990. Parents' unresolved traumatic experiences are related to infant disorganised attachment status: Is frightened and/or frightening parental behaviour the linking mechanism? In *Attachment in the preschool years: Theory, research and intervention*, ed. MT Greenberg, D Cicchetti & EM Cummings, pp 161-182. Chicago: University of Chicago Press.

Main, M., Kaplan, K & Cassidy, J. 1985. Security in infancy, childhood and adulthood: A move to the level of representation. In I Bretherton and E Waters (eds), Growing points of attachment theory and research, *Monographs of the Society for Research in Child Development*, **50 (Serial No. 209, 1–2)**: 66–104.

Matas, L, Arend, R & Sroufe, L. 1978. Continuity of adaptation in the second year: The relationship between quality of attachment and later competence. *Child Development*, **49**, 547–556.

Oppenheim, D, Emde, R & Warren, S. 1997. Children's narrative representations of mothers: Their development and associations with child and mother adaptation. *Child Development*, **68**, 127–138.

Robinson, J, Herot, C, Haynes, P & Mantz-Simmons, L. 2000. Children's story stem responses: A measure of program impact on developmental risks associated with dysfunctional parenting. *Child Abuse and Neglect*, **24**, 99–110.

Schore, A. 1994. *Affect Regulation and the Origin of the Self: The Neurobiology of Eemotional Development*. Hillsdale, NJ: Lawrence Erlbaum Associates.

Shaw, D, Owens, E, Vondra, J, Keenan, K & Winslow, E. 1996. Early risk factors and pathways in the development of early disruptive behaviour problems. *Developmental Psychopathology*, **8**, 679–699.

Spangler, G & Grossmann, KE. 1993. Biobehavioural organization in securely and insecurely attached infants. *Child Development*, **59**, 1097–1101.

Sroufe, A. 1988. The role infant-caregiver attachment in development. In *Clinical Implications of Attachment*, ed. J Belsky & xx Nezworksi, pp. 18–38. Hillsdale, NJ: Erlbaum.

Steele, H, Steele, M & Fonagy, P. 1996. Associations among attachment classifications of others, fathers, and their infants. *Child Development*, **67**, 541–555.

Steele, M, Hodges, J, Kaniuk, J, Hillman, S & Henderson, K. 2003. Attachment representations and adoption: associations between maternal states of mind and emotion narratives in previously maltreated children. *Journal of Child Psychotherapy*, in press.

Steele, M, Steele, H, Woolgar, M, Yabsley, S, Johnson, D, Fonagy, P & Croft, C. 2003. An attachment perspective on children's emotion narratives: links across generations. In *Revealing the Inner World of the Child*, ed. R Emde, D Oppenheim & D Wolfe, University of Chicago Press, in press.

Suomi, SJ. 1999. Attachment in rhesus monkeys. In *Handbook of Attachment*, ed. J Cassidy & P Shaver, pp 181–197. New York: Guilford Press.

Toth, S, Cicchetti, D, Macfie, J, & Emde, R. 1997. Representations of self and others in the narratives of neglected, physically abused, and sexually abused preschoolers. *Developmental Psychopathology*, **9**, 781–796.

Vaughn, BE, Egeland, B, Sroufe, LA & Waters, E. 1979. Individual differences in infant-mother attachment at twelve and eighteen months: Stability and change in families under stress. *Child Development*, **50**, 971–975.

van IJzendoorn, MH. 1995. Associations between adult attachment representations and parent-child attachment, parental responsiveness, and clinical status: A meta-analysis of the predictive validity of the strange situation. *Psychological Bulletin*, **117**, 387–403.

THE VOICE OF THE CHILD IN PUBLIC LAW PROCEEDINGS: A DEVELOPMENTAL MODEL

Dr Gillian Schofield[1]
Co-Director of the Centre for Research on the Child and Family,
University of East Anglia

Summary of paper

Dr Gillian Schofield said that her paper focused on how developmental theory and research can help professionals face up to the challenge of ascertaining the wishes and feelings of children and deciding how to manage the evidence of those wishes and feelings in decision making. She presented a summary model which seeks to capture some of the main themes that can help us understand and integrate different developmental perspectives. She identified the following themes:

- *Affect*
- *Autonomy*
- *Cognition*
- *Belonging*
- *The Developing Self*

Affect

Affect refers to feelings, both about self and others. Dr Schofield stressed the importance of remembering that children have mixed feelings, and that their feelings are going to change and shift, for example between sadness and anger. She said that many children in care proceedings feel confused, even that they are going mad, because their feelings are changing all the time and often the options are complex. So we must reassure children that this is normal and help them to accept and express their mixed feelings.

Autonomy

This involves the idea of using the secure base of relationships to facilitate exploring and learning about the world, in order to become more competent and effective. One of the major developmental tasks is to manage and balance dependency and autonomy. This has an important overlap with the idea of participation. Dr Schofield emphasised the difference between process and outcome. She stressed that, as the Children Act Guidance suggests, although children should feel that they have participated as partners in the decision making process, they should not be made to feel that the burden of decision making has fallen totally on them.

Cognition

A child cannot be autonomous without the capacity to think. A child must develop a flexibly thinking, reflective mind if he or she is to be able to approach new situations with confidence and make choices or choose strategies. Children who have found that their caregivers' minds are not available to them or who have suffered abuse or neglect may find it more difficult to make sense of the past, the present, or to

---

[1] Dr Gillian Schofield, Senior Lecturer in Social Work and Psychosocial Studies, Co-Director of the Centre for Research on the Child and Family, University of East Anglia, Chair BAAF Research Advisory Committee, Member of the President's Interdisciplinary Committee.

consider the options available for their future. This means that such children will need greater help to think through difficult issues before being expected to express their wishes and feelings.

Belonging

Dr Schofield suggested that for many children involved in proceedings, the most important gift they could be given was to be part of a family. Being part of a family brings with it solidarity and support; culture, values and aspirations; as well as an important sense of permanence. The idea of belonging also involves the idea of personal identity, including issues of gender, ethnicity and community. Although families have powerful ties for children it is not easy for children to express this in words, especially when a range of families – birth, foster and adoptive – are possible outcomes.

The Developing Self

These aspects of a child's development are linked in many ways. Ascertaining children's wishes and feelings requires an understanding of these interlocking aspects of development. By focusing on these different themes, and helping the child to develop in the different areas identified, professionals can help children who are the subject of court proceedings to build up their resilience and to feel more hopeful for the future.

Introduction

The duty of courts to take into account the wishes and feelings of children in public law proceedings has presented a number of challenges. Primarily, however, these arise from the possible tensions between on the one hand the child's right to be heard, as enshrined in the UN Convention and the Children Act 1989, and on the other hand the court's paramount duty to make decisions that safeguard the best interests of the child. One way of reconciling the potentially competing but potentially complementary discourses of rights and welfare can be to take an approach that draws on theories of child development. Such an approach can assist in both the task of ascertaining the wishes and feelings of children and the way in which courts manage the evidence of those wishes and feelings in their decision making. It can be argued that not only is it a child's right to participate in decision making, but that increasing the accuracy of the court's understanding of the mind of the child, their thoughts and feelings, will contribute to a more accurate assessment of the likely outcomes of the options before the court. In addition, if it is appropriately and sensitively handled, enabling the child to participate in the process of decision making can also be developmentally beneficial. The need for an appropriate and sensitive approach raises questions about the knowledge and skills of those professionals who ascertain the views of children, those who debate the evidence in court and those who are required to make the decisions that take into account both the wishes and the welfare of children. Even when courts have the benefit of a range of expert witnesses, or perhaps particularly when courts have the benefit of a range of expert witnesses, some knowledge and understanding of the development of children, some appreciation of key aspects of developmental psychology and psychopathology, can be of great assistance to family justice professionals.

Behind our knowledge of the development of children lies a wealth of theory and research evidence. This will be represented in this short discussion paper by a summary model that seeks to capture some of the main themes that can help us understand and integrate different developmental perspectives (see figure 1).[2] Although the model is derived from theory and research on development, it offers the possibility of matching developmental issues with the

---

[2] Adapted from Schofield 'The Significance of a Secure Base: A Psychosocial Model of Long-Term Foster Care' (2002) *Child and Family Social Work* 7 (4): 259–272, also in Schofield *Part of the Family: Pathways through Foster Care* (BAAF, 2003).

dilemmas around both listening to children and taking what they say into account in decision making. The model draws on a number of key developmental theories around attachment,[3] cognitive development[4] and resilience.[5] However, it is a psychosocial model that therefore includes the developmental goals of belonging and identity and so draws also on the literature to do with kinship[6], adoption[7] and foster care.[8]

---

[3] Bowlby *Attachment and Loss: Vol 1 Attachment* (Hogarth Press, 1969), Howe, Brandon, Hinings, and Schofield *Attachment Theory: Child Maltreatment and Family Support* (Macmillan, 1999).

[4] Piaget and Inhelder *The Psychology of the Child* (Routledge and Kegan Paul, 1969).

[5] Fonagy, Steele, Steele, Higgitt, and Target 'Theory and Practice of Resilience' (1994) *Journal of Child Psychology and Psychiatry* 35 (2): 231–257; Rutter 'Resilience concepts and findings: implications for family therapy' (1999) *Journal of Family Therapy* 21: 119–144.

[6] Allan *Kinship and Friendship in Modern Britain* (Oxford University Press, 1996).

[7] Howe *Patterns of Adoption* (Blackwell Science, 1998), Neil 'The reasons why young children are placed for adoption: findings from a recently placed sample and a discussion of implications for future identity development' (2000) *Child and Family Social Work* 5 (4): 303–316.

[8] Schofield, Beek, Sargent with Thoburn *Growing up in Foster Care* (BAAF, 2000), Beek and Schofield *A Secure Base in Foster Care* (BAAF, in preparation).

Figure 1 The Voice Of The Child: A Developmental Model

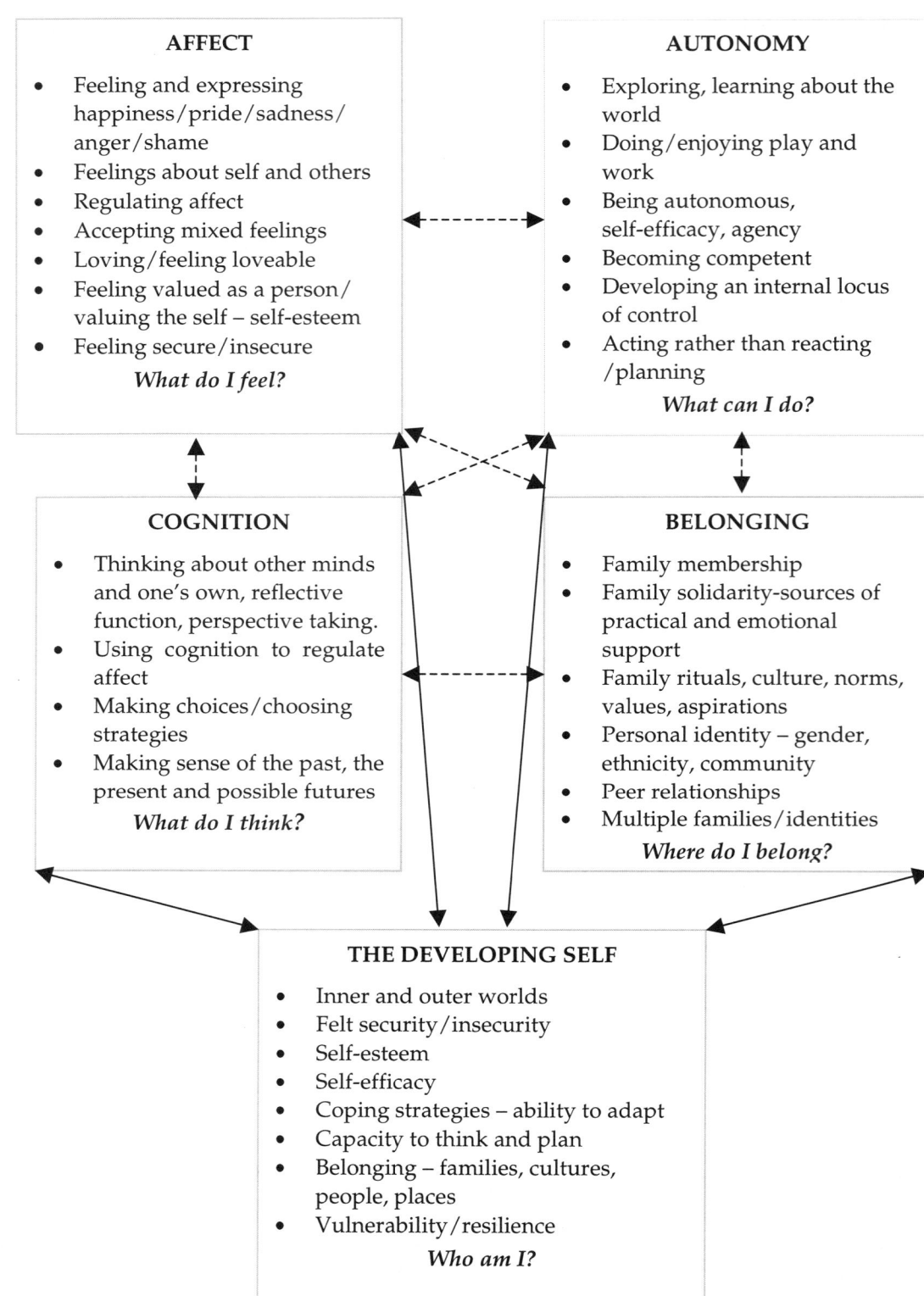

In explaining the model some reference will be made to the types of childrens' cases and decisions in which ascertaining and taking account of childrens' wishes and feelings can be particularly problematic. Case material from practice and from research will be used to illustrate both the developmental model and the practice issues that arise. Each section of the model will be considered in turn with interactions between different aspects being taken into account. The aim is to provide a brief but holistic picture of the development of a child's mind, a framework in which the significance of listening to children can be better understood.

Affect

When evidence is presented to courts about children in public law proceedings, it is expected that children's *feelings* about their birth families, their foster families, their adoptive families, their siblings, their friends and themselves will be described in some detail. Very often their feelings are presented both in terms of what they may have said (whether incidentally or when asked directly as part of the assessment work) and what may be deduced from their behaviour. Neither of these sources of evidence is unproblematic and so it is helpful to start by thinking about children's emotional development and the ways in which feelings are both felt and expressed.

A child's ability to put their feelings into words will vary greatly depending on the child's experience in close relationships. Particularly important will be those experiences in the formative period of infancy, but also through the pre-school years as language develops. The capacity to name emotions relies on the child's developing sense of the meaning and specificity of different emotions, on the child's developing language skills – and on the ability to put those two together in conversation with others. Securely attached children who have experienced sensitive caregiving and attunement will have seen their caregiver's face reflecting back to them from birth those early feelings of joy and sadness, love and anger, trust and fear. There will have been a synchrony between caregiver and infant that allows this mirroring to be precisely timed and accurate. The caregiver's face moderates and contains the infant's feelings in a predictable way that allows the child to continue to feel and express the full range of emotions without fear of being overwhelmed by them. As Fonagy and his colleagues have described, this process enables the child to manage or regulate their feelings through a process of mentalisation, with the result that, 'The infant learns that arousal in the presence of the caregiver will not lead to disorganisation beyond his coping capabilities'.[9]

Where children have experienced a lack of synchrony and accurate mirroring – where for example the infant's happy or anxious or angry face is met with a blank face, as in post-natal depression perhaps, or a fearful face, as in a caregiver struggling with domestic violence or a caregiver frightened by the prospect of the infant's neediness – then the child becomes confused and uncertain about the feelings that they are experiencing and may begin to be overwhelmed by them. The child is picking up the parents' anxiety and defensive strategies rather than being freed up to value and express their own feelings. This is a complex process but its outcome can determine the extent to which a child can accept, express and regulate their own feelings and over time begin to read and negotiate with the feelings of others.

Research has demonstrated the consequences of this developmentally. For example, the difficulty in expressing emotions for children in neglectful or maltreating families often focuses in particular on a reluctance to express negative emotions in the presence of caregivers, since these may prove provocative and therefore dangerous. As early as the second year of life, it has been found[10] that children who have been maltreated will show fewer negative emotions.

---

[9] Fonagy, Gergely, Jurist and Target *Affect Regulation, Mentalization, and the Development of the Self* (Other Press, 2002) at p 37.

[10] Crittenden and DiLalla 'Compulsive compliance: The development of an inhibitory coping strategy in infancy' (1988) *Journal of Abnormal Child Psychology* 16: 585–599.

Insecurely attached children[11] through the pre-school years and into middle childhood need to develop strategies for managing their feelings in order to stay close to caregivers. More defended, avoidant children, for example, will shut down on their feelings to stay close to a caregiver who dislikes emotional demands whereas ambivalent resistant children will use displays of feelings to gain the attention of and control unpredictably available caregivers. Maltreated children, who are most likely to be disorganised in attachment terms, will find proximity to the attachment figure anxiety provoking rather than comforting. In early infancy they may seem helpless and show contradictory, confused behaviours. As they move through into the pre-school years, middle childhood and adolescence, they become increasingly hypervigilant of their caregivers. Such children are likely to develop strategies to control others in order to stay safe. They may use placatory displays of care and affection which work in the short term, but are likely to seem false and manipulative over time. Displays of punitive anger and aggression may frighten others into backing away but leave the child feeling even more isolated.

Because attachment theory proposes that these defensive strategies are associated with the need to reduce anxiety, and particularly anxiety around proximity to and separation from attachment figures, it is likely that children who are separated from attachment figures, for example when they come into foster care, will intensify these ways of expressing or avoiding the expression of emotion, achieving or denying the need for proximity, controlling others or being quietly compliant.[12] Even when children remain in the birth family during court proceedings, it is likely that anxiety about the possibility of separation will intensify insecure organised or disorganised controlling defensive strategies. For many maltreated children such heightened anxiety will have been cumulative in the context of fears of separation and loss generated by domestic violence, parental drug and alcohol misuse or direct threats to the child that the parent will commit suicide or abandon the child in other ways. Once in foster care, children may smile as if nothing has happened, but will be monitoring the carers faces and behaviours in anticipation of danger.

What are the implications of these developmental consequences of maltreatment and separation for the ascertaining of children's feelings in court proceedings? If we look back to the two main sources of evidence mentioned above – the child's directly expressed feelings and observation of the child's behaviour – then it is clear that very great care needs to be taken, even by professionals well-informed about developmental processes. The child who says they do not care about contact with their mother and is rather distant and cool in their mother's presence may yet be gaining some comfort and reassurance from regular contact. In contrast, the child who is effusively sentimental about a father, rushes up to him and gives him a kiss may have been physically or sexually abused and be very afraid. Such behaviours reflect strategies for survival which make sense in the context of their relationship histories, but are very confusing to practitioners. As the case of Kimberley Carlile demonstrated,[13] a child who holds her step-father's hand and skips as she walks across the car park may yet be at risk.

The recognition of this counterintuitive and developmentally complex context is *not* an argument for disregarding children's accounts of their feelings or evidence from their behaviour.[14] A number of separate points need to be made here which reinforce both the benefit to the court of taking into account developmental factors and the developmental benefit to the child of observing and listening to children in order to understand their feelings.

---

[11]   Ainsworth, Blehar, Waters and Wall *Patterns of Attachment: A Psychological Study of the Strange Situation* (Lawrence Erlbaum, 1978).

[12]   Schofield 'Making sense of the ascertainable wishes and feelings of insecurely attached children' (1998) *Child and Family Law Quarterly* 10 (4): 363–376.

[13]   London Borough of Greenwich *A Child in Mind: Protection of Children in a responsible society. The Report of the Commission of Inquiry into the circumstances surrounding the death of Kimberley Carlile* (1987).

[14]   Schofield and Thoburn, *Child Protection: The Voice of the Child in Decision Making* (Institute for Public Policy Research, 1996).

First, children from troubled relationships of the kind most likely to have preceded the case coming to court will almost certainly have complex and mixed feelings about their significant others that need to be very carefully understood. Understanding the developmental context, for example that a particular child tends to shut down on their feelings or to pretend all is well when they are actually highly distressed, allows social workers and others responsible to the court for ascertaining children's wishes and feelings, to understand the more subtle process that is involved. The child who says 'I don't care about my mum' may nevertheless need help in thinking about contact. In contrast the compulsive caregiving of the disorganised child at contact may be reported by professionals as a 'strong attachment', often viewed positively, when in fact it should be understood to be an insecure attachment.

Case example

Amanda (age 13) was excluded from the adoption plans made for her younger siblings when she was six years old because she was deemed to be 'strongly attached' to her very disturbed and aggressive birth mother as a result of her intense preoccupation and concern about her. The court was advised that, on the basis of this attachment, Amanda needed a long-term placement that was not thought of as 'permanent' (ie exclusive) and would allow frequent contact. Five years on and in spite of being in a stable foster placement since the court hearing, Amanda is a young teenager who continues to struggle with endless phone calls from her mother about her problems, including demands that Amanda demonstrate her love for her mother. Amanda is unable to concentrate on school or activities and is already seeming emotionally burnt out, while her siblings are thriving. [15]

The lesson from this case is not about the adoption or long-term foster care choice or about contact per se, but it suggests the ways in which developmental theory can be misused. Notions of 'strong' or 'weak' attachment are very unhelpful and not an accurate use of the theory and need to be consistently replaced by clarity about the behavioural evidence of secure and insecure attachment, especially in the context of care planning for maltreated children.

Secondly, children from maltreating families are likely to have negative feelings about themselves, to have low self-esteem and to believe that they are of little value. The process of court involvement and the many associated anxieties may confirm for children and young people that they are indeed the problem and that it is their badness that has provoked the storm that is now breaking around themselves and their family. Consulting children in this state, although challenging, gives them the message that their feelings are of significance. This is important in itself, but the message needs to be more subtle than that. Children benefit most from the sensitivity of professional listeners who understand that children may both love and hate their mother or father, that they may both need and envy their brothers or sisters or that they may both resent and appreciate the work that social workers are doing on their behalf. Subtlety based on developmental understanding of normal developmental processes and the impact of maltreatment, adversity and separation enables children to give and professionals to receive a more complete picture of their feelings. This is beneficial for decision making, but the process can also be beneficial for children's development.

Autonomy

One of the major developmental tasks from infancy to adolescence to adulthood is to manage and balance dependency and autonomy. Healthy development is often a process of two steps forward and one back, as the toddler and the adolescent may demand the right to make their

---

[15]   Beek and Schofield, op cit, n 8.

own decisions, but are likely the next moment to demand to be picked up – whether in the parental arms as a toddler or in the parental taxi as an adolescent. Negotiating this area of development is one of the many challenges of parenthood, but negotiating around the appropriate degree of autonomy to allow children when decisions are made about their future by courts, causes family justice professionals similar types of anxiety. The risks and benefits of giving or withholding power and choice in situations of very great seriousness lie at the heart of the children's participation rights/children's welfare and best interests debate.

Infants are not born as passive beings, but as unique active individuals who will make an impact on their environment. As Howe et al [16] put it, babies need and enjoy having control and influencing others. Minutes after birth, in the delivery room, babies can make the smallest of sounds, flash a glance or wave a hand and get their parents cooing in satisfaction, gazing fondly back or cuddling them tight. Many of these early interactions, these carefully synchronised behavioural conversations, give the powerful message to infants that they are important and influential people who can make things happen. As a result, even waving the rattle in an apparently random way rapidly becomes a co-ordinated and purposeful endeavour, having the magical consequence of making a sound (on demand) and attracting (on demand) the admiring looks and words of the important people in their lives.

This potential for self-efficacy builds on the secure base established by the predictable availability, interest and emotional and mental containment offered by the sensitive caregiver. The hungry infant learns first that they do not need to keep crying at full volume because the mother's step on the stair means food is at hand. The child is then free to learn the increasingly subtle aspects of relationships and their power within them. The twelve month old in the high chair who smiles engagingly at the father while preparing to drop the eggy toast on the new carpet may not understand the cost of carpets nor the complex feelings of the adult, but is aware that this is a game that will provoke a reaction and in fact does test out the boundaries of the paternal patience. Important lessons are learned but the outcome will depend on the parent's response. The child's striving towards what Sroufe[17] has called agency has risks and benefits for children which adults need to help them to manage. Parents who are themselves secure and autonomous do not just allow but seek to promote children's agency, while providing safe boundaries and safety nets within the context of the relationship. The child acquires an internal locus of control, rather than needing imposed constraints, but this negotiated outcome arises in a relationship. Thus 'autonomy', even in adolescence and adult life, is perhaps most helpfully understood in terms of the negotiated interdependence which family life, friendship groups, romantic relationships, workplace teams and communities can provide.

For children whose early caregiving experiences are characterised by insensitive, neglectful or abusive care, the experience of striving for personal power and efficacy is fraught with difficulties and even dangers. The parent who has unresolved trauma from their own childhood and/or is currently vulnerable and under pressure through domestic violence, drug abuse or mental health problems may experience the crying baby or the toddler in the high chair about to drop the eggy toast as deliberately launching a personal attack. The parent's own sense of helplessness and inability to regulate feelings means that the child's expression of need or assertion of will is seen as behaviour that must be controlled, suppressed or even punished. This response may be to protect the parent, although it may be articulated as a necessary part of firm parenting. The parent who experiences any signs of assertiveness as the child being too powerful may come to feel that giving a child choices would be 'giving in'. In more extreme cases, parents can come to fear the child, even the infant, thus giving the very anxiety-provoking message to the child that the child is a very powerful and dangerous person

---

[16] Howe et al, op cit, n 3.

[17] Sroufe, Carlson and Schulman 'Individuals in relationships: Development from infancy through adolescence' in *Studying Lives through Time: Personality and Development* ed. Funder, Parke, Tomlinson-Keasey and Widaman (Washington DC, American Psychological Association, 1993) at pp 315–342.

who cannot be contained. This makes it almost impossible (in the absence of other caregiving experiences) for the child to regulate feelings or behaviour in order to achieve self-efficacy.

A contrasting but linked developmental experience around autonomy occurs when parents respond to the child's attempt at expressing feelings or developing agency by simply ignoring the child. In these circumstances, children are also likely to feel chaotic and unregulated. Some children may become excessively self-reliant since this seems to be more acceptable to the parent. However, this lacks the interpersonal relatedness which makes the exercise of agency safe. Again, subtlety in assessment is of the essence, since the self-reliant child may be described as 'resilient' at points when such behaviour is developmentally inappropriate.

Throughout childhood children are expected to make decisions, from 'Who shall I play with?' and 'What shall I make from playdo today?' in play group to choosing subjects for GCSE. Children pick from a range of informal or formal options and make those choices with or without external support and consultation. Children's capacity to make those decisions in ways that are realistic and meet their own needs appropriately will draw on a range of innate and environmentally determined factors. When children are invited to participate in decision making in court, they are offered the opportunity to influence decisions that will affect their future in highly significant ways. They may be contributing a general picture of wishes and feelings in relation to certain people and situations or they may be faced with very specific and often stark options – do I want to go home, stay with my foster family, move to another foster family or be placed for adoption? What type/level of contact do I want? Which of my siblings do I want to see most often?

For children who have experienced exercising appropriate autonomy, making decisions is achieved by a combination of careful thinking through and asking advice from key trustworthy others. They can think, act and plan rather than react to events. But for children who have been discouraged from asserting themselves, who feel helpless, who feel that they are powerful but bad or who have had an excessive degree of self-reliance, it is very difficult to know where to start. On the other hand, it is these very children for whom one would most wish to increase the sense that they as people matter and that important decisions in their lives cannot be made without taking their views and feelings into account. These children need most help to ensure that when these momentous decisions are made, the fact that they are children or even children in care does not mean that they are not considered to have views worthy of consideration. This moment in their lives is a point of crisis, but it can also be an opportunity for a different experience. Perhaps the most helpful model for courts is the most obvious – the model of the responsible parent, who both treats the child with respect as an autonomous being *and* has the child's interests in the present and the future at heart. An infrequently quoted part of the Children Act 1989 Guidance[18] offers some wise counsel:

> 'Children should feel that they have been properly consulted, that their views have been properly considered and that they have participated as partners in the decision making process. However, they should not be made to feel that the burden of decision making has fallen totally upon them.'

This guidance stresses the difference between process and outcome. The responsible parent needs to ensure that the child has evidence that they have been heard and the reasons why, if this is to be the case, that a different outcome is proposed from that expressly desired by the child.

---

[18]   Children Act 1989 Guidance, vol 3: Family Placements, para 5.35.

Case Example[19]

Maria was a fifteen year old with mild learning difficulty and a long history of sexual abuse and neglect. Her learning disabled mother had not been able to protect her from a number of abusive partners. Maria was actively involved in the care proceedings, being separately represented and having the opportunity to confer with both the guardian ad litem and her solicitor. Maria's expressed wish to return home was conveyed to the court by her solicitor who tested the evidence with this position in mind. The guardian ad litem also presented the court with Maria's wishes and feelings, several of which were incompatible – such as 'I want to return home and look after my mother but I want myself and my younger siblings to be safe'. Although the court made the care order, Maria had been actively involved and had seen evidence of her wishes being taken into account – for example, she was shown the guardian ad litem report and was informed that the judgement had included reference to her expressed wishes and the reasons why the court had felt that her welfare could not be protected were she to return home.

For Maria, the court proceedings were lengthy and frustrating, with many delays and points at which she had felt powerless, just as she had felt in her birth family. However, the process of consultation, the experience of being treated with respect and listened to by a number of professionals involved and knowing that this distant body called 'the court' had heard her words was probably the first time that she had felt a sense of personal efficacy. The meetings with powerful people like solicitors and being asked for her views at times might have seemed to be a rather too dramatic shift towards putting Maria 'in charge'. But throughout the process Maria was assured by the social worker, the solicitor and the guardian that whatever the expressed wishes of the children or the parents or the recommendations of different professionals in the case, the court would make a decision, based on all the evidence, of what would be in her best interests. This seemed a very developmentally appropriate message for a previously uncared for, previously unprotected as well as previously unheard fifteen year old child.

Cognition

The expression and regulation of feelings and the appropriate development of autonomy in children cannot be achieved without the fundamental development of the capacity to think, about the self, about others and about the world around them. The child's capacity to think has many components: some have genetic roots, such as intelligence; others are associated with age and developmental stage; and others are influenced by environmental factors, ranging from nutrition and teratogens during pregnancy (for example, foetal alcohol syndrome affecting brain development) through to relationship environments. Evidence from research in cognitive development[20] suggests that children's thinking is qualitatively different in infancy, childhood and adolescence, as children move from sensory-motor stages in infancy to more concrete and rule bound middle-childhood and on to the more flexible and abstract thinking of adolescent and adult minds. Although the age boundaries and details of these stages are the subject of some dispute, the shifts towards increasing complexity and abstraction have much significance for professionals and for families. As Brodzinsky[21] suggested, for example, the adopted child

---

[19] Anonymised case from author's previous guardian ad litem practice, Schofield and Thoburn, op cit, n 14.

[20] Op cit, n 4.

[21] Brodzinsky 'A Stress and Coping Model of Adoption Adjustment' in *Psychology of Adoption* ed. Brodzinsky and Schechter (New York: Oxford University Press, 1990), at pp 3–24.

who starts to ask persistent questions about their birth family at the age of seven is less likely to be reacting to a change in feelings about his adoptive family and more likely to be simply showing the appropriate cognitive shift that leads to more questions about social rules, how the world works and where they fit in. These shifts are not automatic with advancing age and will still depend on the quality of experience. Some children never reach the more abstract kinds of thinking, even in adult life. Cognition, like affect and autonomy, is particularly affected by the more extreme experiences of maltreatment. Reaching and understanding the thinking as well as the feeling mind of a child requires a firm foundation of knowledge about nature, nurture and the interaction between the child's mind and the environment in which it is growing and developing.

From birth, the human mind is engaging with, trying to make sense of and adapting to its environment and the environment in the first instance is likely to be dominated by the face and mind of the primary caregiver. When infants gaze into their parents' eyes, they are communicating and seeking not only feelings, but also information about the mind of the parent, the self and the outside world. The child's emerging ability to think about his or her own mind and the minds of others has come to be called *reflective function*.

> 'Reflective function enables children to conceive of others' beliefs, feelings, attitudes, desires, hopes, knowledge, imagination, pretence, plans and so on…. Exploring the meaning of the actions of others is crucially linked to the child's ability to label and find meaningful his or her own experience. This may make a critical contribution to affect regulation, impulse control, self-monitoring, and the experience of self-agency.'[22]

The experience of the caregiver's mind as offering containment and a secure base over time becomes internalised in the child's mind through a process of *mental representation*, so that, for example, the physical presence of the caregiver becomes less necessary as the child moves through the toddler years. These mental representations form cognitive structures known as internal working models,[23] which define children's expectations and beliefs about self and others and will determine the way in which they enter new situations. Where those expectations are positive, children trust new environments and their own capacity to adapt to them.

Where children have found that their caregivers' mind is not available to them, for example in cases of severe post-natal depression, or where caregivers have unresolved trauma from the past, children do not develop the capacity to make sense of others, to make their own experience meaningful and do not learn to 'mentalise'. This leaves children with eruptions of feelings, thoughts and anxieties that cannot be organised or resolved. This in turn contributes to a poorly developed sense of self. Children who cannot understand that other people have ideas, intentions or emotions that are different from their own and are poor at 'mind-reading' will find it more difficult to co-operate, be empathic and negotiate in day-to-day living with other people. Vigilant maltreated children in particular can anticipate and try to avoid parental anger, but with peers and adults outside the family they tend to see hostile intention even in neutral acts, thus creating the potential for wariness, conflict and impoverished relationships.

In neglectful or maltreating families, negative internal working models of the self and others develop, which makes trusting others who may try to offer good care, such as foster carers or adoptive parents, too risky. Such children have mental representations which are so distinctively distorted that far from being able to accept or welcome appropriate care when it is offered by new carers, they will misinterpret what is happening, reframing it to fit their own expected model.

---

[20] Fonagy and Target 'Attachment and reflective function: Their role in self-organisation' (1997) Development and Psychopathology 9, 679–700 in Fonagy *Attachment and Psychoanalysis* (Other Press, 2001) p 165.

[23] Bowlby (1969) op cit, n 3.

'The individual may so distrust both affect and cognition that even discrepant information may not trigger the mind to re-explore reality. Instead the mind may determine that this too is trickery and deception or that the risk of mistakenly responding as though it were true is too great to be tolerated. In such cases, the representation of reality is like a false, inverted mirror image in which good and bad, true and false are reversed.'[24]

This quotation summarises well the way in which maltreated children are not able to process new information about reality (eg that the loving foster carers are not like previous adults and that perhaps the concept of 'adult' might need to be changed) because when driven by anxiety about survival it is safer to believe that this is just another trick.

Alongside the developing intersubjectivity of infants and caregivers, the child's thinking capacity is also enhanced by the predictable shape of events provided for the young child by the caregiver. The soothing voice, gentle touch, ritual and regularity around such events as feeding, bathing and bedtime provides the child not only with a positive sense of self, but also a cognitive scaffolding, a view of the world as a reliable place that makes sense. The running commentary provided by parents when caring for a child will reduce anxiety and enable the child to have a sense of the pattern of events. As the child acquires language, time – yesterday, this afternoon, after the parental cup of tea, tomorrow, next week – acquires helpfully structured meaning. Again, where caregiving is chaotic and uncertain, where the availability of care and the pattern of events are unpredictable, children may become anxious and unco-operative or anxious and helpless.

The importance of the development of a flexibly thinking, reflective mind that can approach new situations with confidence and adaptive strategies highlights the risks and difficulties for those children who do not have this capacity. This is highly relevant for those who seek to ascertain, understand and take into account the wishes of children. The challenges for professional practice operate at several levels. Problems with children's thinking interact with problems in naming feelings and exercising autonomy. Key here is the fact that a relatively high order of thinking is required when children are asked to offer a view on the big questions before the court (eg adoption or long-term foster care?), when children are invited to share something of what they are thinking about aspects of the options available (eg how much contact? move of school? separation from siblings?) or even when the assessment simply needs to establish how the child makes sense of the fact that they are now in foster or residential care (eg was I taken away, given away, rescued or kidnapped?[25]). Children and young people cannot exercise autonomy without having some understanding of the options. Those whose thinking is at a very concrete level because of age and lack of mentalising experience or who are anxiously confused because of the lack of the experience of a containing mind and cognitive scaffolding find it very difficult, if not impossible, to engage easily with a discussion about hypothetical situations. Given that trained professionals in the family justice system often struggle to hold simultaneously in their minds all the details and ramifications of different options as they weigh the merits of each, it is hardly surprising that children find this well beyond their developing capacities. Additionally for these children, thinking about the risks and benefits of possible futures is not only a very difficult but also a very painful process. Engaging with thinking about feelings and choices in the context of survival needs requires emotional strength as well as cognitive coherence.

However, as with affect and autonomy, the more that psychology teaches us about the complexity of children's thinking, the impact of adversity on young minds and the challenge for children of thinking in the court situation, the more effort needs to be put into using psychological knowledge to help promote children's appropriate participation and to ensure that as accurate a picture as possible of the way children think about their world is available for

---

[24]   Crittenden, 'Attachment and psychopathology' in *Attachment Theory: Social, Developmental and Clinical Perspectives* ed. Goldberg, Muir and Kerr (Analytical Press, 1995) at p 401.

[25]   Fahlberg, *A Child's Journey Through Placement* (BAAF, 1994).

the court. Although Maria in the case example given earlier had limited intelligence as well as a traumatised past, it was nevertheless possible to support her and engage in a debate with her that recognised that she as a person and her ideas were valued and respected.

Belonging

For children facing separation from birth families or moves into different kinds of substitute care, it is important to include in our model a more psychosocial dimension of development, the significance of belonging. Although understanding the quality of close relationships within families is an essential part of listening to children in family proceedings, decisions before the court almost invariably have to deal with options that will potentially reorientate the child in terms of their family membership and their identity. Although 'belonging' may seem easier to make sense of than the complex subtle theorising around expressions of feelings and thought described above, it is not at all straight forward for children to think about or express their ideas and feelings about where they belong currently or would like to belong in the future. The value of family membership is at the heart of family law and yet it becomes a more contested concept when the court is weighing the quality of family membership associated with different biological, legal or procedural ties, as happens regularly when decisions are made about the birth family, adoption or foster care. Such a weighing process, even more than in respect of the quality of relationships, takes place with a lifespan perspective in mind – an even greater challenge for courts and for children and young people participating in decision making.

The power of family membership and its effect on children's thinking helps explain a number of phenomena. Children expressing a wish to remain with a neglectful or abusive caregiver, for example, can be explained in terms of the psychology of trauma and insecure attachment relationships, but for children in middle childhood and adolescence, there is also a strong sense of both the familiar culture, norms and values of *their* family and the cultural norm of living with your *'real'* family in a society in which family remains our primary identity. Family is often linked to a number of other identities, such as ethnicity, religion, school and community, but all of these areas of belonging may also be affected by decisions in family proceedings.

Allan[26] suggests that a useful way of understanding kinship ties in families is to think in terms of 'diffuse enduring solidarity'. Solidarity, he says, is reflected in the persistence of 'obligations, rights, privileges and responsibilities' across the life-span. Although this theory is developed in relation to birth families and kinship networks, fostered children[27] and adopted children[28] can also articulate vividly the meaning of this sense of solidarity and family membership as it affects them in families with no biological ties. Adopted children have legal ties which support this sense of family, but many adults who grew up in foster care will still say of their foster parents, 'They are my real parents. I don't care what anyone says!'[29]. Long-term foster carers and adoptive parents reciprocate by talking about their children as being definitely 'part of the family'.[30] Outcomes for fostered and adopted adults demonstrate the power and importance of family membership across the lifespan. This quotation is from a twenty-nine year old man, who is talking about how he would describe his relationship with his foster mother, with whom he was placed at the age of four.

'Mother and son. She looked at me as her son and I looked at her as my mum sort of thing. Even though when you're 18 you officially leave care but we kept in touch. We go round there for dinner, she comes round here. She classes my children as her grandchildren.'

---

[26] Allan, op cit, n 6.
[27] Beek and Schofield, op cit, n 8.
[28] Thomas and Beckford with Lowe and Murch, *Adopted Children Speaking* (BAAF, 1999).
[29] Schofield, 2003, op cit, n 2.
[30] Beek and Schofield, 'Foster carers perspectives on permanence: a focus group study' (2002) 26:(2) *Adoption and Fostering* 14–27; Howe, *Adopters on Adoption* (BAAF, 1996).

Increasingly as we look to foster care to provide permanence and as adoption becomes more likely to include some form of contact, looked after children's family membership will be in multiple families, often offering different kinds of meanings in children's lives. Although this will always represent a challenge, it appears from research to be entirely possible to have ties and resources of different kinds within a number of 'families' in adult life, including former residential care placements. Adults from successful placements are most likely to take their primary membership, rituals, norms, values and aspirations from their adoptive or long-term foster family, but may still appreciate receiving a 'congratulations on the new baby' card from the birth family, a former foster carer, a key residential worker or a social worker.[31] In very great contrast, however, as the leaving care literature suggests, care pathways that do not provide any family for young people to belong to and turn to as of right in adult life leave vulnerable young people socially dislocated and very much adrift.[32]

In court proceedings where wishes and feelings about family membership may need to be taken into account, children are often being invited to comment on both current families and options which are based on hypothetical family situations – whether in a changed birth family situation or in a substitute family that may yet to be located. For reasons described above, it is rarely easy for a child to evaluate mixed feelings and uncertain thoughts about current or hypothetical future family ties. In many ways it is easier to talk about feelings, about loving or falling out with or worrying about family members, than it is for the child to capture the essence of what it means to belong, to feel part of the close family, the extended family, the friendship group, the neighbourhood, the area of the country. As children are increasingly moved to different parts of the country for fostering (partly as a result of the rise of the independent fostering sector) and adoption (partly as a result of the Adoption Register) the impact of dislocation – even at the level of just 'talking funny' – may need to be thought about by the child if they are to contribute in an informed way to decision making.

As with other aspects of the model, conversations with children and young people about belonging during proceedings provide an opportunity not only to gather evidence for the court, but to help the child think about and evaluate aspects of their family memberships as part of the process of refining their sense of self. Although evidence before courts regularly refers to 'roots and identity' it seems that 'belonging' is an area of developmental health and risk that needs to be more subtly defined and understood.

Conclusion: The Developing Self

These different aspects of children's development are inevitably linked in myriad ways. Feeling loved and lovable and knowing that caregivers are predictable and available, for example, liberates the child's capacity for autonomy and increases the likelihood of a sense of family membership. This in turn can bind the family together in ways that promote emotional commitment. This is a psychosocial model in which inner and outer worlds also interact, so that the experiences of school and peer groups will be both affecting and being affected by the child's capacity to think and manage affect.

The developmental goal of resilience[33] is built from these same building blocks – regulating emotion, self-esteem, autonomy, self-efficacy, reflective function and, it is possible to argue, identity and a sense of belonging – which fortify the child in times of stress. Children are not born resilient, although genetic and prenatal environment factors can help or hinder the process of successful adaptation in circumstances of adversity. Environments will be interacting with these different factors in the child.

Listening to children as part of this decision making process entails taking account of this

---

[31]　Examples from stories provided in Schofield, 2003, op cit, n 2.

[32]　Biehal, Clayden, Stein and Wade *Moving on: Young People and Leaving Care Schemes* (HMSO 1995); in Schofield, 2003, op cit, n 2.

[33]　Fonagy, Steele, Steele, Higgitt and Target, op cit, n 5.

rich developmental picture and being aware of the challenges and subtleties of establishing what children 'really' think or feel. Children themselves will not be aware of or be keeping this complex picture in mind, but professionals in the family justice system need to be doing so on their behalf. The process of listening, making sense of and taking into account the wishes and feelings of children needs to arise from a full assessment, which includes the broader task of understanding how the world looks through the child's eyes, from infancy to adolescence.

PLENARY TWO

PLENARY DISCUSSIONS

Panel: Dr Jonathan Green, Dr Miriam Steele, Dr Gillian Schofield

The panel was asked to comment on the inter-relationship between attachment status and personality disorder in adults, and infant attachment status and personality disorder.

Dr Green advocated a separate approach to attachment status and personality. He said that treating them as if they were independent is a starting point. Adults with personality disfunction do have difficulties in parenting. There are links between parenting style and both personality and attachment status. He said that he thought that they were not completely co-terminus, but that they were partly co-terminus. Looking at attachment representation, the inner understanding towards attachment, is a particular way of understanding the way adults think. Personality is much broader then that, they are bound to overlap but are not the same thing. He reiterated that he was suggesting that they are worth looking at independently. He said that the same is true of infancy. We know that way they look at attachment does have an inter-relation with other aspects of functioning, but, for example, childhood temperament seems not to relate to attachment, they seem to be different. What we know about attachment is that it does have widespread ramifications.

Dr Steele said that borderline personality disorder leads to mixed attachment classifications. There is an inter-relation between personality and attachment status, for example a teenager suffering from anorexia commonly has a dismissing attachment status, whereas a bulimic will have a preoccupied status.

The panel was asked what can be done with methodologies in cases of children in isolation, particularly refugee children who are alone?

Dr Green said that it was a real challenge for us to try to understand a child's mental state when they come from such a different context. Care must be taken not to jump to conclusions too quickly.

Dr Steele said that just because a child is alone in this country, it does not mean that the quality of parenting before they left their country of origin would have no impact on how they are now. She said that research carried out with children who had survived the Holocaust showed that children who had experienced difficult relationships beforehand, went on to experience difficulties, more so than those who had experienced good relationships.

The panel was asked about the fact that in many private law cases, decisions must be made on the basis of a single CAFCASS report and such perceptions as parents feed in. In view of the emphasis on the context of assessments which emerged from the papers, there is a concern that we may have to rely on assessments which are very incomplete.

Dr Schofield said that any decision based on a single observation of contact is very dangerous. A single observation is very difficult to interpret. Much depends on the CAFCASS officer and the child. One of the tricky things is whether a single encounter can be relied on, especially when a child says something contradictory to what they have said in the past. She said that some sort of balance must be struck between a single snap shot and endless interviews with a child who does not want to make a decision.

Dr Green said that there had been some research carried out about children who were caught up in divorce proceedings, particularly in relation to young pre-school children. One of the things the research shows is how sophisticated children's thinking is and how well they understand the role of different people: people who are safe to talk to and people who are not. So it is important to ask who the child will be able to trust. Another important factor is the child's understanding about what is going to be said.

The panel was asked whether the fact that the instruction of experts who are instructed to assess primary care rarely extends to the assessment of alternatives (eg foster carers, aunts, grandparents) was something which lessens the validity of the assessment.

The President said that it does worry her if the judge is not getting the same sort of information about each of the prospective carers. If, for example, an aunt turns up at the last moment, the question of delay must be considered, but if she is a serious contender then she should be assessed. She said that she had got experts to see someone at very short notice, and that it was very unsatisfactory to have a situation where the expert does not see all of the prospective carers. They ought to be identified extremely early and the expert ought to assess everyone.

Dr Green spoke of the position of evidence from social workers. He said that there are different forms of expertise, and that we should be used to working with the presumption that we are able to train up professional groups and work with mutual respect for the information they can bring. There should not be an assumption that an expert needs to do everything.

The panel was asked how much weight a judge should put on diagnostic techniques.

Dr Steele said that techniques like the story stem should never be the only assessment, there must be a much more comprehensive assessment, including for example, assessment by the child's teacher and social worker. Nevertheless, the story stem technique has been used thousands of times and the databases are structured so that they can be reliable. It is possible to compare one child's responses to those of all those other children, you cannot do that if you wait until the child comes up with information spontaneously. She said in relation to sexual abuse, it is almost impossible for a child to express that using the story stem technique if they have not experienced it.

Dr David Jones raised two points which had arisen in his group discussions.

We should be encouraging all who work in the family justice system to be critical consumers of the research and literature. That means knowing that we do not have all the evidence about which schema to use in different circumstances, we do not have a gold standard story stem. It is very powerful, but we must be careful.

There is a general problem about care with converting research paradigms to clinical practice. If we are using story stems we must use all the other information too, and tell the court about the positive *and* the negative.

Dr Green said that the story stem technique gives us something to hold on to, but warned that we must resist the temptation to hold on too hard. It is very valuable but the more evidence there is from different sources and the more convergent the evidence is, the better chance there is of being right.

Dr Schofield emphasised that we should look at way the person using the story stem has been trained to use it.

Professor June Thoburn said that her group had raised the issue of how messages from the research carried out by Dr Steele could be brought into the court arena.

Dr Steele said that it is not always the case that a securely attached parent is best for a child. We do know that parents who are unresolved need more support; we should not turn them away from adopting children, but give them more support.

Judge Donald Hamilton asked about attachment therapy and whether it needs to be the subject of a wide warning?

All the panel members agreed that there had been some alarming developments in respect of so-called 'attachment therapy' and that it was very worrying. Dr Green pointed out, in particular, the fact that some 'attachment therapists' are holding themselves out as offering adoption support. The panel felt that the public ought to be informed of the possible dangers of attachment therapy.

Mr Justice Wall expressed his own concern in relation to attachment therapy and said that he was alarmed to think that there is a school of thought which is out to make money by offering a quick fix for children who suffer poor attachment. He said it seemed to him that often, where children have been to lots of placements, they appear to lose the capacity to form secure attachments. He asked the members of the panel whether they thought that the earlier one is able to place a child the better the prospects of re-forming attachments and asked how much damage was done by the process of care proceedings which may last 6–9 months.

Dr Schofield said that all of the evidence indicates that the younger the child is, the more successful the placement is. However, her research about older children in foster care is that some children of 15 to 17 can and will take advantage of late opportunities. She said that older children should have the opportunity of a family, even in their teenage years. She has seen children of 15 or 16 who have had horrendous childhoods and then go into a foster family and 10 years later that family provides them a real anchor in adult life. Children can be extremely resilient and the panel felt that we should be promoting resilience as part of the court process.

Dr Green expressed his view that we should avoid the tendency to treat the group of children who go into alternative care as a whole. They are very diverse and we do need more understanding about why some are more at risk and do not seem to develop new relationships.

Dr Jones said that his group had raised the issue of the 'overegging' of the use of the term attachment. He said that lawyers sometimes use the term too liberally and refer to all warm relationships as attachment. Experts have a responsibility if they are asked to do something that is not framed in a reasonable way to send it back and ask for more specific instructions.

PLENARY THREE

COMMUNICATING WITH CHILDREN

Dr David Jones
Consultant Child Psychiatrist, Park Hospital for Children

Summary of paper

Dr David Jones explained that his paper is a distillation of his book about communicating with vulnerable children, and he invited the conference to consider three main issues:

(1) How the material contained in his paper and his book can be of use and value to the different professional groups involved in communicating with children, and what may need emphasising for particular groups.

(2) The issue of communicating verbally in relation to non-verbal communication. We communicate emotions particularly, but a good deal else, through non-verbal means. Furthermore, verbal communication involves inflection, pause, eye fixation etc, and many of those factors can be lost in transcripts of words. He invited the conference to consider how best to describe and convey non-verbal communication, bearing in mind that there must be transparency of the distinction between observations and opinion or interpretation of the meaning of those observations.

(3) Making sense. Dr Jones said that it was of interest to find out how each of us makes sense of what is in front of us and how we convey that to another group. He asked delegates to discuss the question of what each group needs from the other and how communication between professional groups could be improved. Experience has shown that multi-disciplinary teams work best if people understand and celebrate the differences between the different professions.

Lastly, Dr Jones explained that the whole notion of getting to know what a child really means, thinks, and wants to say is a process of finding out what is behind the mask. However, behind the mask there may be lots of contrasting views pointing in different directions; there may be a mass of disorganisation and not one single view. He warned that any over-simplification of that process may impede our efforts to communicate.

Introduction

The ability to communicate with children and young people is a key skill for front line practitioners who work with this age group. Teachers, social workers with children and families, youth workers, nurses, health visitors, child and adolescent mental health professionals communicate with children each day. Most of these conversations are either general in nature or task specific. This publication is mainly concerned with the skills required for communicating with children and young people about difficult subjects.

Difficult subjects may prove a challenge for adults, children or for both. Sometimes the professionals' work is centrally concerned with communicating with children about very difficult issues.

For example, social workers working in assessment teams may often be in the position of doing direct work with children, undertaking initial or in-depth assessments (DoH et al, 2000).

For other professionals, difficult or challenging subjects arise less frequently and may not be a core aspect of their work, eg teachers who occasionally need to communicate with a child presenting with personal difficulty.

Some examples of subjects which are *difficult or challenging*

Listening and/or obtaining information from a child:

- Situations which involve children's personal experience of adverse events (child abuse and neglect);
- Where children are knowledgeable about or witness to significant violence (eg, inter-parental violence, but also other forms of family violence, including being witness to murder);
- Children's views, wishes and feelings concerning contact and residence;
- A child's capacity to consent to treatment.

Telling

- Life-threatening illness, affecting self, or a loved one. Where children have knowledge or may require to have knowledge about illness in another family member. Physical or life threatening illness within themselves;
- Secret or shameful occurrences, eg, past abuse, HIV/AIDS;
- Where a parent has been involved in serious crime;
- Knowledge about parentage (eg genetic origins, in relation to the new reproductive technologies; or knowledge about genetic origins derived from DNA examination). This is particularly relevant where one carer is a non-genetic parent, and where the child may reasonably expect that s/he is a genetic parent.

Why communicate with children at all?

One reason is that studies have found that children want to. If lines of communication are not opened up with children in similar circumstances to those listed above, then, later on, children wish that they could have and that somebody would have communicated with them earlier.

Secondly, it can be argued that children have a right to know about or understand certain matters that involve them, such as their parentage.

Thirdly, sometimes it is necessary to enquire about the child's situation where there is a possibility that they may be suffering harm and that the child therefore needs safeguarding.

Fourthly, children may need information in order to prevent future distress, harm or disadvantage. Examples include: knowledge about prior abuse or neglect to the self, (eg children who when younger were abused and who need information about what occurred), illness, significant information about self or a loved one which would be harmful if delayed, eg parentage, which may result in lack of trust if withheld.

How this is done is of course all important. There is an obligation on adults, therefore, to provide opportunities for children to communicate, though it is important that children are not coerced.

Communication

The word communication means the act of imparting, transmitting, and receiving information. With respect to communication with children, it refers to the range of activities involved in imparting, sharing, and receiving information between adults and children. It is a two-way process.

Necessary preconditions include being receptive, whether through listening, hearing, or alternative means. Much is communicated non-verbally. Even when words can be found we convey added meaning through reliance on non-verbal techniques as well as verbal, eg timing, accompanying gesture, and body language.

For some children other forms of language are preferred, for example, sign or other types of augmentative communication.

What additional areas of knowledge or skill are required?

Some knowledge of the particular area which presents difficulty or a challenge for the child and adult, eg:

- child abuse and neglect;
- inter-parental conflict and domestic violence;
- children's knowledge of death;
- life-threatening illness either in the child or family members;
- the field of divorce, post-divorce conflict;
- contact and residence;
- implications for child and family health of the new reproductive technologies.

To these may be added:

- Sufficient knowledge of developmental psychology, including memory, suggestibility, language development in children;
- Attachment and attachment disorders;
- Mental health needs of looked after children;
- Parental mental health and child welfare.

Further areas in which it can be helpful to understand:

- Aspects of difference and disability in relation to children's communication;
- The law in relation to childhood;
- A systemic understanding of disciplines which work with children and families;
- Psychology of violence and victimology;
- The psychology of disclosure – how children communicate about personal adversity and what factors contribute to delay or sustained silence.

Child abuse and neglect

Overall approach

These are particular points and principles to bear in mind when communicating with children about the possibility of child abuse and neglect.

The approach necessary for communicating with children effectively in this area can be summarised in terms of those qualities most likely to lead to successful communication, though with an accurate and full account obtained, contrasting on the other hand with those qualities likely to lead to a poorer outcome.

Positive qualities

- Listening to and understanding the child;
- Maintaining a non-biased approach;
- Maintaining personal neutrality about any issues raised;
- Managing oneself in relation to potentially distressing material which the child may communicate;
- Adopting the perspective that it is the child or young person who is the expert, not the adult;
- Conveying genuine empathic concern, to a degree that is congruent with the child or young person's situation;
- Using open-ended and non-biased approaches to communication with the child;
- Bearing in mind that if the adult does not ask, it is unlikely that they will be told;
- Allowing children to freely recall their experiences;
- Operating within a context of continuing professional development and critical review of personal practice;
- Plan the best way to record the exchange.

In addition, when undertaking Initial Assessments (Department of Health et al, 2000) the following aspects should also be added:
- Identify the aims of the work, including who has asked for the assessment and what plans have been decided upon, and why;
- Record the exchange, including both its content and duration;
- Clarify any ambiguous information arising from the child or any other adult;
- Report the content of communications afterwards, as appropriate, to any agency or group of professionals, where necessary obtaining consent to do so (Department of Health, 2003).

Qualities to avoid or discourage:

- Maintaining assumptions or biased views may influence the interchange between the child and adult;
- Employing leading questions or other techniques that are prone to error;
- Using coercion or pressurising methods of enquiry.

Consent and confidentiality

It is useful to distinguish between giving consent to communicate with the child, and subsequently sharing information.

Impromptu first responses to children's concerns are not pre-planned, formal interviews but immediate responses to children's presentations. Therefore, consent is either implied, because it is inferred from the circumstances in which the communication occurs, or it is not practicable to obtain because it is necessary at the time to determine whether the child needs safeguarding.

These first responses contrast with communications which are planned in advance, which do raise issues of consent. Generally, it is important to obtain informed consent from children or their parents in relation to any procedures that affect them. Similarly with younger children they should be involved as far as possible and their assent or agreement sought, even if they lack capacity to provide consent.

If there are clear cut concerns about the child's safety then the child should be referred to the appropriate agency (social services or police).

Social workers may need to do initial or core assessments. They should obtain consent from someone with parental responsibility for the child, unless to do so would place the child at risk of harm (however, recommendation 65 of the Victoria Climbié inquiry seeks to lower this threshold).

The child's consent or, if not capable of providing it, their assent should be sought too.

Information sharing

Generally personal information acquired during the course of working with children and families is confidential and one has to take particular care about sensitive information (Department of Health et al, 2003). However, information may need to be shared either with consent, or sometimes without the consent of either the person who has proved the information (a child), and/or the person about whom the information relates. Normally these exceptions to confidentiality involve circumstances where information is necessary to disclose on a 'need to know' basis so that the child's welfare may be protected. This has to be proportional to the nature of the information itself and potential harm to the child involved. The Department of Health document 'What to do if you are worried that a child is being abused' (DoH et al, 2003) outlines the legal constraints on the disclosure of confidential information, summarising the common law duty of confidence, the Human Rights Act 1998, and the Data Protection Act 1998. Broadly, professionals are not prevented by law from sharing information if, either consent is given or, the public interest in safeguarding the child's welfare overrides the need to keep the information confidential, or, lastly, if disclosure is required under a Court order or other legal obligation.

First responses to children's concerns expressed to front line practitioners

Any professional working with children can be faced with a situation where either a child wants to communicate, or the professional senses the need to respond to a child. Often the child initiates these situations unexpectedly, during the context of everyday services provided for children, such as education, primary health care, social and health care.

All practitioners working with children should make themselves available to respond to concerns expressed by children and young people. These professionals are often in a position of trust vis-à-vis children and therefore the ones to whom the child or young person turns in their search for a listening ear, or for help. It is vitally important from the child's perspective that the professionals convey verbally and non-verbally that they can listen and respond to the child or young person. At the same time it is important for the professional to avoid overpowering or pressurising the child.

It can be difficult to decide whether the child should be seen on their own. Sometimes children find the presence of other children inhibiting, or may find settings such as a head teacher's office one which is associated with discipline. Therefore practitioners such as teachers may need to find an opportunity to communicate with a child away from the main class group.

Paediatricians or general practitioners normally see children with their parents. Sometimes raising the issue of the child's possible reluctance with a parent and child together can allow a parent to withdraw temporarily if the child appears to want to communicate without the parent present. At other times it may be possible to talk with a child directly, even though the parent is, perhaps, to one side or out of the child's direct line of vision.

The professional choice of approach taken would depend on how the concern has been raised. Possibilities include something that the child has just said, physical disease or findings, or a change in the child's behaviour or emotional state.

A child's word

In these circumstances the practitioner can invite the child to elaborate on the matter that has just caused the concern. An alternative would be to see whether the child would prefer to talk to a colleague. For example, in a school this might mean talking to a designated teacher or one with whom it is known that the child has a positive relationship.

The professionals' approach should be open ended and consist of an invitation to talk if the child so wishes. For example, children can be asked to say why they are concerned about a particular place or person (if they have just told the teacher about such a concern).

Similarly, a child might be asked to say a bit more about an expressed concern or worry (for example, where a child is reluctant to be collected by a particular adult). In these situations specific questions are avoided and the question is phrased in an open-ended way, without conveying either verbal or non-verbal pre-supposition about harm.

Physical disease or findings

A doctor or health visitor can ask how a child became sore or bruised, or marked in a particular part of their body, while examining them. A similar approach can be used when a child has a sexually transmitted disease, or one which is frequently common but not always transmitted through direct sexual contact.

Behavioural or emotional change

Ask more about the child's sadness or apparent anxiety. Or, ask about behaviour change, especially that involving violence or sexualised behaviour towards another.

General considerations

It can be helpful to practice potential responses to situations such as those above, discussing these with colleagues or child protection advisors. Discussion with colleagues from other disciplines in multi-disciplinary training events can also prove useful.

First responses are very important because suggestive practice by professionals can jeopardise future responses to the child's situation. By contrast good initial practice lays the foundation for future work and helps establish the child's trust in professionals.

The professional's role in first responses is simply to listen, note the conversation as soon as possible afterwards, and then respond appropriately. The professional should not attempt to investigate the situation independently if concerned about the child's safety, but instead arrange referral to a designated child protection service for further action.

Recording communications

It is important to record conversations which have raised suspicion about possible harm having occurred, just as soon as possible. The professional needs to record not only the full sequence but also the events which preceded the conversation, as well as subsequent events. Practitioners should also note non-verbal elements of communication as well as verbal ones, and include, as far as possible, everything they can recall about what they said as well as the words of the child. Normally these impromptu communications are not planned and therefore only rough jottings would be likely to be made during or immediately after. These jottings should be kept along with any fuller record which should be completed as soon as possible after the event. These records become especially important in situations that progress to formal assessment procedures.

What happens next

The possibilities range from concerns about the child being allayed through to a revelation that the child's safety is seriously compromised. For other children the situation remains unclear, notwithstanding the professionals' best efforts. In these latter circumstances it is important to keep a line of communication open with the child, while perhaps also arranging for other services to help respond to any needs for extra help that the child may have.

The professional will have to decide whether local child protection procedures need to be set in motion through sharing information with social services departments. If in doubt, advice can be sought either through colleagues or through channels set out in local child protection procedures. Many professional concerns are allayed through these first responses, or alternatively a much lower level of need is identified, rendering formal child protection procedures unnecessary,

Initial assessments

These are undertaken by social workers or sometimes by other professionals when a component of their first assessment includes initial enquiry about the possibility that the child may have suffered harm.

Initially decisions need to be made about who to see, and in what order. The child's age is likely to affect this decision. Teenagers are likely to seek greater independence in the arrangements, compared with younger children who will probably want to be seen nearby, or even with their parent. Younger children may need more than one session in order to establish trust with an unknown professional from outside their family if they are to communicate effectively. Similarly disabled children are likely to expect professional adults to do things for and to them and may therefore require more extensive preparation to enable them to communicate their concerns freely without adult directional prompting. Race and cultural expectations may also affect decision making. Specialist help may be required in order to communicate effectively.

The starting points, under 'First Responses', can be developed further in initial assessments, by elaborating on initial comments made by children, exploring reasons for physical findings or changes in behavioural or emotional state.

Other approaches to initial assessment include the following.

Using general opportunities

There are likely to be many opportunities to raise the possibility of adverse experiences. For example, assessments often include general discussion about sleeping routines and arrangements, and with older children, issues of privacy and discussions about their living space. These provide opportunities for concerns to be expanded upon, if children wish. Similarly, discussions concerning discipline often bring out accounts of excessive punishment as well as routine disciplines. Further, discussion about family structure and relationships are an integral part of specialist assessments. This allows for questions about who the child likes to spend time with, and those with whom they do not. Similarly, to whom the child is close and vice-versa. Answers to these questions can be followed up with open-ended enquiry to further explore the basis for these preferences.

In general a useful approach is to pair positive experiences with potentially negative ones. Thus, discussions might be initiated about who the child is close to and then alternatively to whom they do not feel so close; or 'the best thing that has happened to you', followed by 'the worst thing that has happened to you'. Similarly, the person 'you like being with' versus the person 'you don't like being with'.

Exploratory questions

Below are suggestions for exploratory questions, which could be adapted for different aged children. They are intended to supplement the approaches already outlined. As a general principle, if questions such as these are used, it is important that if the child responds in the affirmative, subsequent questions should consist of open-ended prompts and invitations to describe any adverse experiences in more detail. In this way the possible objections to exploratory questions are addressed, but at the same time the child is given the opportunity to raise their experiences with the interviewer, if they wish to.

Exploratory questions

Has anybody done anything to you, which upset you? *[await response]*; or made you unhappy?

Has any person hurt you? *[await answer]* or touched you in a way that you didn't like?

Or touched you in a sexual way, or in a way that you didn't like?

A circular, permission giving question can be useful in some circumstances, eg:

Some children talk about being upset or hurt in some way – has anything like this happened to you? *[In circumstances where the possibility of victimisation or adversity seems quite strong, yet the child appears to be inhibited]*.

Responding to concerns raised unexpectedly

Sometimes concern about maltreatment arises unexpectedly during the course of an assessment. The child should not be prevented from communicating, but equally, the professional should be careful not to adopt an investigating role, deferring to mandated agencies for this purpose. The child should be allowed to finish raising whatever issues they wish to and then an opportunity found to refer on to relevant professionals.

Adult suspicion and vulnerable children

Adults may be concerned about a child, even though the child in question has expressed no concerns him/herself. The practitioner may be able to capitalise on general situations, but exploratory questions may also be needed in order to initiate communication about possible adversity. It is important to maintain a balance between leading the child and failing to provide the child with an opportunity for communication. Provided exploratory questions are limited to one or two, and tentatively framed, they are unlikely to lead to a false account.

At the end of an initial assessment the practitioner should prepare the child for what might happen next, whether no further action, provision of services, review later, or progression to a more in-depth assessment or even an investigative interview (*Achieving Best Evidence*, Home Office et al, 2002).

A full record should be made, together with any observations about the child's non-verbal communications.

In-depth interviews with children

In-depth interviews are undertaken by social workers or others as part of core assessments. Other professionals may undertake in-depth interviews too, when requested to in order to assist social services, or if requested to undertake an assessment in Family Proceedings.

Sometimes some elements of an in-depth interview are required when adversity or possible maltreatment emerges in response to open ended enquiry, often unexpectedly during a first assessment. Practitioners should follow the guidance set out in Achieving Best Evidence (Home Office et al, 2002), where a crime is thought to have been committed.

Planning

Interviews such as these require advance planning in order to establish the main purpose, specific objectives, and to identify issues particular to this child and family. Specific objectives might include; the child's psychological condition, or to understand the child's views, wishes, and feelings about particular persons or contact arrangements.

Planning should also cover the following:

- A review of existing information;
- The specific aims and objectives of the session;
- Children's and parents' rights particularly with respect to consent and confidentiality;
- Whom to interview;
- Who would undertake the assessment?
- The approach to the child and introductions;
- Collecting information;
- Recording;
- The site for the interview;
- Resources (with respect to age, special needs, impairments or disabilities);
- What time scale is anticipated;
- Analysis of any information obtained and feed back to family and other professionals.

Preparation

The child may need preparation, for example to allay or address excessive fearfulness, to attend to special needs or impairments, or to respond to an older child's concerns about confidentiality and the consequence of disclosing their experiences. Other children with significant mental health problems or where children are very young may also need special preparatory time. Sometimes carers require preparation too.

A schema for undertaking in-depth interviews

1. Introductory, rapport gaining phase;
2. Enquiry into suspected adverse experiences;
3. Further exploration;
4. Closure.

Rapport gaining phase

The main aims of this phase of the interview are to establish a working relationship with the child, to engage their interest in the session, and at the same time to place the child or young person at ease. If a preparatory session has not occurred previously it would be necessary to deal with some of these items in this phase of the main interview. Even if there has been a successful preparatory session, the interviewer can use this phase of the interview to talk about a neutral matter in order to practise the ground rules of the interview which will follow. That is, the central ethos of an in-depth interview is that the child is the expert, whereas the adult is not. Hence, to choose a neutral subject, which the child has knowledge of, but the interviewer does not, provides an excellent opportunity for practising the style of the session which follows.

Possible approaches might be to discover how the child travelled to the interview, particular interests, or activities recently participated in.

The practitioner generally avoids the areas of concern which led to the interview unless the child or young person appears to find this irritating and wants to progress more rapidly.

It may be necessary for the practitioner to explain who they are, if this has not been done at a preparatory stage. Such introductions should be brief and avoid specific reference to matters of concern. It is perhaps best to avoid identifying oneself as someone who protects children or ensures they are safe because this establishes a particular agenda for the session. Equally, it would be inappropriate for the practitioner to educate the child about correct words for parts of the body, or personal safety issues, or to pass an opinion on what adults should or should not do.

Once rapport has been established, the interviewer's aim is to encourage the child to freely recall their memories and perceptions of adverse experiences. The aim is to do this without introducing or suggesting any version of events that emanates from the practitioner (leading questions). Many children will be aware for the reason for the interview, either because they have previously expressed their concern, or because the broad purpose of the interview has been discussed during a preparation phase. A single open-ended prompt from the practitioner is often sufficient to enable the child to start talking freely about areas of concern. This particularly applies to those children who have disclosed information previously (Sternberg et al, 1997). Some sample questions of open-ended prompts are:

- Do you know why you are here today?
- I want to talk now about why you are here today.
- Tell me the reason you came here today.

Clearly, if children pre-empt the practitioner and launch into an account of their concern, it would not be appropriate to stop or discourage them while they are spontaneously recounting memories. If this happens before there has been a chance to set out the ground rules for the session, these can be returned to at a later stage in the interview, if necessary (Poole and Lamb, 1998).

Sometimes these straightforward approaches do not lead to the child communicating anything. In these circumstances the practitioner may feel there is sufficient concern to justify further exploration, and some means will need to be found to gently explore these further, without introducing any new information. We explore such situations next.

Enquiry into suspected adverse experiences

There are circumstances when practitioners decide there is sufficient concern to talk to the child about possible adverse experiences. Examples of this include where it has been decided after a strategy meeting, that the child's situation does not fulfil criteria for a joint investigation (Department of Health et al, 1999, at paras 5.31 and 5.32); or circumstances where there has already been an *Achieving Best Evidence* interview, and where a decision not to press criminal charges has been made, yet where there is sufficient concern to justify further exploration. These are the grey areas, which appear to be quite common in practice. The approach that the practitioner follows depends on what kind of concerns led up to the current assessment. The following possibilities are quite frequently encountered:

- The child may have already spoken to someone about his or her concerns.
- The child may be considered to be at risk of some form of adversity or maltreatment.
- The child may have been found to have a physical condition which raises the possibility they have been exposed to adversity or maltreatment.
- Behavioural change in the child may have led to concerns expressed by parents, teachers, or some other adult.

The following are some suggested phrases for managing the transition and introducing enquiry about adverse experiences. They are organised according to the mode of presentation and the origin of concern. Within each category, the questions are set out first with relatively open enquiries, progressively moving towards more direct questions.

When the child has already disclosed information of concern

'I understand something may have happened *[which upset you, which scared you, which made you sad]*. Please tell me every detail that happened, from the beginning to the very end'.

'I understand that some things have been happening in your family *[or school, another house, etc]*. Tell me about them'.

'I have spoken with *[your mum, your teacher, mummy]* and it sounds as though a lot of things have been happening in your *[family/school/etc]*. Tell me about that'.

'Your *[mum]* said she had talked with you – about some things that had upset you. Tell me about that'.

Adult suspicion about a place or person

'Tell me about *[place/person/time of incident causing concern]*'.

'Tell me who looks after you when your mum goes out. *[Pause]* What things do you like to do with *[name of baby-sitter/childminder]*…anything that you don't like when X comes to your house / looks after you?'

'I've been talking to *[your mum]* and she told me she was worried about you *[at place or time of witnessed incident]*. Tell me everything about what happened'.

'*[Your mum]* told me that you *[don't like it/get upset]* when Uncle John comes to stay at your house. Tell me about that'.

At risk of harm

First, introduce general enquiry about the situation in which the child is considered to be at risk. For example, initiate discussions about school when the concern relates to bullying, punishment for wrong doing where the concern is possibly about physical abuse in the home, family relationships or household arrangements, likes and dislikes where the concern is about possible sexual maltreatment within the household.

In other circumstances a child may have described some adverse circumstances and the practitioner is concerned about other possible forms of adversity:

'You've told me that *[summary of adverse events already disclosed, such as witnessing interparental violence, being bullied, and experiencing physical or sexual abuse]*. Has anyone *[hurt, upset, or harmed]* you in any other way?'

Or, 'has anybody done anything else to you that you didn't think was right'?

Or, 'did anything else happen to you at *[place or time of already disclosed incident]*.

Or, 'Did any other person hurt you'?

'Your *[brother/name of different child about whom there is concern]* has told me about some things that happened to him. Tell me what you know about that'.

Then, after pause, 'and she *[your mum]* was worried about you'.

Or, 'did anyone do something to you that you didn't think was right'?

Or, 'did anything happen to you at *[place or at the time of the abuse disclosed by another child]*'?

Interparental violence

Enquire about home, in general.

Then, 'what's the best thing about being at home?' followed by;

'What's the worst thing about being at home?'

'Your mum told me that she and your dad have been arguing – getting upset. Tell me everything about that'.

'Have there been any times when your mum hit your dad, or dad hit your mum?'

'Your mum told me that she had to go to the hospital/doctor after she had an argument with your dad. Tell me everything about that time'.

Physical disease/change

'I've been talking to Doctor X. She told me that *[brief reference to condition, eg you've had trouble going for a wee-wee, or a sore bottom, or trouble going to the toilet]'* *[in the case of a young child with suspicious repeated urinary tract infections]*

'I've been talking to Doctor X, she told me that you've had to have some *[medicine/tablets/injections]* because of a problem in your bottom *[eg, for a child with unexplained sexually transmitted disease]* – can you tell me everything about that'?

Behaviour change

Enquire directly about the child's symptoms *[anxiety, depression, nightmares]*:

For example, 'I hear you've been worrying a lot. Tell me all about that'.

'I hear you've had a lot of very scary dreams. Tell me what happens when you have them'.

'You've told me you're very *[depressed, worried, upset]* – tell me all about that'.

Enquiry when child displays sexualised behaviour problems:

'Can you think about the time when you were *[playing with/having sex with – repeat essence of presentation of sexualised behaviour]* like that with Fred? – Tell me everything about that'.

Followed by: 'Have there been any other times when things like that have happened?'

Or, 'has anybody done things like that with you'?

Specifically concerning aggressive behaviour:

'I want to talk with you now about *[aggressive episode]*. Tell me everything about that time.'

Followed by, 'have there been other times when things like that have happened?'

'Do you know why that *[aggressive episode]* happened?'
'Have there been any things that have been upsetting you?'
'Has anybody done things like that to you?'

Specific questions following deliberate self-harm:

'Do you know why that happened?'
'Have any things been upsetting you?'

Follow this with general enquiry about school, friends, family members, for example:

'Sometimes young people *[hurt themselves, take tablets]* if they have something very upsetting which they have seen, or has happened to them and they don't know how to talk about it' – *[Pause]* – 'has anything like that happened to you?'

Then, direct questions about possibility of maltreatment (see further approaches, below)

Further approaches for raising issues of concern

If the child says 'yes' to any direct questions then the next one should be along the lines of 'tell me a bit more about that', or, 'I think I understand, but just help me by telling me a bit more about that'.

Sometimes further sessions may be required. Providing the child is appropriately prepared and anxieties are contained, repeated interviews, per se, do not lead to inaccurate accounts. However, if interviews are conducted inappropriately and a pre-determined 'answer' relentlessly sought, erroneous accounts can emerge. A properly conducted repeat interview, with due attention to what happens between sessions, is better than attempting to prise an account from a child in one session.

Sometimes more direct, focused questions will be appropriate because there are other strong indications that a child has been harmed. Examples include:

About place and time

'Has anything happened to you at [*place or time of alleged incident*]'?
'Did anything happen to you at [*place, or actual time of abuse disclosed by another child*]'.

About physical assault

'Has anyone hurt you or hit you'… [*Pause*]. 'Either another young person, or an adult?'

About domestic violence

'Have there been any times when your mum hit your dad, or dad hit mum?'
'Have you heard your mum and dad fighting?'
'Have you seen your mum hurt your dad…? [*Pause*] or your dad hurt your mum?'
'Your mum told me that she had to go to the hospital/doctor after she had an argument with your dad. Tell me everything about that time'.

About bullying

'Have you been hit or hurt by another child, either at school or on the way to and from school?'
'Have you been hurt in a sexual way by another child?' (*For an older child*)

About possible sexual assault

'Has anyone touched you on your body in ways that you didn't like'?
'Your mum said that you had some worries… about being touched on private parts of your body – tell me about that'.
'Has anyone touched the private parts of your body, and made you feel uncomfortable?'
'Did anyone, even a grown up who you are close to, ever touch the private parts of your body'?
'I talk to a lot of children, and sometimes to children who have been touched on private parts of their body – it can help to talk about things like that. Has anything like that every happened to you?'
'Some children are touched on private parts of their body, sometimes by people they know very well. It can help to talk about things like that. Has anything like that ever happened to you?'

These latter two involve permission-giving statements, initially, but end with a direct question. Questions of this kind are clearly potentially suggestive and would only be of value therefore if suspicion of adversity was high, and the nature of the concern being assessed was severe.

Further exploration

The direction at this stage would depend upon whether professional concerns have been allayed by the sessions so far, or uncertainty continues, or alternatively, concerns are confirmed.

If professional concerns are allayed the interview would need to be closed before the child returns home and parent or carer informed of the outcome. Arrangements for follow up should be made and possibly other plans for further assessment of the child's needs.

If concerns about adversity are confirmed by the interview the practitioner will need to consider whether, on the basis of the information revealed the child should have an investigative interview to gather evidence for criminal proceedings, bringing the interview to a close and making the appropriate arrangements. Alternatively, the decision may be made to clarify any details about adverse experiences particularly if any ambiguities remain outstanding (see Jones, 2003, pp 140–142).

In other situations, concerns remain unclear. Although professionally frustrating, it is preferable to close the session, without having pressurised the child, rather than become drawn through professional anxiety into a hectoring or coercive stance. Plans can be made for a review or reassessment in the future, with time to reflect on any possible impediments to successful communications so far. Children, their parents, and other professionals would probably need advice as to how to handle any interim phase (Jones, 2003, pp 139–140 and Chapter 13).

Closing the interview

This is a very important part of an in-depth session. It serves to orientate the child to the next steps and also to recognise and vindicate the child's communication and, where appropriate, expression of emotion. The practitioner should convey appreciation and empathy for the child's situation. Congratulation, personal perspectives of the professional, or promises which cannot be delivered are all inappropriate. The child should be asked if there is anything which they want to know or raise. Contact numbers for future help are important, especially for older children. Some children want to know about what information will be shared.

The child's communications need to be set in the context of their overall needs and welfare status.

References

Department of Health et al, 2000. *Assessment Framework*. London: TSO.

Department of Health et al, 2003. *What to do if you are worried that a child is being abused. Summary*. London: DoH Publications.

Jones DPH, 2003. *Communicating with vulnerable children: A guide for practitioners*. London: Gaskell.

MAKING SENSE OF WHAT CHILDREN SAY: CONTRIBUTIONS FROM DEVELOPMENTAL PSYCHOLOGY

Dr Jan Aldridge
Clinical Child Psychologist,
University of Leeds

Summary of paper

Children are not inferior or lesser adults and, although there are qualitative differences in the cognitive processes of children and adults, children do have considerable competencies: this was the main point made by Dr Jan Aldridge in the introduction to her paper. Dr Aldridge emphasised the need for professionals to move away from the false dichotomy between 'foolish child' and 'wise adult' and to consider the extensive empirical research which has demonstrated that the presumed gulf between the witness abilities of children and adults has been seriously exaggerated.

Dr Aldridge's paper examines the contribution of developmental psychology to communication with children in the context of language, attention, memory and suggestibility. In her introduction to her paper she focused on examples from one area, specifically language, giving examples from the structure of language, the use of 'opaque' words, sources of misunderstanding, and concepts of time and temporal terms:

(1) Structure

Adults' speech structures can pose difficulties for children. Questions to children should be simply phrased, active-voice sentences with few modifying verbs. Dr Aldridge gave an example of a barrister who asked a child, 'Do you say you are telling the truth, or do you say you are not?' which elicited the response, 'Yes.' Sometimes structures that pose difficulties for children are less obvious. An example of such an apparently simple structure that causes problems for young children is the tag question (For example, 'He went into house then, didn't he?) This is a common way of formulating a question, but young children do not fully appreciate it as a question form which can be challenged, rather regarding it as a statement of fact from the adult to be accepted.

(2) Words

Words are not always used in the same way by adults and children. They do not always have the same shared meaning. In addition a commonly used word which can seem simple to an adult can be nevertheless be opaque to a child. Dr Aldridge gave the example of the word 'any' – as in 'Did anything else happen?' An adult would think its meaning is obvious; however to a child its meaning can be quite opaque.

(3) Sources of misunderstanding

Words may have different meanings to different children. One must be careful about making assumptions, for example abusers will often deliberately distort their use of language or talk to a familiar child in a shared code that seems innocent to outsiders. Professionals must make sure that they share the child's understanding of the words. Children can both over-extend and under-extend the meaning of words. This means that they can use words in slightly different, but potentially significant, ways from adults.

4) *Concepts of time and temporal terms.*
    Certain concepts which seem straightforward to adults are often not so for children. One such example is time. The placing of events accurately in time is difficult for children. Other concepts, such as speed, can be difficult for both adults and children to report on accurately.

Children's accounts do not always conform to adults' expectations and provide the information that adults consider important. For example, in narrative accounts adults attach significant weight to information about location and date. However pre-school children have difficulty placing events in locations and time, but to them actions are very important and these are matters they are frequently able to remember well and accurately communicate about (often non-verbally). In court a not uncommon strategy is to use discrepancies in children's accounts of what the children regard as minor and peripheral details to discredit their central account. Dr Aldridge illustrated this point with an example from a case involving two sisters, where the five year old was the alleged victim of sexual abuse and the nine year old a witness to the abuse. The five year old said, 'He took my clothes off.' The lawyer summarised with 'So he took all your clothes off and then what happened?' The child did not correct the lawyer. One possible reason for this might have been because children do not find it easy to correct unfamiliar adults in formal settings and in any event she was not given an opportunity to do so because the lawyer went straight after the inaccurate summary to the next question, '...and then what happened?' Another reason, and perhaps why the child did not correct the lawyer was because in her mind the distinction between 'taking clothes off 'and 'all your clothes off' was not a relevant one. The main point to her was that he took her clothes off and that was something that he should not have done. Then the child's sister said, 'I came in and she had no trousers and pants on.' The discrepancy between 'all' the child's clothes being off and just her trousers and pants being off was used against the sisters to undermine their credibility as reliable witnesses.

The role of question type was noted. Questions posed need to be comprehensible and neither leading nor confusing. Dr Aldridge cautioned against bombarding a child with questions, and pointed out the need to allow a child the time and space to answer a difficult or important question. It is important to support a child who is answering a tough question, without intervening too quickly. Dr Aldridge emphasised that the quality of the information we receive from a child interviewee is crucially dependant on the skill of the adult interviewer.

In conclusion she reminded those professionals tasked with interviewing children to be aware also of the impact upon communication of all the other emotional issues which a child may be wrestling with. Communicating with children is not just a cogitative question.

Introduction

In 1984 Margaret Donaldson observed:

> 'Much of the research carried on in the first half of this century seems to have been curiously preoccupied with young children's incapacities.'

At this time I was a fledgling clinical and academic psychologist and this preoccupation puzzled me, especially as in my own research (including my newly completed PhD on the neurodevelopment of 244 six month to five year olds) I was being struck by the capacities of young children (Aldridge, Bidder, Gardner and Grey, 1980; Aldridge and Wallace, 1982; Hanson and Aldridge, 1987).

However, Donaldson was right in her observations and from searches of the published literature it is clear that until the 1980s much research on children's intellectual capacities focused on their deficiencies, limitations and inabilities. This traditional focus contributed to the polar opposition that was at times postulated between the stereotypical nature of adults and children; the adult being portrayed as logical, rational, competent and reliable compared with the child as illogical, irrational, lacking in perceptual and cognitive structures and unreliable. In line with this generally perceived gulf between the behaviour of adults and children was portrayed a similar gulf between adults and children as witnesses.

However, the more recent research over the last twenty years, however, in the field of developmental psychology and the study of cognitive processes, has produced an explosion of empirical findings that have allowed a reappraisal of children's cognitive skills and intellectual strengths. Over the same time period the eye-witness testimony research has abundantly and repeatedly demonstrated that the presumed gulf between the witness abilities of children and adults has been seriously exaggerated.

Wider society, including our judicial system, is increasingly drawing upon and incorporating into knowledge bases this more recent work. I think Judge Pigot would be pleased with this progress, especially as it was only thirteen years ago in 1990, that he noted:

> 'Courts still prefer to rely on the accumulated wisdom of the past and have not absorbed or applied the fruits of modern research into child psychology.'

Current research is clear that children are not inferior or lesser adults. There are qualitative differences in the ways children and adults think and understand. Some of those differences have important implications for better understanding the communications of children.

In this paper examples of the contribution of developmental psychology will be drawn from four broad areas. This will be done by integrating lessons learned from clinical and legal cases with up-to-date research.

1   Language

Some of the significant and potentially confusing differences between children's and adults' use of language will be explored. Examples will include:

- Syntactic structures that pose difficulties for children;
- Words that appear simple to adults but are 'opaque' to children;
- Sources of misunderstandings (for example, in everyday life children will attempt to make sense of questions that are put to them, even apparently unintelligible ones, and answer at least a part of them);
- Concepts of time and temporal terms.

2   Attention

- The development of attention;
- Changes in attentional capacity with age;
- Children's focus on different aspects of events from adults (for example, children are able to report details but they do not conform to adults' expectations of what is salient or interesting); and
- Influence of children's knowledge base on attentional strategies.

3   Memory

- Types of memory;
- Reliability of recall;
- Accuracy and structure of children's reports;
- Inter-interview consistency?

4   Suggestibility

- The effects of suggestion on children's and adults' accounts;
- The influence that suggestive questioning might have on later recall;
- The role of cognitive and social factors.

Finally, the complexity of ascertaining children's wishes and feelings will be discussed and the role of interviewer style and the wider influences on children that can complicate their communications.

Conclusion

As a society we are increasingly questioning our assumptions that our youngest members are always the least able witnesses or the ones who can provide the least. Much is known about children, their cognitions, their behaviour, their memory and how to work with them to maximise the value of their testimony. If this body of knowledge is used effectively then the gains are potentially enormous. However, in order for children to give their best they remain heavily dependent on the adults who interview them.

Summary of comments from the groups

Group A

The group very much supported the David Jones publication and considered it would be of immense value in improving communication with children throughout the disciplines.

Their group discussion considered various action points:

Training

- The group identified a need for members of the judiciary and the Bar, and solicitor advocates to receive training in how to interview and/or question children, with an emphasis on practical training. It was emphasised that there is no substitute for interactive role-play. Skills do not change unless they are practiced.
- It was felt that where children's evidence is given by video, that children should always see the video before being cross-examined.
- It was felt that criminal trials were a particular problem and that training should therefore be particularly directed at criminal practitioners.

CAFCASS Training

Charles Prest and Amanda Finlay offered to make enquiries into the training module for CAFCASS officers. It was felt by the group that it is extremely important to ensure that the training received by CAFCASS reporters will be of the highest quality and that the appropriate expertise is tapped into.

Reporting Interviews with Children

- The group suggested that where interviews are not videoed or audio-taped the following method of reporting should be adopted:
  - There should be two columns on the page, one recording the verbal questions and answers, and the other recording the interviewer's observations of non-verbal communication. The two columns should be linked temporarily so that the relationship between the child's verbal and non-verbal communication is clear. There should be a general convention about what goes into the second column.
  - There should also be a third space where the inferences which the reporter or interviewer draws from the question and answer, and from observations, should be clearly written. Clearly this would only apply in cases in which the interviewer has the expertise to draw those inferences (the need for the third column). It was recognised that it is important to distinguish between observation and inference and to understand that not every interviewer will have the expertise to draw inferences.
  - It was suggested that in some cases, in which videotaping may not be suitable, the use of audio taping could be considered, supplemented by a written note which records the demeanour of the child. This would enable the interviewer to concentrate more on non-verbal communication without needing to worry about taking an exact note of verbal communication at the same time. It was recognised that in some cases this method might not be suitable, because it might be inhibiting and uncomfortable for the child. In all cases the child's consent would have to be obtained.

Group B

The lawyers

- Indicated that it would be most useful particularly where solicitors were working with children where no guardian had yet been allocated but were quick to point out that the book alone is not the answer and we don't become experts simply by reading the book.
- It would however be useful particularly in determining wishes and feelings.
- The book was thus commended but only as a guide – we still need professional and expert assistance and the government must not expect us to use the book instead of the professional help and guidance we need.
- Also extracting information from children is different to obtaining information about their wishes and feelings and explaining the court process to them – we were anxious about the differentiation between the two things. A child's wishes and feeling may be inchoate – it is important that we do not automatically expect them to be.
- Also there must be a message that we don't ignore what the child says when the information has been given – it will stop the child from saying anything if they are consistently ignored.
- Also guidance is important on preparing statements for child – whose language should be used – that of the child but often we see that of the author of the statement.

Social Work Response

- The book is enormously useful but highlights the level of skill needed in communicating with vulnerable children and the need for training, practice and rehearsal. There was concern that social workers do not get enough training.
- The book can not be regarded as a substitute for training and experience but is clearly a resource that a social worker can use.

Experts

- The book is a useful 'aide memoire' but the key for social workers and children's guardians is 'time'. It takes a long time to listen to children in all their complexity. Increasingly work is being done with children by unqualified professionals.
- The key to working with children is trust and independence – the big question is what the person will do with the information the child provides.
- There is concern about information sharing and whether and how the child's consent is obtained. It places experts in a dilemma when asking children questions because they cannot guarantee to the child what one will do with the information obtained – the difficulties of explaining confidentiality (at the outset) to a young child were highlighted.
- The need for core skills when training different disciplines was highlighted.
- However, there was also concern that some research suggests that training doesn't automatically improve some professionals in their communicating skills, or in techniques of Memorandum interviews, whether police or social workers.
- It was felt that we have laboured for too long in the Family Justice System with a Memorandum Interview system designed to deal with the criminal justice system – *Achieving Best Evidence* should be seen as a tool for the Family Justice System.
- The difference between verbal and non-verbal communication was highlighted. A child might say one thing but observance may show that the child actually means another – there is a need to convey both in a report which then becomes a subjective document.
- In the absence of a video recording of the interview a judge is entirely dependant upon what is then subjective reporting.

General discussion

- It was a generally held view that the court system as presently structured meant that too many people were trying to communicate with children within the process – some of them unskilled and untrained.
- There was a plea from the experts that there should be more interdisciplinary planning of assessments at an early stage to avoid if at all possible duplication of interviews and questions.

Group C

- How can good practice and/or training in the field of interviewing children be disseminated to a wider range of disciplines? This particularly in the light of references in the Green paper to the co-location and interdisciplinary working?
- Full implementation of Pigot apart, how can Judges and lawyers be educated to be sensitive to the needs of the child?
- Are there any particular lessons from any other jurisdictions about the way children are interviewed and questioned and/or cross-examined in the forensic context?

Group D

Some of the issues and dilemmas for courts were outlined:
- How to bring the words of the child to the court in a meaningful way.
- Reports which make clear the context within which the child's voice was relayed are the most helpful. Such reports would clarify the relevance and significance of the content and process of the communication with the child. It would be important to know how many times a child had been interviewed.
- The adult who is reporting the child's words and demeanour has a great responsibility. The court will be interested in the reliability and credibility of that adult person, be they lay or professional. If professional, their qualifications, experience and reputation would be considered. Even more important, however, is the quality of the work actually done in the individual case. This would be the central plank on which to ascribe weight.
- The court will place great emphasis on the quality of the detail of the child's words. This will include how the information is gathered and to what extent the report includes direct reference to the child's words.
- The court will place considerable emphasis on the rigour of the report. The quality and specificity of the source material and the degree to which it is properly based on evidence from the child. Needs to be specific and evidence based, and distinguish between observation, the words spoken and, the interpretation made. The voice of the child had to be cogent and compelling to be of value. This led to a discussion about what makes a report about the voice of the child cogent and compelling, from a legal perspective:
- Explanation of the significance of the words.
- Context.
- Too little and too short a report, or observations, were unhelpful.
- The adult who reported the words needed to be assessed with respect to what weight to be ascribed to their report.
- There also needed to be great clarity about non-verbal communication.
- Spontaneous utterances from the child were much more compelling than answers to direct questions etc.
- It was felt that the one interview pressure was essentially a flawed model.
- The language used was very important and the use of jargon was especially eschewed by courts.

- The voice of the child needed to be specifically reported and reports should be very specific and evidence based with clear accounts of the source material used so that courts can evaluate its quality.

Further issues discussed:

- Many of the issues above would be of importance in terms of training and continuing professional development to the CAFCASS reporter.
- All professionals – judiciary, social workers, Guardian, mental health, should have access to information such as David Jones' book, as well as training on communication. This should be part of continuing professional development.
- The group emphasised the importance of reflective practice and the need for the professionals involved in this work to have the opportunity to discuss, with one another, the fine detail and difficulties encountered, together with finding appropriate solutions to these, with peers.
- It was agreed that the area of evaluating children's wishes and feelings was particularly difficult.
- Maintaining an open-minded stance in all work with children. Nowhere does this seem more important than in the context of communicating with and interviewing children.

Group E

- The group emphasised the need for training of judges in the criminal justice system in listening to the voice of the child. (The training course run by the JSB for serious sex cases does not include this, let alone the induction course for new Recorders).
- The need for such training to be included in the basic advocacy training, which is a professional requirement for pupil barristers (plus also for solicitors).
- Reports should start with a chronology or statement of the facts, followed by a distinct opinion interpreting these. The opinion section should include, as appropriate, a range of possible interpretations/opinions, with reasons for preferring the one that is preferred. The group felt that the above was basic but at the same time still needed to be iterated.
- A mechanism for feedback to experts after the Court decision aimed at drawing lessons for professional practice should be found.

Group F

The group thought it important to be clear why we are listening to the child.
- Ascertaining wishes and feelings, or
- for therapeutic purposes, or
- forensic enquiry into what the child can tell us about what has happened.

Important for interviewer to be clear as to what hopes expectations he/she brings to the interview.

Key issue is the first interview.
- Often done by the least qualified.
- Can impact adversely on all further work.

Important needs.
- To allow child time to speak.
- Constantly to check that the child and interviewer understand each other and using language in the same way (for example, three different meanings of 'fence'!).
- To recognise child's different perceptions of speed, time, and distance.

PLENARY FOUR

LISTENING TO AND SAFEGUARDING CHILDREN FROM MIXED HERITAGE BACKGROUNDS

Beverley Prevatt-Goldstein
Director, BECON

Summary of paper

Beverley Prevatt-Goldstein began the introduction to her paper by outlining the challenges she faced in preparing it. There was the challenge of isolating, from the wealth of information available, the most useful for this conference. Another challenge was to specifically address the topic by taking note of language. She emphasised that the clarity of our language is very important. Indeed, the term mixed heritage itself is a challenging one. Did it mean mixture of class or religion? Did it mean mixed ethnicities? If so, did it include mixed white ethnicities or mixed black ones? She concluded that she was probably being asked to discuss mixed 'racial' ethnicities. Despite the mixed racial group being only 1.2% of the population the majority of published literature and research, as well as the national census, refers to mixed 'racial' groups not mixed heritage. It is an important group because children belonging to it can be peculiarly (not necessarily disproportionately) disadvantaged.

She accepted the challenge of focusing on people from black and white parentage but within the context of wider mixed heritage, and mixtures within ethnic groups. She explained that there can be an undue focus on mixed 'racial' children, and felt that it would be helpful to shift the focus onto the wider mixed heritage group, including mixed white ethnicities and mixed black ethnicities.

She considered the use of the terms race and racial, and explained that she uses 'racial' with care and avoids using the term mixed race, as there is one race, the human race, and you cannot mix it.

Ms Prevatt-Goldstein identified four main issues for consideration:

1) Experiencing mixed heritage
We may assume that children who are mixed heritage have access to and experience of more than one heritage, but many who may have the potential for enjoying a mixed heritage are denied it. Sometimes a child's experience of their non-dominant heritages may be limited or even absent. In being sensitive and attuned to the voice of the child, and during the process of re-centering we must listen to the gaps in what the children are telling us, and hear what is not said. Children have a right to have access to all of their heritages and it is necessary to safeguard that right.

2) Valuing mixed heritage
We need to consider the fact that some children may not value some of their own diverse heritage, and it may be necessary to re-centre their experience of their heritages. We may have to take care that we do not pathologize the child who may have learnt from society or from the experience of abuse to undervalue particular heritages. When we re-centre a child's heritages by making space for the most devalued we must remember to do so in a balanced way, and not in a way that detracts from the other heritage(s); it is about combining difference.

3) Accepting identity as process
Ms Prevatt-Goldstein warned of the need to avoid overly focusing on one statement at a particular point

in a child's life. The issue of their heritage is often not problematic but our focus on it can make it a problem. Children achieve their identity in a gradual manner. The process of developing an identity is a continual one, not something that happens at a certain age, it grows and changes, and this can be difficult because court processes have deadlines. The court does not want undue delay, and we have sometimes to make quick decisions. We need to think about how, as far as possible, we allow space for ambiguity and indecision. We need to choose placements which also allow this space and avoid placements which confirm the passing preferences for the easier identities.

4   *Understanding identity outcomes*

One of the reasons we may rush into a concern about identity is that we have fixed personal ideas about outcomes. These may be influenced by our own experiences, our family make-up, or our politics. We ourselves may value or undervalue particular identities. We might rush the process because of what we value. Ms Prevatt-Goldstein explained that there is a polarisation in views about the most favoured outcome of children with mixed 'racial' heritages. One is in favour of a black public identity, the other in favour of mixed public identity. However the children themselves are saying that it is not so simple. Some children may have a clear public black identity and wish to stick to that. Others may have a black identity with other identities subordinate, others a mixed identity, a few, particularly at a young age, may have a white identity. We need to accept diversity while recognising the political significance of identity in a racialized world.

In listening to and safeguarding children from mixed heritage Ms Prevatt-Goldstein recommended that we stay sensitive and attune to the voice of the child while recognising its context; centre the most marginalized and devalued identities in a balanced way and recognise that identity formation is both a process and has psychological and political significance.

Introduction

Children from mixed heritage backgrounds are neither 'children first' nor 'of mixed heritage' first. Their experience of being children is textured by their being 'of mixed heritage' and vice versa. This chapter addresses the common likely experiences, challenges, strengths and needs of children of mixed heritage, particularly in the looked after sector. The individual experience of being 'mixed heritage' is itself textured by a range of factors such as gender, age, experience of poverty or affluence, style of parenting and so on. Hence this chapter on listening to and safeguarding children from mixed heritage backgrounds will need to be adapted in practice to each specific context.

'Mixed heritage background' can be used to refer to mixed *ethnic* background, where heritage or ethnicity means 'a common culture, language, religion and origin (territorial or ancestral) shared by a group of people' (Prevatt-Goldstein and Spencer, 2000). It therefore refers to all children of mixed ethnicities, including mixed white ethnicities such as Irish and English, mixed black ethnicities such as African Caribbean and South Asian and mixed 'racial' ethnicities. However, the term 'mixed heritage' is often a euphemism for 'mixed racial' ie children of one black and one white parent. For example, the 2001 Census in its mixed ethnicity section only specifies white and black Caribbean, white and black African and white and Asian. Mixed black ethnicities are covered in its 'any other' category and mixed white ethnicities are not even in this mixed ethnicity section but included in the category of white ethnicities. Additionally, the great majority of published literature and research is focused only on mixed 'racial' children. Because of this common interpretation of mixed heritage as mixed racial heritage and because of the high representation of children of mixed 'racial' heritages in the care system[1] (Butt and Mirza, 1996), this chaper will focus particularly on children of mixed 'racial'

---

[1]   The Labour Force Survey 1997–9, like Barn (1993), challenges this common finding and suggests that children with one or two African or African-Caribbean parents are equally likely to be over-represented in the care system.

heritages. But it will do so in the context of the wider mixed heritage group, as this draws needed attention to the common experiences and needs of the wider group, and relieves mixed 'racial' children from being singled out as abnormal.

The context of mixed heritage background

Children of mixed heritage background including mixed 'racial' heritages have a long history in Britain and should not be perceived as a new phenomenon or problem (Fryer, 1984; Prevatt-Goldstein, 1999a). The mixed 'racial' population has been estimated in the 2001 Census at 15% of the black population and 1.2% of the total population of the United Kingdom.[2] It is predominantly a young population (55% under 16 compared to 19% under 16 in the white population) with the predominant group being of African-Caribbean fathers and white mothers (Barn, 1999; Modood et al, 1997). The limited research on this group suggests that the majority experience racism, maintain a high level of self-esteem and that a minority have difficulty accepting themselves as black mixed heritage, particularly when younger (Tizard and Phoenix, 1993; Fatimlehin, 1999). Research on this group in the care system is even more limited but suggests that they are likely to be placed with families, mainly white families (Barn, 1993; Barn et al, 1997) and that the outcomes are less satisfactory than for other groups (Berridge and Cleaver, 1987; Fratter et al, 1991; Charles, 1992). In much research, particularly on adoption, this group is subsumed in the larger black group where the overall findings include some satisfactory outcomes (Gill and Jackson, 1983; Thoburn et al, 1999), some experience of racism and some unmet racial and ethnic identity needs (Kirton and Woodger, 1999; Richards and Ince, 2000).

It has not been possible to identify the figures for mixed black ethnicities accurately from the latest census as these are subsumed under 'other mixed', which is 0.3% of the population of England and Wales. Mixed white ethnicities are not specifically identified in the census but are considered to be a very small proportion of the 'other white group' which are 2.6% of the total population of England.

The lack of attention in the 2001 Census and in the research literature generally suggests that being of mixed mono-'racial' heritage is publicly perceived as 'not an issue' except, as with Dutch-German children, in the aftermath of a major conflict involving the two countries of heritage (Ifekwunigwe, 1999). Conversely, the evidence suggests that children of mixed 'racial' backgrounds have consistently been perceived and treated negatively, at best suffering from identity conflict and confusion, at worst as 'a little race of mulattoes, mischievous as monkeys and infinitely more dangerous' (Thicknesse, 1788). Currently however there are also more positive competing discourses such as, that black mixed racial children experience the same challenges and joys of black children with two black parents (Small, 1986) or possess 'a wealthy and multi-faceted heritage which needs to be celebrated and positively acknowledged' (Fatimlehin, 1999).

In listening to and safeguarding children of mixed heritage through the court processes we need to hear the voice of the child and place it in the context of their likely experiences and challenges. We need to safeguard them from neglect, physical and sexual abuse (see Dutt and Phillips, 1996; Dhir, 1999 and Prevatt-Goldstein, 1999b). We also need to listen to and safeguard their heritage and potential as children of mixed ethnicity through being attuned to experiencing mixed heritage; valuing mixed heritage; accepting identity as process and understanding identity outcomes.

---

[2]   These figures are likely to be an underestimate as many may still, as in the 1991 census, choose to be recorded as Black or, as in the Labour Force Studies, are recorded by their parents as White (Aspinall, 2000). The figures are also likely to be unstable as 'those of mixed ethnicity may well respond differently at different times' (Haskey, 2003).

Experiencing mixed heritage

Children of mixed heritage backgrounds may be assumed to have greater *personal* access to more than one heritage than other children. Yet this may not be the reality. Other children, for example, those of non-dominant heritages accommodating to both their own heritage and that of the dominant heritage in the United Kingdom, and some children of the dominant heritage living in multiracial areas with multiracial networks, may experience diverse heritages while children of mixed heritage backgrounds may be living in mono-cultural worlds. This may be particularly so if they are being parented largely by a white parent or/and living in largely white communities. Dual/multi-ethnic children require access to the lived aspects of their heritages, the languages, the daily experiences, the extended family, the ability to feel at home, to pass and be accepted within the ethnic groups in order to easily realise the potential of their multi-ethnic backgrounds. This is available to some children only:

> 'I am British/Scottish, my daughter is Scottish/Chinese and her other parent is Chinese. We live in a white Scottish community... An issue has been that there are not enough people in Central Scotland who speak Mandarin Chinese. Unfortunately she is therefore not equally bilingual.' (EYTARN, 1994, p 41)

> 'I could say that I am half Iranian but I don't know any Iranian people, I don't know anything about the culture... Culturally I am white. I cook and eat white food... There should be more to me than there is. You should be part of another culture but you are not. Instead of being half a person you would feel more whole.' (Richards, 1995, p 67)

> 'I am Maltese, my children are Pakistani/European and their other parent is Pakistani/European. We live in a racially mixed community. Being of mixed parentage, my children have gained the best of two cultures...' (EYTARN, 1994, p 33)

As well as being potentially enriching, a child's access to their diverse heritages is also a right.

> 'In those states in which ethnic, religious and linguistic minorities or persons of indigenous origin exist, a child belonging to such a minority or who is indigenous shall not be denied the right, in community with members of his or her group, to enjoy his or her culture, to profess and practice his or her own religion, or to use his or her own language.' (UN Convention, Art 30)

In our conversations with mixed heritage children we need to recognise that their experiences of both/all their heritages may be limited. The experience of a 'void', of a lack of one cultural inheritance, may only be voiced in adulthood when there is awareness, confidence and support structures to do so: 'once able to face [my mother's racism] (and I still deal with the effects) I have made conscious efforts to find out about and value both parts of my heritage' (EYTARN, 1994, p 59). Late disclosure is now well understood in the experience of abuse and similarly it is important not to assume that children are able easily to communicate the whole story of their heritage experience and needs during their childhood. We need to understand the constraints experienced by the child due to a lack of familiarity with one of their heritages and an understandable reluctance to invite change. This lack of familiarity may be compounded for the child by the negative messages they receive from society about any one of their heritages. We need to undertake the conversations that can help the child acknowledge the heritages with which they may be less familiar. Conversations which acknowledge and value without stereotyping or exoticizing the non-dominant heritage, which are clear about racism and ethnocentricism without allowing this to dominate conversations or overwhelm the child appear to be the most helpful (Tizard and Phoenix, 1993; Wilson, 1987). This is equally important for children of non-racially mixed heritages (black or white) as for children of racially mixed heritages. This may be a challenge for some professionals who may also be unwilling to invite change, themselves be unfamiliar with or not value the non-dominant heritage. It may be easier to ignore the fact that the child is mono-cultural or accept this status-quo rather than invite those conversations which can demonstrate to the child that some adults can acknowledge and value all their heritages, thus enabling the child to consider this option.

Our ability to acknowledge and value non-dominant heritages is demonstrated by the efforts we make to secure placements where these can be safeguarded. In placing a child to safeguard their personal access to their non-dominant heritages it is important to go beyond the external to everyday practice. As one parent commented, 'My 5 children were split up – none in Muslim homes. Eventually they got to go to a mosque once a week. But nothing, nothing about their daily practice' (Richards and Ince, 2000, p 66). Adult respondents in the Kirton, Feast and Howe research (2000) suggest the lived practice of the non-dominant heritage is critical and that this does not negate the dominant heritage because 'you have that side of you all the time because you live in this country' (p 14). Placing children where access to their non-dominant heritage is safeguarded can seem a herculean task, particularly where there are multiple heritages. Prevatt-Goldstein and Spencer (2000) suggest some guiding principles:

- Ensuring that the child is well placed to positively develop those heritages that are most minimised or devalued.
- Ensuring that the valuing and reflection of these heritages does not diminish the promotion of, or access to, other identities of the child (p 14).

Failure to make these placements can have long-term consequences. Some of the respondents in Kirton, Feast and Howe's research (2000) indicate that while this was a major reason for seeking out their birth parents, finding them was disappointing as the cultural divide between their birth and adoptive families was too wide. Our approach to safeguarding the experience of mixed heritage therefore needs to be sensitive and attuned to the voice of the child and the context of that voice, as well as focus on the most marginalised and devalued of their heritages in practical everyday ways.

Valuing mixed heritage

Our conversations and actions to safeguard children from mixed heritage backgrounds may also need to take on board the fact that some children may not value some of their own diverse heritages. This is not pathological but a participation in the common prejudices as well as a rational response to racist abuse and alienation. There is considerable evidence on black children experiencing racist abuse (Barter, 1999) and that this is equally so for black children with one white parent (Tizard and Phoenix, 1993). Garrett (2000) and Smith (2000) provide evidence of anti-Irish and anti-Jewish prejudice and the racist abuse experienced by some of the children. Evidence from ChildLine suggests that racist/ethnocentric abuse is likely to be exacerbated by isolation and the census indicates that children of mixed 'racial' heritages are more likely to be scattered within dominant communities than children of a single minority heritage (Aspinall, 2000). Isolation and undue public and professional attention also contribute to the feeling of not being normal, a feeling that challenges the well-being of children and adults.

'People used to ask me. That made me realise that it isn't normal, or they think it isn't normal for someone to have a black dad and a white mum. That made me different. I never used to like it.' (Tizard and Pheonix, 1993, p 91)

'We are always in a goldfish bowl ... We have never been allowed to feel normal.' (Alhibai-Brown, 2000)

'All these people are trying to define who you are, tell you that you can't be Black. Look how light you are! Your mother's White so how can you be Black?' (Ifekwunigwe, 1999, p 114)

Many children will be aware from the experiences of their parents and the media that the prejudice and abuse they experience as children because of one of their heritages, be it black, Irish, Jewish, is likely to continue throughout their life and that this diminishes their chances of success in education, employment, social and political inclusion. It is therefore not surprising that some children, particularly at a young age, are negative or ambivalent about some of these heritages. However, it is a tribute to their resilience and to their parenting that this is a minority feeling that is often overcome with age and wider experience:

'Being of mixed parentage has given me a strong sense of my own identity though developing it has been a struggle but with a sense of victory at the outcome'. (EYTARN, 1994, p 59)

In listening to children of mixed heritage backgrounds, we need to take on board the possibility that any particular child may have been protected from negative messages and experiences, may have experienced these and internalised them or experienced these and resisted them. Importantly, in listening we need to move beyond an acceptance of any negative views to an active engagement which understands the reasons for negative views, challenges these views at the appropriate depth and pace for the individual child and gently provides the child with alternative perspectives which are grounded in reality. It is equally important to challenge the racism and racist abuse that may have contributed to the negative views.

Furthermore, it is essential that countering negative views about some aspects of a child's heritage does not lead to negative views on other aspects of a child's heritage. This may require particular skill where there have been historic power imbalances and injustices between specific groups, for example, Irish and English; African-Caribbean and English; African and African-Caribbean; African-Uganda and South Asian. An awareness of the complex political history is helpful but what is essential is to convey to the child that injustice is not inherent in any heritage, though it may have been expedient, and that there were individuals of each heritage who did not participate in and who challenged these injustices, for example, Africans and English people who challenged the slave trade. Moreover, it is important to convey that there are individuals of all heritages who are currently challenging injustice (Derman Sparks et al, 1980). While this balancing act may seem overwhelming, it is similar to the skills required in assisting children to be confident in their gender, recognise gendered inequality or sexual abuse while remaining positive about both genders.

Professionals also need to ensure that their conversations do not contribute to the alienating attention which has historically been focused particularly on mixed 'racial' heritages. They themselves need to perceive having diverse ethnic heritages as normal, and recognise that many children positively manage their diverse heritages despite the hurdles of abuse and alienation placed in their way (Durojaiye, 1970; EYTARN, 1994; Fatimhelin, 1999; Tizard and Phoenix, 1993; Poston, 1990; Wilson, 1987). It is possible that professionals, in seeking to 'normalise' mixed heritage, may become over-enthusiastic, seeing the combination of ethnic/racial differences as exotic or special. This may please the child in the short-term but may prolong the feeling of alienation and contribute to the child feeling better than those of a single heritage and not participating in those groups. The testimonies of children of mixed 'racial' heritages indicate that as well as experiencing racism from white peers some may also experience some exclusion from black groups.[3] The way to manage this is by understanding it as an attempt to reverse racism based on colour and particularly on the darker shades of colour (Featherston, 1994; Gorham, 2003), challenging it and assisting the child in feeling 'equal to' rather than 'better than'.

---

3   Mixed 'racial' people have historically been accepted by black groups in the United Kingdom (Fryer, 1984) with exclusion being both recent and relatively limited (Ifekwunigwe, 1999).

In order to safeguard children's positive views on their heritages and consequently of themselves, it is necessary to place them, not only where these heritages are valued, but also where they can be buffered from alienation and abuse, the major barriers to valuing background heritages. Neighbourhoods and schools which are mixed 'racially', parents who acknowledge the child as both black and of mixed heritage and parents with a political awareness of racism have been recommended by Fatimhelin (1999), Richards (1995), Tizard and Phoenix (1993) and Wilson (1987). Wilson and Fatimhelin add that living with their black parent can supply a richer and more tangible experience of being black and one of the respondents in Ifekwunigwe (1999) affirms the contribution of a black extended family. This suggests that the minimum positive placement for children of mixed heritage backgrounds is in areas that reflect ethnic diversity and mixed heritages including their own, and with parents who positively acknowledge and value the diverse heritages. If one of the heritages is devalued or marginalised in society the parents need to particularly reinforce that heritage and reflect that heritage within the home.

Accepting identity as process

There is a breadth of thinking on 'racial' identity as process, as developing gradually and erratically over time (Cross, 1978; Mama, 1995; Plummer, 1996; Poston, 1990) and not necessarily in a linear fashion (Parham, 1989). This is borne out by the testimony of many of mixed heritage:

'I am Asian/white British ... I use a number of terms depending on the purpose of the definition. Usually I say my father was Indian and I am of mixed descent but I have used mixed race, mixed parentage and sometimes Black.' (EYTARN, 1994, p 59)

'Children need to feel okay about both/several facets of their personality/identity and taught that it is okay if they identify more with one than another at different points in their lives.' (EYTARN, 1994, p 62)

and by the research:

'the notion that mixed-origin children are essentially black is understood to a greater degree by the children themselves and their parents [than by white social workers]. However, this black identity does not exist from the start but emerges in later adolescent years.' (Barn, 1993, p 74)

'It is clear that mixed parentage adolescents are able to develop a positive racial identity [black] and simultaneously claim dual identification. This ability increases with age and is associated with high self-esteem.' (Fatimhelin, 1999, p 315)

Professionals need to avoid negative attention to the identity development of a child at one particular stage. Conversations around identity can pathologise and fix a changing process unless they are open-ended and directed by the child. The additional uncertainty and instability these conversations may create is similar to a situation in which young children are constantly being asked to choose their gender or having different professionals and the media debating their gendered identity. Richards suggests that 'work with young people [before late adolescence and early adulthood] would therefore address the abuse and alienation that they experience rather than identify problems of racial identity' 1995, p 69.

Professionals equally need to avoid making permanent decisions based on a passing stage of a child:

> 'I ended up with a white family at 9 years old because I specifically requested it. My social worker was fine about it. It made life easier for her … and it made my life easier. Today I struggle to reconcile living with a white family. I think my biggest regret is that I wasn't with a black family.' (Richards and Ince, 2000, p 44.)

This is not a mandate for ignoring the wishes and feelings of a child, rather for both seeing identity as process and also the context in which the child may be expressing those wishes and feelings. This context may include the experience of generalised racist abuse and alienation or in some instances abuse from a black adult. Dhir (1999) suggests that communication which conveys to the child that abuse by a black person occurred because of one person and not their entire cultural and familial systems challenges the racism that the child may have internalised. Prevatt-Goldstein and Spencer (2000) remind us that:

> 'the majority of white children who are abused or neglected by white parents do not enter public care stating that they do not want to live with another white family … The fact that black children are said to express such negative views about black families should be considered an indictment of the racism prevalent in wider society as well as in public care … A plan of work needs to be undertaken which can help the young person begin to unlock the negative messages they have internalised about black people, their relatives and ultimately themselves.' (Prevatt-Goldstein and Spencer, 2000, p 18.)

Professionals can collude with racism in using 'the wishes and feelings' of the child to place the child with white parents without undertaking this plan of work. The need for this conversation and work plan may be less obvious when the diverse heritages are mono-'racial' but professionals need to be aware that abuse and alienation can be experienced and internalised by children of diverse ethnicities. This understanding of identity as process is a challenge to court timetables but is essential in avoiding placements which fail to meet the child's long-term needs.

As many children will experience some ambivalence, particularly when younger, placements need to be sought which safeguard this space for conversations, which understand identity as process and can tolerate ambiguity and negativity while providing the building blocks for the development of positive identities. Prevatt-Goldstein and Spencer (2000) suggest the following building blocks:

- Carers who can acknowledge and continuously, in natural and uncontrived ways, give positive messages to the child about all aspects of their identity;
- Placements where the child experiences a positive role modelling of significant aspects of their identity, including ethnicity and 'race';
- Placements where the above are readily available in neighbourhoods, schools and places of worship (p 11).

Children holding strong negative views on one of their identities may benefit from bridging therapeutic placements which begin the process of centering the more marginalised identities before being placed with carers of those identities (Dhir, 1999). However, Rashid's work (2000) demonstrates that many black carers, using their own support networks, have been able to help children deal with their internalised racism.

Understanding identity outcomes

Our concern about identity may be rooted not only in mistaken assumptions about the extent of identity conflict and in a lack of recognition that identity development is a process, but also in our beliefs about the preferred identity of children of mixed 'racial' heritages. This appears to be less publicly contested for children of mono-'racial' mixed heritages, which enables the space for fluidity as recommended in the previous section. Those of mono-'racial' mixed heritages, either within black ethnicities or white, may have the opportunity to:

- Develop an individual expression of what it means to be of that particular ethnicity, eg Irish, Hungarian, Sri Lankan, Angolan;
- Experiment with the balance of belonging to any one group, changing and re-changing the prioritised group as needs, moods, circumstances change;
- Eventually hold identities in tandem with one or two dominant as signified by choice of neighbourhood, choice of associations, language spoken at home, daily routines, main traditions handed down while retaining some sense of belonging and residue of traditions of the other(s).

The situation becomes more complex for children of mixed 'racial' heritages as the political and professional interest in their public identity can reduce the space for the private development of identity as recommended above. Brah (1992) has suggested that 'changing identities do assume specific concrete patterns against particular sets of historical and social circumstances' (p 141). The reality of racism, exclusion from the white group and acceptance by the black group has led to the specific concrete pattern of a black identity for children of 'racially' mixed heritages. This identity can be fluid if it avoids the essentialism of the Black Power Movements (Prevatt-Goldstein, 1999a) and the stereotypes of a racist society (Kirton, 2000). Wilson's statement that 'the white/non-white line is a heavily guarded social barrier, and having one white parent is not deemed a sufficient entitlement to cross it' (1987, p 36) seems to be borne out by the fact that, notwithstanding the advanced publicity about the new mixed category in the 2001 Census (Aspinall, 2000), this category is still officially counted as within the black minority ethnic group.

There are now two main competing professional positions regarding the most favoured identity outcome and placement of children with mixed 'racial' heritages. The first reflects the reality of the census categorisation with black children with one white parent remaining as a subset within the black group, and promotes placement with one or two black parents. Within this position there are variations as to the extent to which a black public identity is shared with a mixed racial identity:

'I will be Black till the day I die, no matter how many White people want to tell me who I am and what I am.' (Akousia, in Ifekwunigwe, 1999, p 112.)

'I identify as Black but I am not ashamed of my non-black ancestry. I should be allowed to be who I am and so should everyone else. Just let's do it with enough awareness to know where we are really located.' (Camper, 1995, p xxiv.)

'I am Black British…I would like to be called Black because it is a political term for me. I do not mind mixed race/mixed parentage.' (EYTARN, 1994, p 62.)

Nevertheless, these variations all reflect an acceptance of the value of a black public identity that recognises the reality of public perception, offers a group identity in which to feel secure, offers an enriching cultural and political tradition, retains the integrity of a group that needs the numbers and support to challenge racism and recognises that a new racialized group will not dismantle racism.

The other main professional position, though this is not reflected in the census, is in favour of a mixed public identity which appears to balance the diverse heritages and to take an optimistic, non-racist position:

'My brother and I are Asian-European. We live with my mother who is Maltese. My father is Pakistani/German. I would like to be called Human.' (EYTARN, p 67.)

'I would like to be called mixed race. That way I feel part of all races.' (EYTARN, 1994, p 63.)

'I wouldn't call myself black. I feel that is denying that my mother is white.' (Tizard and Pheonix, 1993, p 47.)

This position seems less exclusive of and to the white parent though ignores the gendered experience where children's acknowledgment of their gender is not interpreted as excluding the parent of a different gender. It can reflect less direct experience of racism or/and a lack of a political understanding of racism. Professionally, it is linked to the promotion of placement with one or two white parents (Tizard and Phoenix, 1993):

'When they want to consider where to place children for adoption it lets them off having to look for a Black family. They can ignore our Blackness and focus on our whiteness.' (Banks, 1992, p 35.)

Each research project produces a different pattern of identification, perhaps because of the different age and neighbourhood of the respondents. For example, the adults in the EYTARN (1994) sample chose a black public identity more frequently than the teenagers; in Wilson's (1987) research, those in multi-racial areas identified as black mixed parentage more than those in white areas. The different findings may also be a consequence of the fact that some research probes further into private identities. For example, the adolescents in Richard's (1995) survey first self-identified as black, and then subsequently as with a white parent and some of Tizard and Phoenix's respondents (1993) expanded their identifications later in the conversations. Additionally, physical appearance (Poston, 1990 and Tizard and Phoenix, 1993), political understanding of parents (Tizard and Phoenix, 1993), experience of racism, and psychological value of this identity to the individual (Mama, 1995) may also play a part in determining the dominant identity. In listening to the voice of the child, professionals need to be aware of the context of those voices, accept identity as process and be aware that in a racialized society with continuing racial abuse and institutionalised racism (Macpherson, 1999) racial identity outcomes have political consequences in terms of group strength[4] and psychological consequences in terms of a group identity that matches public perception and provides access to cultural heritages and traditions of challenging racism.

Conclusion

We have drawn attention to safeguarding the diverse heritages of children of mixed heritage and most particularly of mixed racial heritage. This process requires being attuned to the experience of mixed heritage, valuing mixed heritage, accepting identity as process and understanding identity outcomes. Throughout it is necessary to be sensitive both to the voice of the child and to the context of that voice; to centre the most marginalised and devalued identities in everyday life without devaluing the more dominant; to accept mixed heritage as normal and non-problematic while taking account of and challenging the racism, ethnocentricism or exclusion that society may impose on some children of mixed heritage; to accept identity as process while understanding that in a racialised society racial identity has both political and psychological implications. These skills in attending to both the individual and the context, in working with difference and in looking at long term as well as short term outcomes are widely transferable and likely to benefit not only children of diverse heritages but all children and young people.

---

[4]   1% of white people are in relationships with black people while between 3% and 66% black people, depending on gender and ethnic group within black, are in relationships with white people (Modood et al, 1999).

References

Alhibai-Brown, Y. 2000. *Mixed Feelings,* London: Women's Press.

Aspinall, PJ. 2000. Children of Mixed Parentage – Data Collection Needs. *Children and Society,* **14,** 207–16.

Banks, N. 1992. Some consideration of 'racial' identification and self-esteem when working with mixed ethnicity children and their mothers as social services clients. *Social Services Research,* **3,** Birmingham University.

Barn, R. 1993. *Black Children in the Public Care System,* London: BAAF/Batsford.

Barn, R. 1999. White mothers, mixed parentage children and child welfare. *British Journal of Social Work,* **29,** 269–284.

Barter, C. 1999. *Protecting Children from Racism and Racial Abuse,* London: NSPCC.

Berridge, D and Cleaver, H. 1987. *Foster Home Breakdowns,* Oxford: Blackwell.

Brah, A. 1992. Difference, diversity and differentiation. In *Race, Culture and Difference,* ed. J Donald J and A Rattinsi , London: Sage.

Butt, J and Mirza, K. 1996. *Social Care and Black Communities: A Review of recent research studies,* London: HMSO.

Camper, C. (ed). 1994. *Miscegenation Blues,* Toronto: Sister Vision.

Charles, M, Rashid, S and Thoburn, J. 1992. The placement of black children in permanent new families. *Adoption and Fostering,* **16(3)**: 13–9.

Cross, WE Jnr. 1978. The Cross and Thomas Models of Psychological Nigrescence. *Journal of Black Psychology,* **5(1)**: 13–19.

Derman-Sparks, L, Higa, TC and Sparks, B. 1980. Suggestions for developing positive racial attitudes in *Council on Interracial books for children,* **11(3)**: 4.

Dhir, B. 1999. Anti-disciminatory issues in child protection. In *Working with Black Children and Adolescents in Need,* ed. R Barn, London: BAAF.

Durojaiye, MOA. 1970. Patterns of friendship choice in an ethnically mixed junior school. *Race,* **12(2)**: 189–99.

Dutt, R and Phillips, MC. 1996. Race, Culture and the Prevention of Child Abuse. In *Childhood Matters: Report of National Commission of Inquiry into the Prevention of Child Abuse,* Vol 2, Background Papers, pp 149–21, London: The Stationery Office.

Early Years Trainers Anti-Racist Network (EYTARN). 1994. *The Best of Both Worlds: Celebrating Mixed Parentage,* London: EYTARN.

Fatimlehin, IA. 1999. Of Jewel Heritage: racial socialisation and racial identity attitudes amongst adolescents of mixed African-Caribbean/White parentage. *Journal of Adolescence,* **22,** 303–18.

Featherston, E (ed). 1994. *Skin Deep,* The Crossing Press: USA.

Fratter, J, Rowe, J, Sapsford, D and Thoburn, J. 1991. *Permanent Family Placements: A Decade of Experience,* London: BAAF.

Fryer P. 1984. *Staying Power,* London: Pluto Press.

Gill, O and Jackson, B. 1983. *Adoption and Race,* London: Batsford.

Garrett PM. 2000. Responding to Irish Invisibility. *Adoption and Fostering,* **24(1)**: 23–33.

Gorham, C. 2003. Mixing it, *Guardian,* 22 February 2003.

Haskey, J (ed). 2003. *National Statistics: Population Projections by Ethnic Group,* London: The Stationery Office.

Ifekwunige, JW. 1999. *Scattered Belongings,* London: Routledge.

Kirton, D. 2000. *Ethnicity and Adoption,* Buckingham: Open University Press.

Kirton, D, Feast, J and Howe, D. 2000. Searching, Reunion and Transracial Adoption. *Adoption and Fostering,* **3,** 6–18.

Kirton, D and Woodger, D. 1999. Experiences of Transracial Adoption. In *Assessment, Preparation and Support,* London: BAAF.

Macpherson, W. 1999. *The Stephen Lawrence Inquiry,* London: The Stationery Office.

Mama A. 1995. *Beyond the Masks,* London: Routledge

Modood, T, Berthoud, R, Lakey, J, Nazroo, J, Smith, P, Virdee, S and Beishon, S. 1997. *Ethnic Minorities in Britain, Diversity and Disadvantage,* London: Policy Studies Institute.

Parham, TA. 1989. Cycles of psychological nigrescence. *Counselling Psychologist,* **17,** 187–226.

Plummer. 1996. *Journal of Black Psychology,* **22(2)**:175.

Poston, WSC. 1990. The bi-racial identity development model: a needed addition. *Journal of Counselling and*

Development, **69,** 152–155.

Prevatt-Goldstein, B. 1999a. Black with one parent: A positive and achievable identity. In *British Journal of Social Work,* **29,** 285–301. London.

Prevatt-Goldstein, B. 1999b. Direct work with black children with a white parent. In *Working with Black children and adolescents in need,* ed. R Barn, London: BAAF.

Prevatt-Goldstein, B and Spencer, M. 2000. *BAAF Practice Guide: Ethnicity and Placement: Good practice with specific reference to black children,* London: BAAF.

Rashid, SP 2000. The strengths of black families: appropriate placements for all. *Adoption and Fostering,* **24(1):** 15–23.

Richards W. 1995. Working with Mixed Race Young People. *Youth and Policy,* **45,** 62–72

Richards, A and Ince L. 2000. *Overcoming the obstacles, Looked After Children: Quality Services for Black and Minority Ethnic Children and their Families,* London: Family Rights Group

Small J. 1986. Transracial Placements: Conflicts and contradictions. In *Social Work with Black children and Their Families,* ed. S Ahmed, J Cheetham, J Small, London: Batsford

Smith, G. 2000. Meeting the placement Needs of Jewish Children. *Adoption and Fostering,* **24(1):** 40–47.

Thicknesse, P 1778. A Year's Journey through France and Part of Spain. In *Staying Power,* Fryer, P, Pluto Press, 1984, p 161.

Thoburn, J, Norford, L and Rashid, SP. 1999. *Permanent Family Placement for Children of Minority Ethnic Origin,* London: Jessica Kingsley.

Tizard B and Phoenix A. 1993. *Black, White or Mixed Race,* London: Routledge

Wilson A. 1987. *Mixed Race Children: A Study of Identity,* London: Allen and Unwin.

CHILD PROTECTION, THE COURTS AND MINORITY ETHNIC FAMILIES

Ashok Chand
Centre for Social Work
University of Nottingham

Summary of paper

Ashok Chand began his introduction to his paper by reiterating the view expressed in Ms Prevatt-Goldstein's paper that it is important that professionals take into account the fact that children's identities may change over time, depending on their experiences, preferences and personal development.

In researching his paper, Mr Chand said that he tried to look at the research into child protection, courts and experiences of minority ethnic families. He was surprised to find that there is very little literature in this area. Consequently, his paper discusses in detail the few research studies that are available.

The Children Act makes specific reference to the needs of minority ethnic children, for example Part III of the Act states that 'a local authority shall give due consideration ... to the child's religious persuasion, racial origin and cultural and linguistic background'. Mr Chand asked whether the Act, agencies and professionals go far enough in protecting the rights of children from minority ethnic families? He pointed out that there are concerns amongst professionals that the needs of such children are being ignored or minimised in child care policy and practice. He also asked whether the needs of minority ethnic children are any different from those of other children? All things being equal their needs are no different, but all things are not equal, since there are indications that some minority ethnic children and their families are likely to experience particular difficulties related to their ethnicity, for example racism.

Mr Chand argued that the family justice system needs to demonstrate fairness, trust and confidence. Parents need to observe that the system is fair and that account is taken of diverse lifestyles. Indications from various studies suggest that this is not the case. Four main themes were highlighted from his paper:

1) *A study by Hunt et al (1999), looked at children who were at risk of significant harm, and the research included an analysis of the families who entered care proceedings. In relation to the adults, it was found that those from minority ethnic backgrounds were half as likely as white adults to have drug, alcohol, and/or learning disabilities, and were almost three times more likely to have an adult in employment. Fewer minority ethnic adults had experienced abuse, or had a criminal record. In short, the white UK families presented a more troubled profile, yet overall one in two non-European families reached court within three months of their involvement with social services.*

2) *The overuse of emergency powers and orders with minority ethnic families, was the second theme Mr Chand raised. A recent study by Brophy et al (2003) found that 64 (35%) out of the 182 children in their study, were subject to an Emergency Protection Order (EPO) prior to an application for a care order. The minority ethnic breakdown indicated that 19% were children from the white group, compared to 36% for the black group and 60% for the South Asian group, with Indian children being the most vulnerable. Of the 64 EPOs in total, only 14% (9) involved white children, the remaining 86% were minority ethnic children including those from mixed parentage backgrounds.*

3) *Regarding language barriers, Mr Chand suggested that one reason for the more punitive practices experienced by some minority ethnic families, may be due to language barriers not*

effectively being bridged. For example, it can be difficult for a social worker to explain to some minority ethnic families whose English is not their first language, why social services are involved. Where language problems limit a parent's ability to understand the proceedings, it may contribute to experiences of being unfairly blamed and feeling that they have suffered discrimination (Brophy et al, 2003).

4) *'Enforced' accommodation was the fourth theme highlighted. A study by Packman and Hall (1998) explored the implementation of s 20 of the Children Act 1989, including whether voluntary accommodation was now being used instead of emergency and/or care orders. Minority ethnic children were most significant in the 'at risk' group, which was the group most susceptible to practices where the voluntary nature of the accommodation was at times a 'sham', and parents were seen to feel obliged to go along with the s 20 admission for fear of something worse.*

Mr Chand concluded by suggesting that if we are truly committed to listening to the voice of the child we must ensure that the child protection and family justice systems are fair and equitable, and do not in any way disadvantage children further.

Introduction

'... the family justice system needs to be able to demonstrate fairness. It needs to generate trust and confidence within ethnic minority communities both with regard to the degree to which British institutions respect alternative lifestyles and value systems and afford appropriate protection to minority ethnic children who are ill-treated by their parents or carers ... Such parents need to be able to observe that 'the system' is fair, and that justice can be 'seen too be done' in the account taken of diverse lifestyles and belief systems.' (Brophy et al, 2003, p 253.)

'It sometimes feels as if, the moment a person who is black, Asian or from any other ethnic minority group enters the family court system, they are seen as possessing pathological traits.' (Hawkes, 1999, p 206.)

The first statement was taken from a recent study by Brophy et al (2003) which encapsulates perhaps the ideal that needs to be strived for if minority ethnic children and families are to receive a fair and equitable service in the family justice and child protection system generally. The second statement in contrast, is the view of a psychotherapist's observations of what is ascribed to some minority ethnic families when they enter the family court system, and is obviously far from the ideal. The aim of this paper is to consider whether minority ethnic children and their families experience disadvantage or barriers, due to their ethnicity being afforded insufficient attention or perhaps inappropriate attention in family legal issues. The paper highlights a number of key research studies which serve to illustrate some of the ways such families may be discriminated against, either intentionally or otherwise, by social workers, guardian ad litems, and other legal personnel including magistrates and judges, when faced with care proceedings. The themes covered include a profile of cases that enter family proceedings courts with comparisons made between those involving white families and those involving minority ethnic families. An analysis of the different routes to court follows, again with comparisons made between different ethnic groups. The paper then considers the language barriers for minority ethnic families; highlights the notion of 'enforced' accommodation; considers the use of Emergency Protection Orders (EPOs) and Care Orders between different ethnic groups, before finally moving on to how policy and practice might be improved.

Before exploring these themes in turn, it is important to first consider the Children Act 1989, which makes some important references to the assessment, services and/or interventions, that specifically address the needs of minority ethnic children and families. For example, Part III of the Act which includes the duties of local authorities in relation to children looked after by them, states that:

'In making any such decision [regarding a child looked after or proposing to be looked after] a local authority shall give due consideration ... to the child's religious persuasion, racial origin and cultural and linguistic background.' (Section 22(5)(c).)

The accompanying Guidance also states that:

'A child's ethnic origin, cultural background and religion are important factors for consideration. It may be taken as a guiding principle of good practice that, other things being equal, and in a great majority of cases, placement with a family of similar ethnic origin and religion is most likely to meet a child's needs as fully as possible and to safeguard his or her welfare most effectively.' (*Guidance and Regulations*, vol 3, *Family Placements*, para 2.40–242, cited in Jones and Gnanapala, 2000, p 149.)

Other aspects of the Children Act 1989 which indicate that children and families from minority ethnic backgrounds may need particular attention in the decisions made about them, include s 1(3)(d) of the Act whereby a court, in making any decisions around either a section 8 order or an order under Part IV of the Act, shall have regard to 'his age, sex, background and any characteristics of his which the court considers relevant'. In this context, it could be argued that a child's ethnic background might be a relevant characteristic. Similarly, when deciding whether harm suffered to a child is significant (s 31(10)) the child's health and development should be compared to the health and development of a similar child. This comparison, according to the Guidance (Vol 1, para 320) advises to consider cultural background when considering the notion of similarity (Jones and Gnanapala, 2000, p 149).

Despite these significant sections within the Children Act 1989, the important question is whether the Act goes far enough in ensuring the needs of minority ethnic children and families are fairly met. Indeed there are some concerns by various researchers and writers that the particular needs of minority ethnic children and families in the UK, are either ignored or minimised in child care policy, practice and/or decision-making. As Morgan and Taylor (1987) note '...the success or failure of the Children Act 1989 in meeting the needs of ethnic minority children and their families depends upon the willingness of local authorities to use resources in and for the ethnic minority community' (cited in Parry, 2000, p 22).

Protection through the legal process

As noted earlier, this section is concerned with a profile of cases that enter the family justice system, with comparisons made between different minority ethnic groups. Specifically, Hunt et al (1999) looked at children who were at risk of significant harm, and whose interests required compulsory protection through the legal process. Part of their study involved 133 case children from 83 families of which 45 of the cases concerned white families, and 37 were families from minority ethnic origins. The largest group of minority ethnic origin were those of mixed parentage (25).

An analysis by the researchers of the main differences between white and minority ethnic children, were that the latter tended to be older: cases involving children of 11 years and older were much more likely to involve non-European families, even more so when the child was a teenager. Children from non-European families were also recorded as having more special educational needs but were less likely to have health problems or disability. The adults from minority ethnic families were half as likely than white families to have problems around drug and/or alcohol abuse, learning disabilities, and to a lesser extent a psychiatric disorder. They were almost three times more likely to have an adult in employment and the mothers tended to be older at the birth of the first child. Fewer were known to have experienced abuse or were in local authority care as children, and less had a criminal record. In short, '... on almost every one of a range of indicators of social morbidity it was the white UK families who presented the more troubled profile' (p 23).

	Case involves non-European Family	Other Cases
	%	%
Case current	74	84
Continuous involvement> 3 mths	48	73
Non-case child care experience	4	23
Previous court experiences	37	46
Seriously considered for proceedings only	29	50
Current CPR registration	52	70
(N=)	27	56

Hunt et al (1999)

The researchers go on to note that:
- Non-European families were less likely to be known to welfare agencies;
- 95% of white families were currently being worked with (47 cases) or had had previous substantial involvement (6 cases). In comparison, only 74% (20) of cases involving non-European families were current, and the remainder had little more than a brief involvement;
- Of the current cases involving European families, 61% had been continuously worked with for over a year compared to 55% for other families, and 87% for more than three months compared to a poor 35% for non-European families.

The researchers found that overall '... one in two non-European families reached court within three months of their involvement with social services' (p 30), which was twice the rate noted in the rest of the sample. The non-European families were also less likely to have had their other children either looked after by the local authority, involved in previous care or related proceedings, or to have been seriously considered for such proceedings (Hunt et al, 1999).

The findings from this study raise a number of concerning questions: do minority ethnic families experience more punitive measures like court proceedings, rather than agency support services to address their problems? In short, are they heavily weighted to the 'control' rather than 'care' side of the social work spectrum? Or perhaps child care cases involving minority ethnic families were more serious, which meant that the legal route was the preferred option? Were such parents more uncooperative, which meant that compulsory intervention was necessary? Hunt et al (1999) go on to say that '...despite their general shorter continuous involvement with the welfare system, these families were in receipt of around the same level of service provision as the rest of the sample. They were also much more likely to have refused services' (p 30). It is not clear from the research findings how these services were measured or determined to be the same. The issue of co-operation will be considered later in this paper.

Another study looking at minority ethnic groups and care proceedings was by Brophy et al (1999). The first stage of the study involved a national postal survey of guardians, and in a later publication Brophy (2000) looked specifically at issues affecting minority ethnic families in care proceedings. One early indication was that minority ethnic children, particularly those from

African, African-Caribbean and mixed parentage backgrounds, may be over-represented in family proceedings. For example, it was noted that 16% of the 558 cases involving nearly 1000 children from the survey, concerned children from minority ethnic households.

Another finding identified by Brophy (2000), was that very few minority ethnic children had a guardian that was matched for ethnicity; all of the children of South Asian origin had a white guardian as did most of the other black children. This was particularly relevant given that only 57% of the guardians had undertaken equal opportunities training, though many wanted more training specifically looking at representing minority ethnic children. Furthermore, there was very little use of cultural advisors/advocates in the cases involving minority ethnic children. This latter finding is particularly relevant, when some of the views of minority ethnic parents involved in the family justice system are considered later in the paper.

Routes to Court

So far this paper has identified at least two important issues affecting minority ethnic families subject to the family justice system: firstly, that minority ethnic families may be more susceptible to court action and secondly once there, are unlikely to have an ethnically-matched representative. Returning to the first issue in more detail, this paper now considers whether there any differences in the routes to court between minority ethnic families and white families. The study by Hunt et al (1999), identified seven different routes to court which are as follows:

- Route 1 involved removal of a child at birth, due to serious concerns about the parents' care of their previous children, who were also more often than not removed.
- Route 2 involved crisis situations with knowledge often scanty, none of the families were being worked with before the events leading to proceedings, and cases often involved emergency orders/powers and were in courts within days.
- Route 3 involved new cases where the child remained at home while a range of services was offered. Court action followed when either these services did not address the concerns or further problems emerged.
- Route 4 focused on using voluntary services to keep families together while assessments were carried out, for example, by using mother and baby units.
- Route 5 required separation between the child and family while further work was carried out, since it was not felt safe for the child and parent to remain together.
- Route 6 involved both a separation and a supervised setting, and
- Route 7 concerned children who were subject to previous court proceedings during the continuous period of social work involvement.

When we consider minority ethnic families and their routes to court compared with other cases, we find that they were more likely to go through route 2 (22% v 9%) and route 6 (11% v 7%), and less likely to go through route 1 (4% v 13%) and route 4 (4% v 9%). The rest were broadly similar. The most concerning finding from this analysis of routes, is the use of emergency powers/orders with minority ethnic families. Is it the case for example, that this is simply more evidence of social control than social care? Hunt et al (1999) found that there were three broad factors that often precipitated court action: 'maltreatment' [of children in the past], 'behaviour or circumstances of significant adults' and 'condition, development or behaviour of case children'. With regard to minority ethnic families, the researchers found that these families were more likely to reach court, despite '... presenting a rather less pathological profile than other families subject to the same proceedings ... suggesting that they may be disproportionately vulnerable to statutory intervention' (p 87 and p 103). Furthermore, in a follow up study by Hunt and Macleod (1999), looking at whether families received an appropriate level of service provision, the researchers found that three of the five cases that concerned Asian families were particularly disadvantaged. Where these families needed specialist resources there were serious deficiencies, and none of the Asian families had an ethnically matched worker.

Language barriers and minority ethnic families

'[Minority ethnic families] ... are quite seriously disadvantaged in a court setting where the language used is precise, formal and sometimes impenetrably legalistic.' (Duncan, cited in Wilkinson, 1985–1986, p 482.)

If minority ethnic families are perhaps experiencing more punitive practices as suggested in the previous section, the prognosis is unlikely to improve once they are involved in care or related proceedings. One reason is that some minority ethnic families may be further disadvantaged due to language barriers that are not effectively bridged. There have been a number of studies that have raised concerns about this issue in child protection generally (see Brandon et al, 1999; Humphrys et al, 1999 and Farmer and Owen, 1995). A recent study by Brophy et al (2003) included language difficulties within the context of family proceedings and found specific issues affecting minority ethnic families. They noted that 'there were numerous documented instances of failures to use interpreters at crucial points in interviews with parents both prior to, and after the instigation of court proceedings' (p 138). Some of these examples are highlighted below:

One case concerned children of Indian origin where it was noted 'there were some anxieties about the mother's understanding of the concerns put to her since English was not her first language' (p 93). In another case, there was a view that the family had not comprehended the seriousness of the situation as noted by a new social worker:

'... the failure of all agencies to recognise and address the cultural and language issues resulted in agencies (example the local authority, the hospital, the health visitor etc) becoming concerned resulting in proceedings.' (p 105.)

'There were also reported instances of interpreters arriving late and not matched for language or dialect, and indications of the use of family members rather than professionals.' (p 138.)

The researchers conclude that these and related findings '... raise some serious questions about access to justice for parents whose first language is not English' (p 139).

With regard to the use of interpreters in courts, Brophy et al (2003) found that magistrates were facilitative in their efforts to enable the process of interpretation, for example by asking advocates to speak more slowly. However as proceedings progressed, advocates were observed reverting to the more traditional approach of speaking directly to the Bench. There were further observations where minority ethnic parents tried to speak for themselves, having become angry or upset over a particular exchange between a judge and an advocate. The responses noted ranged from stern reprimands to more measured responses. Another study on language and specifically the guardian ad litem service found that:

'...guardians had considerable professional discretion in deciding how and when to take account of language, and this raises some important questions about what sorts of knowledge they might have used to inform their practice.' (Pugh and Jones, 1999, p 536.)

Given the problems around poor interpretation provisions in some of the cases involving minority ethnic parents, it is perhaps not surprising that as a consequence, their experiences and understanding of the child protection and litigation process is at times negative. For example, Brandon et al (1999), identified one young mother who found the interference of the authorities outside her experience and comprehension:

> 'I was so worried and unhappy. First it was my mother-in-law and all of that, and then the Social Services. I don't know the law and the language. I'm very worried about the court. I class it all as racism and that goes on. I only want to bring my children up. It's the only thing I can do. I can't fight with the government and the court. I am a mother and I am worried for my children.' (p 202)

Brandon et al (1999) noted that:

> '... it was extremely difficult for the social worker to explain why Social Services were involved, and it took time and patience to establish with both parents the basis for intervention. Had this been possible earlier, recourse to the courts might have been avoided, or better understood.' (p 112.)

In another case the guardian ad litem reported that the Bangladeshi parents found the use of state powers shocking '... the local authority's involvement appears to have been more an alien concept to them [parents], at times they felt not just hostile and resentful, but somewhat bemused' (cited in Brophy et al, 2003, p 127). With regard to how parents might experience court hearings 'in some highly charged situations some minority ethnic parents clearly felt marginalised and somewhat bewildered while professionals tried to resolve issues – sometimes not very well, at least from the parent's perspective' (Brophy et al, 2003, p 202). The researchers continued that:

> 'where language problems limit a parents' ability to understand proceedings, this may contribute to feelings of not being fully understood and perhaps unfairly blamed. Where language problems are coupled with considerable 'cultural distance' between parents and judges and magistrates, this may result in parents feeling they have suffered a form of discrimination.'

Hence the reseachers concluded that 'some parents left court bemused and anxious, others were visibly upset and angry' (p 203).

The above examples demonstrate that minority ethnic families, perhaps in particular those who are have settled in Britain only recently, are likely to find the child protection system an alien concept as well as anxiety-provoking. This may not seem that different to the experiences of some white families involved in the child protection system who also have difficulties around communication. However, as Pugh (1996) maintains 'In the wider social setting of British society, attitudes to bilingualism are inconsistent and often suffused with racist assumptions about superior and inferior languages' (cited in Pugh and Jones, 1999: 536), with those from Africa and the Asian sub-continent ascribed a negative value.

'Enforced' accommodation and minority ethnic families

One issue that has dominated social work research and writing over the decades concerns the over-representation of some minority ethnic children in local authority care. (For early studies see Foren and Batta, 1970; Batta and Mawby, 1981; Rowe, 1989 and Barn 1990). Despite the findings by the various studies of the over-representation of African-Caribbean and mixed-heritage children in particular, there have been disagreements about whether these necessarily signal discriminatory practices or services. Some researchers for example, have suggested that Black people have sought this type of support from local authorities due to experiencing problems associated with housing, employment and poverty, and that this explains their over-representation. Other researchers and writers have argued that prejudice and racism may have played a part in the over-representation of Black children in local authority care, (see Chand 2000, for a fuller discussion). More recently, concerns have been expressed about how voluntary 'voluntary accommodation' is for children and their families under s 20 of the Children Act 1989. The relevance of this issue within the context of family proceedings, becomes obvious when we consider the following studies.

Packman and Hall (1998) carried out a study which aimed to explore the implementation of s 20 of the Children Act 1989 along a number of dimensions. This included whether voluntary accommodation was now being used instead of emergency and care orders. The researchers analysed 177 admissions (153 cases) into local authority care under s 20 of the Children Act 1989, and found that of the 153 children in the cohort, 74 (48%) children were seen to be at risk of significant harm to some degree, and 58 (38%) were either on or had been on the child protection register. Ethnic minority children were clearly seen to be over-represented in this cohort: of the 14 minority ethnic children in the study, nine (64%) were in the category of 'at risk', (the rest were in the 'difficult adolescents' category). The researchers noted that 'the numbers are obviously too small to claim any statistical significance, but inevitably this raised the question of whether some form of discrimination was at work' (p 89).

Packman and Hall (1998) go on to question whether agencies are quicker to perceive risk when dealing with unfamiliar situations or families, or whether these families are only drawn into the social services system when their problems have reached an advanced stage. More importantly, they continue that in some cases, the *voluntary nature of the accommodation* (my emphasis) for the 'at risk' group of children was a 'sham', '… a pretence that parents felt obliged to go along with, for fear of something worse' (p 95). The researchers further noted that

'… the old power to assume 'parental rights' over a child in 'voluntary care' under the Child Care Act 1980 was being replaced by the threat of immediate protective action should parents fail to agree to admission, or should they attempt to exercise their right under Section 20 (8) of the Children Act 1989 to withdraw their child whenever they wished.' (p 96.)

The complexity around the use of s 20 accommodation to perhaps circumvent the application for EPOs or care orders are summed up in the following two quotes by a solicitor and a guardian respectively:

'My main anxiety is accommodation, I feel that it is not really working. I don't know how you get around it; there's nothing illegal about it but social services are in such a strong position that parents have little option, if they don't comply with various conditions then the local authority will take proceedings. So social services manage to achieve the same result without actually going through court proceedings. In theory parents have complete parental responsibility; in reality they are quite powerless.' (Cited at Hunt et al, 1999, p 36.)

'Accommodation is for those situations where parents need help and ask for help But if the local authority would take proceedings if the family don't agree then they should take proceedings. I feel legal proceedings can protect families. I know they're very stressful and that has to be taken into account but they can also protect families against local authorities abusing their power.' (Cited in Hunt et al, 1999, p 36.)

Brophy et al (2003) carried out a recent study on minority ethnic families and child protection litigation, based upon an analysis of case files, observations in court and interviews with court personnel. One important finding relevant to this section, is that at the start of court proceedings, the ethnic breakdown of children's residences at the point of proceedings revealed that only 10% (4 out of 42) children of South Asian origin were still living with their mother at the point of application. Specifically, 38 out of 42 children from Indian, Bangladeshi or Pakistani origins were already living away from their birth parents at the date of application. It is not clear from the study how this particular finding might be explained, though barriers due to language difficulties might have played a part. I would suggest that though language may have been a factor, it seems highly improbable that it is the only explanation. The majority of these South Asian parents, who did not have their children living with them at the point of proceedings (90% of which only 17% were subject to a court order), I would suggest may have been subject to some form of enforced accommodation. It should also be noted, that with regard to the other ethnic groups, 50% (13 out of 26) of African children were either living with their mother or both parents at the start of legal proceedings, compared to 33% of children from other Black groups (including mixed heritage), 20% of children of Caribbean origin, and 19% white children. As the above studies indicate, minority ethnic families may be subject to enforced methods of accommodation to perhaps circumvent other legal routes. However, where other routes are used like emergency orders, the situation for minority ethnic families continues to look grim.

The use of emergency orders

Earlier findings from Hunt et al (1999) have already indicated that compared to white families, the route to court for minority ethnic families is more likely to be through the use of emergency orders/powers. This issue is now considered in more detail by returning to the study by Brophy et al (2003). The researchers analysed the orders that were in force at the point of care proceedings and found that 64 (35%) children out of 182 were subject to an EPO immediately prior to an application for a care order. The minority ethnic breakdown indicated that children from the white group accounted for 19% of EPOs prior to care proceedings, compared to 36% for the Black group and a significant 60% for the South Asian group, with Indian children being the most vulnerable at 77% (that is 10 out of the 13 cases involving Indian children were subject to EPOs prior to a care order). Whilst an ethnic breakdown is useful, it should be noted that in total *81% of minority ethnic children were subject to EPOs immediately prior to care proceedings* (my emphasis).

Is the above an indication that minority ethnic families are pathologised in the family justice system as suggested in the earlier quote by Hawkes (1999)? Some form of structural discrimination towards minority ethnic families, becomes increasingly likely when we consider that family co-operation, or the lack of it, with local authorities did not differ significantly between the different ethnic groups (had there been significant differences based on ethnicity, this might have explained the varying results in the use of EPOs). Similarly, if we consider the possible relationship with children who are on Child Protection Registers (CPRs) and that are subsequently involved in care proceedings, we find that of the 178 cases where this information was known:

- 81% of white children had been or were on the CPR during proceedings;
- 84% mixed parentage;
- 67% the aggregated black group; and
- 65% South Asian children who were the least likely to have been on the CPR during proceedings (Brophy et al, 2003).

When comparisons are made with the applications for EPOs, it is interesting that South Asian children were most likely to be subject to them, yet least likely to have been on a child protection register. Perhaps this indicates that these families presented to social services in emergency situations and little was known about them, as suggested by Hunt et al (1999) in their study. The findings from Brophy et al (2003) indicate that this is unlikely, since the vast majority of the families were well known to social services at the point of proceedings (p 30) and this included 92% of the Indian families.

The evidence so far then presents a worrying picture whereby particular minority ethnic groups largely appear to be experiencing punitive practices, like being subject to EPOs, with little evidence for why this might be. Instead this raises concerns about structural racism and oppression, in particular in the application and granting of emergency orders under the Children Act 1989. Whether this practice then continues into Part IV Care Orders and Supervision Orders needs more research (see Brophy et al, 2003 for some of their findings).

Conclusion

This paper has raised a number of concerns about how minority ethnic families may experience discrimination and disadvantages in child welfare and court systems. However, it would be wrong not to highlight some of the many examples of excellent practice with minority ethnic families that have been noted in the various studies already mentioned. To stay with the most recent study, Brophy et al (2003) demonstrated that various professionals like social workers and guardians went to great lengths to try and meet the cultural needs of some of the families they were involved with. For example at times advice was sought from specialist minority ethnic teams or workers; relatives from Asia were contacted regarding the needs of a particular child; independent specialist workers were used at times, and so on. Hence, there is little doubt that good practice goes on, but appears to occur inconsistently throughout the different local authorities and courts. As the researchers noted '… the family justice system has a complex task in understanding and addressing allegations of discrimination and racism. Parents and professionals start from very different socio-political contexts' (p 188).

This paper has presented many key findings concerning minority ethnic families that could be used to contextualise improvements in policy and practice. However, due to a limited word count, I am only going to focus on one of the key findings noted from the research studies in this paper, which was that ethnically matched guardians, advocates or expert witnesses were rarely used or available for minority ethnic families. I would suggest, that for a court system or indeed any other system, which is largely white in appearance and values yet advocates a recognition and respect for diversity (LCD, 2002), it is important for minority ethnic parents to feel there is the opportunity for someone from their own ethnic background, who understands their culture and language, to represent them in family proceedings. This may not only help in the communication and understanding of cases involving minority ethnic groups, but may also enable such families to challenge any feelings or experiences of racial discrimination within the courts, given the current system where '[p]arents and their advocates would be unlikely, and arguably unwise, to openly criticise lawyers or courts…on these grounds… (Brophy et al, 2003, p 226).

Related to the above point, the questionable views, attitudes and beliefs of some court personnel, including magistrates and judges, towards racial issues, should be open to challenge if minority ethnic parents are to feel that the system is in any way fair. As Jones and Gnanpala (2000) note '[t]he essentially male, white middle-class judiciary is not always impartial towards the new ethnic minorities and some judicial comments are insensitive' (p60). Some examples of these insensitive comments include a magistrate who said in an open court that most migrants 'come to this country just to thieve' (Daily Telegraph, 10 April 1973, cited in Jones and Gnanapala, 2000: 61). While another magistrate warned a black defendant:

> 'whatever you do in your country I don't know, but you don't tell lies in this country, get that into your thick head … If you're going to live in England you're going to behave like an Englishman and tell the truth or you can leave … we are sick of you and your like.' (In Cain and Sadigh, 1982, p 92.)

Although these particular examples are dated, and relate to the criminal justice system, they nevertheless serve as powerful reminders of the potential damage such comments or beliefs might cause to the delicate interface between minority ethnic families and the family justice system. Until these types of comments and beliefs are seen to be stamped out, the criminal and civil justice systems will struggle to demonstrate their fairness and equity towards all minority ethnic children and their families, that come before their courts.

References

Barn, R. 1990. Black Children in Local Authority Care: Admission Patterns, *New Community*, **16**, 229–246.

Barn, R, Sinclair, R & Ferdinand, D. 1997. *Acting on Principle: An Examination of Race and Ethnicity in Social Services Provision for Children and Families*, London: BAAF.

Batta, I & Mawby, R. 1981. Children in Local Authority Care: a Monitoring of Racial Differences. In *Policy and Politics*, **9**, 137–149.

Brandon, M, Thoburn, J, Lewis, A & Way, A. 1999. *Safeguarding Children with the Children Act 1989*, London: The Stationery Office.

Brophy, J. 2000. 'Race' and Ethnicity in Care Proceedings: Implications from a National Survey of Cases containing Expert Evidence. *Adoption and Fostering*, **24 (2)**: 70–72.

Brophy, J with Bates, P, Brown, L, Cohen, S, Radcliffe, P & Wale, CJ. 1999. *Expert Evidence in Child Protection Litigation: Where Do We Go From Here?*, London: The Stationery Office.

Brophy, J, Jhutti-Johal, J & Owen, C. 2003. *Significant Harm: Child Protection Litigation in a Multi-Cutural Setting*, London: Lord Chancellor's Department Research Unit.

Cain, M & Sadigh, S. 1982. Racism, Police and Community Policing: a Comment on the Scarman Report. In *Ethnic Minorities in English Law*. 2000. R Jones & W Gnanapala. Stoke: Trentham Books Ltd.

Chand, A. 2000. The over-representation of Black Children in the Child protection System: possible Causes, Consequences and Solutions. *Child and Family Social Work*, **5**, pp 67–77.

Department of Health **(???)**

Farmer, E & Owen, M. 1995. *Child Protection Practice: Private Risks and Public Remedies*, London: HMSO.

Foren, R & Batta, I. 1970. Colour as a Variable in the use made of a Local Authority Child Care Department. *Social Work*, **27**, 10–15.

Gibbons, J, Conroy, S & Bell, C. 1995. *Operating the Child Protection System*, London: HMSO.

Hawkes, B. 1999. Are Black and Ethnic Minorities on Trial? Thinking, Psychoanalytically about Family Court Work: a Forensic and Intercutural Approach. *Psychodynamic Counselling*, **5(2)**: 205–218.

Humphreys, C, Atkar, S & Baldwin, N. 1999. Discrimination in Child Protection Work: recurring themes in work with Asian Families. *Child and Family Social Work*, **4**, 283–291

Hunt, J & Macleod, A. 1999. *The Best-Laid Plans: Outcomes in Judicial Decisions in Child Protection Proceedings*, London: Stationery Office.

Hunt, J, MacLeod, A & Thomas, C. 1999. *The Last Resort: Child Protection, the Courts and the 1989 Children Act*, London: The Stationery Office.

Jones, R & Gnanapala, W. 2000. *Ethnic Minorities in English Law*, Stoke: Trentham Books Ltd.

Lord Chancellor's Department (2002) *Race Equality Scheme* at *www.lcd.gov.uk/dept /equality/raceequal.htm*

Morgan and Taylor. 1987. A Study of Young Black People Leaving Care. In Parry, ML (2000) Local Authority Support for Ethnic Minority Children in J Murphy. 2000. *Ethnic Minorities, their Families and the Law*, Oxford: Hart Publishing.

Packman, J & Hall, C. 1998. *From Care to Accommodation: Support, Protection and Control in Child Care Services*, London: The Stationery Office.

Parry, ML. 2000. Local Authority Support for Ethnic Minority Children. In *Ethnic Minorities, their Families and the Law*, J Murphy. Oxford: Hart Publishing.

Pugh, R. 1996. *Effective Language in Health and Social Care*. In Language and Practice: Minority Language Provision within the Guardian ad litem Service, R Pugh & E Jones. 1999. *British Journal of Social Work*, vol. 29, pp 529–545.

Pugh, R & Jones, E. 1999. Language and Practice: Minority Language Provision within the Guardian ad litem Service. *British Journal of Social Work*, **29**, 529–545.

Rowe, J. 1989. *Child Care Now*, London: British Association of Adoption and Fostering.

The Children Act 1989, London: HMSO.

Thoburn, J, Wilding, J & Watson, J. 2000. *Family Support in Cases of Emotional Maltreatment and Neglect*, London: Stationery Office.

Wilkinson, JP 1985–86. Why magistrates need race relations training. In *Ethnic Minorities in English Law* R Jones, R & W Gnanapala. 2000. Stoke: Trentham Books Ltd.

THE MENTAL HEALTH NEEDS OF REFUGEE CHILDREN AND THEIR FAMILIES

Dr Guinevere Tufnell
Consultant Child & Adolescent Psychiatrist, Traumatic Stress Clinic

Summary of paper

Dr Tufnell stated that over the last two years, she and her team have seen more than 100 refugee children aged between 2 and 18 years. The children have typically described mass killings, rape, torture, and terror. Having arrived in the UK, the families' expectations of hope and security are often disappointed. Language and cultural problems make it difficult to understand the system. Racism is not uncommon. Worries about family members left behind compound the effects of loss of occupation, social status, family support and familiar culture.

Mental health difficulties are common and can significantly affect the ability of parents to provide the support and care which children need. Fathers often become depressed and withdrawn, or irritable and violent. They may attempt to numb their pain with drugs or alcohol. Many mothers suffer from anxiety, depression and post-traumatic stress disorder (PTSD).

Children are affected very differently, depending on their age, understanding, type of experience they have suffered and the support available to them. Once settled in the UK, many children adapt quickly, and settle well in school. However, the children seen at the clinic often describe severe mental health symptoms on returning home.

The exact prevalence of psychiatric disorder in refugees in the UK is unknown, but it is probably 30% or higher. There is a greater risk of mental health problems in situations which combine multiple risk factors – in the child, in the parent, and in the environment.

Almost all children seen at Dr Tufnell's clinic have had severe psychiatric difficulties. Of the children seen by her and her team, some are referred for treatment and others for expert witness reports.

Where children are referred for expert reports, referring solicitors usually request answers to three questions:

- *What has the child experienced?*
- *How has the child been affected?*
- *What effect will it have on the child to return to their country of origin?*

Solicitors are often reluctant to interview a traumatised child themselves. Psychiatric assessment involves interviewing the child and also obtaining information from a variety of other sources in order to optimise reliability.

The Home Office often raises concerns about the credibility of applicants for asylum. Discrepancies are often cited as evidence that the applicant has not been truthful. However Dr Tufnell said that it is important to remember that discrepancies may also be caused by emotional or cultural pressures, as well as by mental health problems.

In relation to the third question – the return of children to their country of origin, Dr Tufnell raised the following issues:

- *Children who have been traumatised need safety and security above all. If they are sent back to their country of origin and experience further trauma there is a likelihood they will develop chronic PTSD and long term mental health problems.*

- *They may be exposed to powerful reminders of past trauma. These can trigger post-traumatic symptoms.*
- *The disruption of a major move is a well-known cause of stress. For refugee children, another move is likely to be particularly stressful and could result in further losses (eg education) and disruption.*
- *If the child suffers from a disorder which requires specialist treatment, it may not be available in the country of origin; even if it is it may be impossible for the child to access.*

Concluding, Dr Tufnell said that refugee children and parents have a high risk of mental health problems. Mental health problems reduce parents' ability to care for their children. Environmental support as well as specialist treatments has a crucial role in alleviating such mental health difficulties. Psychiatric reports can help to ensure that the court is fully informed when making decisions about a family's right to remain in the UK.

Abstract

Refugee children and their families are vulnerable to mental health problems that can be severe, disabling and long-lasting. Post-traumatic stress disorder (PTSD) and depression are particularly prevalent. However, exposure to life-threatening traumatic experience is not the sole determining factor. There are multiple risk factors for developing mental health problems, or for perpetuating such problems. Some of these risk factors occur after the family has arrived in the host country. Many of them are preventable. Those that are not could be alleviated by early intervention. This paper presents a brief review of the research and examines some of the practical issues facing the clinician who is instructed to give evidence in relation to court proceedings related to asylum claims.

(1) Refugee Families – the figures

Approximately 110,000 people applied for asylum in the UK in 2002/03 and of these 3,600 were unaccompanied minors. Of those who applied for refugee status, 26% were recognised, but only 9% received refugee status, with 17% receiving Exceptional Leave to Remain. This rose to 42% following appeals.

At the Traumatic Stress Clinic in the last two years the Child & Family Team has seen more than 100 refugee children, ranging in age from 2–18 years, some completely alone. These children originate from Eastern Europe, Africa, South America, and the Middle East. Children and their parents who come from countries engaged in war or civil conflict, typically describe seeing mass killings, rape and torture inflicted on their families and communities, as well as harrowing tales of how narrowly they themselves escaped with their own lives. It is often only after many years of persecution and terror that they have been able to leave their country, alone or with their families.

(2) Prevalence of psychiatric disorder in refugee children and families

No one knows the exact prevalence of psychiatric disorder in this population in the UK. Hodes (2000) estimated a rate of 40%. A study by Turner et al (2003) of 842 adult Kosovan refugees in the UK found that just under half of the group surveyed had a diagnosis of PTSD and less than one fifth had a major depressive disorder. In a longitudinal study of 94 children aged 6–18 followed up two years after the 1991 Gulf War (Dyregrov et al, 2002), found that a high proportion of those exposed to various stressors (including seeing dead bodies and body parts, hearing screaming, smelling burnt bodies, separation from parents, being without food and drink for long periods, loss of close family members and friends) continued to experience fear of loss of family, grief, and depression, with around 80% having a probable diagnosis of PTSD. A recent review of studies from around the world of children affected by war (Smith et al,

2002), shows that rates of PTSD, depression and anxiety are significant.

(3) Stress as a risk factor in refugee children and families

Stressful experiences occur not only during the conflict situation, but also during the flight to safety. Less well understood are the major stresses that occur later, during the period of adjusting to life as refugees in the host country. All of these may have an impact on mental health. Several studies suggest that post-migration stressors may be as powerful as events prior to flight (Pernice & Brook, 1996; Van Velsen et al, 1996; Gorst-Unsworth & Goldenberg, 1998; Steel et al, 1999). These stressful experiences affect the family system as a whole, as well as having a major impact on the individuals within it. For example, a woman who has been raped by soldiers may, in addition to the physical and psychological effects of this, face cultural imperatives which condemn her to being ostracised by family and community and compelling her husband to take murderous revenge.

Effects of stress on the family unit

The children who we see have endured interrogation and torture, witnessed their parents, siblings and neighbours tortured and killed in front of them.

The flight to 'safety' often involves enormous and protracted difficulties which affect both children and parents. The journey is difficult and costly to arrange, hazardous in transit and often involves relying on unscrupulous carriers.

When the family arrives in the host country, they face many uncertainties about what will happen to them. The contrast with what they expect and what occurs is often stark. The safety and security that they have imagined are replaced by anxieties arising from delays in the legal system, dispersal, and financial difficulties (Ekblad, 1994; Hodes, 2000). Language and cultural problems make it difficult to understand the system and feel in control. Poor accommodation and social isolation can contribute significantly to depression (Van Velsen et al, 1996). Racism and stereotyping by the host community is not uncommon. Worries about family members who have been left behind and absence of contact, compound the effects of loss of occupation, social status, family support, and familiar culture.

Effects on the adults as parents

What effect do these experiences have on the capacity of the adults in the family to provide the care and protection that their children need? We find that parents often convey a sense of uncertainty, incompetence and helplessness in relation to parenting which is linked to a profound loss of the sense of personal identity and purpose.

Non-verbal indications of sadness, estrangement and lack of intimacy in their relationship are striking in the couples that we see. The physical distance maintained between husband and wife, the avoidance of eye contact, the profoundly withdrawn behaviour of one, and the plaintive desperation of the other. Facial expressions often reflect an inner sense of desolation and hopelessness. Such behaviours are often accompanied by a stark tale of separation, abandonment and terror. For example, one Kosovan mother described how her husband was forced to leave the family home, in order to avoid being killed. She and her children then experienced repeated interrogation and torture by police searching for her husband. Just before fleeing to this country, she was repeatedly raped in front of the children, and the home was destroyed by fire. Now reunited with her husband, she says that if he ever finds out that she was raped, her life will be over. And what of the parent-child relationship here? The child who has witnessed his mother's rape will never be able to talk to either parent about what has happened, and bears a terrible burden of responsibility. These dangerous secrets become the emotional landmines of later years, creating profound lack of trust and insecurity. Furthermore, attempts to avoid remembering or talking about past trauma may prevent emotional resolution and set the scene for chronic mental health problems.

Parents may be too preoccupied with their own problems to meet the child's needs. Many are unable to provide ordinary details of the child's developmental history, and the narrative that they do provide is fragmented and confusing. Lacking support and comfort themselves, they are unable to provide these for their child. In addition, child and parent may try to avoid discussing or remembering past trauma, only to find themselves triggered into re-experiencing as though for the first time. A family member waking screaming from a nightmare is a common example of such triggering. Physical tiredness, pain and ill-health can also prevent parents caring for their children as well as they would wish.

Fathers often experience a painful loss of status and role in the family, as well as the loss of occupational and social identity. Some appear depressed, withdrawn and unengaged and may feel that 'my life is over – I care only about what happens to my child', whilst others are highly irritable and given to outbursts of violence, or attempt to numb their distress with alcohol or drugs. Mothers who have lost their network of support from family and relatives and speak only their own language can become very dependent on their children to provide a focus for their life and a link to the outside world. There are high rates of depression, anxiety, post-traumatic stress disorder among such mothers, and these further reduce their resourcefulness as parents for their children. Such mental health problems in parents are also a risk factor for mental health problems in the children (Yehuda et al, 1997).

The effects of stressful experiences on the child

Children are affected very differently by stressful and traumatic experience, depending on how old they are at the time. A very young child who witnesses events that it cannot make sense of in cognitive terms, will respond to the physical sensations and emotional quality of the experience. If exposed to repeated traumatic experience the child may show long–lasting signs of disturbance (Perry, 1999). For the very young child, loss of safety may also mean the loss of conditions for forming a secure attachment. For an older child, their general level of understanding will do much to determine how they interpret the meaning of what has happened and their response to this. For them, multiple bereavements and other losses have the effect of disrupting attachments, education and a familiar way of life. For unaccompanied children, the often dangerous journey from their country may end in being left destitute and alone.

Once settled in their host country, many pre-adolescent children make remarkably swift adaptations, becoming competent in speaking the language and settling well into school, where they thrive on the security of a familiar routine and the presence of other children. Teachers often report excellent academic progress. The children that we see at the clinic, however, often experience significant post-traumatic symptoms after school and in the holidays.

For adolescents, it is more difficult to acquire a new language and to find a peer group. Unaccompanied adolescents may find themselves extremely isolated, accommodated in a hostel where there is little or no support and with little to occupy them during the day. Some are pregnant as the result of rape. Social Services may offer little more than basic accommodation, and the child's social worker may only be able to visit very infrequently. Local education resources can also be very meagre. For these youngsters, there is a considerable risk of depression and of suicide as well as post-traumatic symptoms. Those that are pregnant, lacking most of the resources that they need to look after their baby, require a great deal of practical and emotional support. In particular, the risk of depression in a vulnerable young mother with PTSD signals safety concerns about both mother and child.

(4) Risk and resilience factors for mental health problems in refugee children

Risk factors for mental health problems are now well recognised. They include characteristics of the events experienced, factors in the child or parent, and factors in the post trauma environment. These are summarised in Table 1.

Table 1. Risk Factors for mental health problems in refugee children. (Adapted from Fazel & Stein 2002)

Child factors

Number of traumatic events experienced or witnessed (Punamaki R, 1989)

Expressive language difficulties (Montgomery, 1998)

PTSD leading to long term vulnerability in stressful situation (Realmuto et al, 1992)

Physical health problems resulting from trauma or malnutrition (Westermeyer, 1988)

Older age (Garmezy & Masten, 1994)

Parental factors

Mental illness in either parent (Sack et al, 1986; McCloskey & Southwick, 1996)

Observation of torture of parents, especially mother (Montgomery, 1998; Garmezy & Masten, 1994)

Death of or separation from parents (McCloskey & Southwick, 1996; Zivcic, 1993)

Unemployment of parents (Garmezy & Masten, 1994)

Underestimation of stress levels in children by parents (Hodes, 1998)

Lack of emotional support from parents (Dyregrov et al, 2002)

Environmental factors

Poverty (Hodes, 2000)

Time taken for immigration status to be determined (Ekblad, 1994)

Cultural isolation (McCloskey & Southwick, 1996)

Period of time in refugee camp (Montgomery, 1998)

Time in host country – risk may increase with time (Kinzie et al, 1989)

Re-activation by news of war (Nader & Pynoos, 1993)

The available evidence suggests that where there is an accumulation of risk factors, there are greater risks to mental health (Espino, 1991; Ford & Kidd, 1998; Garbarino and Kostelny, 1996, Mollica et al, 1997, Sack et al, 1996).

Resilience factors

It is important to bear in mind that there are many young refugees who cope well, in spite of the terrible events to which they and their families have been exposed. There is now a substantial literature on resilience, showing that, rather than being a trait of personality or genetic endowment, it derives from a combination of factors. These factors operate by a variety of processes before, as well as during and after, the stressful event. Many people exposed to traumatic events do not develop mental health problems, while of those who do, some will gradually recover and others will develop a more chronic condition.

A variety of individual, family and social factors can affect resilience as well as risk (Elbedour et al, 1993). Consistent evidence exists for the protective effects of family support. Children tend to receive stronger social support when parental distress is low (Gorst-Unsworth & Goldenburg, 1998). Greater family cohesion and adaptability are associated with fewer symptoms in young children (Laor et al, 1996). Support provided by the wider community also appears to be important (Hodes, 2000). Factors that protect against the effects of traumatic experience are summarised in Table 2.

Table 2. Protective Factors

Perceived safety and security – stage of legal process

Parental support

No previous psychiatric history

Supportive environment – parents and school

Understanding of situation

Feeling in control

Good self esteem

---

(6) What can the psychiatrist contribute?

It has been argued by some that the distress suffered by refugee children and families is normal, given what they have been through, and that a psychiatric diagnosis merely adds stigma to their difficulties (Summerfield, 2001). However, it is clear that there is a significant population with mental health needs that require attention. What kind of services are there? In order to give a flavour of what can be offered, I will draw on the experience of our team at the TSC. Almost all the 100 children and young people referred in the last two years have severe psychological difficulties. Some are referred for treatment, others for expert witness reports. Let me deal first with the issues raised by expert witness reports. I will then deal briefly with issues of treatment.

a) Questions for the Expert or Professional Witness

Referring solicitors basically ask for the answer to three questions:

- What has this child experienced?
- How has the child been affected psychologically?
- What effect will it have on the child if they return to their country of origin?

I will take each of these in turn, starting with what the child has experienced.

Question 1. What has this child experienced?

Solicitors are often reluctant to interview a child who is obviously vulnerable or traumatised. Many say that they lack adequate training in interviewing vulnerable children. As a result of this, they are not sure that they will be able to obtain adequate instructions from the child. They often have questions about whether the information that the child has given is true or reliable. When children are obviously distressed and speak no English, some solicitors are concerned that an interview might cause severe emotional upset, retraumatise the child, or precipitate dangerous or suicidal behaviour. Feeling concerned that a child is too vulnerable to undertake the normal Home Office interview, solicitors may ask us both to provide the detailed information they need about what the child has experienced and for an opinion about how the child's experiences of rape or torture are likely to affect their ability to cope with the Home Office interview or with the process of giving evidence in court.

Our approach to answering these questions relies upon gathering detailed information about the child's past and present functioning from as many sources as possible, and then forming an opinion which accounts for this information. We like to see children both with their families and separately. Because parents are often unable to give accurate information about what their child has witnessed and the consequent psychological impact, it is important to see the child separately. The interview format will depend on the child's developmental level, but basically follows the semi-structured format described by Pynoos and Eth (1986). This is summarised in Table 3.

Table 3 Trauma Interview (adapted from Pynoos & Eth, 1986)

Introduction and explanation

Identifying traumatic event(s)

Describing child's responses at the time

Child's responses up to present

Child's attributions/meanings about event(s)

Child's thoughts about the future

Wind down

When interviewing children, especially unaccompanied adolescents, it is important to anticipate the support needed both during and after the interview. Sometimes youngsters come for their assessments alone and unprepared. We make sure that the purpose of the interview has been understood, explain the information we need, and try to put them both at ease and in control. We try to ensure that someone they trust will be able to accompany them to the interview and offer support.

Concerns about the credibility of the applicant's story or of the child witness is frequently mentioned in Home Office letters explaining the reason for refusal of the asylum application and may be the main factor leading to the request for an expert opinion. The interviewer therefore needs to be aware of the specific issues in question, and to address these during the assessment, clarifying apparent inconsistencies in the child's narrative. In addition, we seek to establish whether the symptoms and behaviours described to us and observed by us are consistent with the narrative of events and with other, more neutral information provided. Particular care is needed when there are apparent inconsistencies with statements given by others, or apparent discrepancies in relation to other legal documents. For example, a child or mother may disclose to the solicitor that she has been raped as part of persecution and torture. If she did not disclose this in her Home Office interview, the court may interpret the discrepant information as evidence that the individual has not been truthful. However, there may be **many** reasons why the information was not given in the initial interview, including shame, avoidance, dissociation, amnesia, or cultural pressures. Herlihy and colleagues (2002) suggest that the more traumatised the witness, the more likely they are to give discrepant accounts. A child's eye witness account of the events described by the parents may provide a new perspective on the story given by a parent. A very young child's play and other behaviour may show more clearly than words what has happened.

Question 2. How has the traumatic experience affected the child psychologically?

The answer to this question involves not only providing a diagnostic opinion as to whether or not the child suffers from any psychiatric disorder, but also to what extent the child's mental state can be attributed to their experiences, whether there are any associated mental health needs and if so, what help is required.

In relation to the diagnosis of psychiatric disorders, there may be questions about the *degree* to which a child has been affected and the *reliability* of the diagnostic opinion. Standard instruments such as the Children's Post-Traumatic Stress Disorder Inventory (Saigh, 1989), the Impact of Event Scale (Horowitz et al, 1979) and the Birleson Depression Rating Scale (Birleson, 1981) may be helpful in establishing a baseline and reliability. However, these instruments are mostly in English, and may be difficult for the children to respond to even with the help of an interpreter. Furthermore, they have been standardised with children from a very different educational, cultural and linguistic background from the refugee children that we see. Therefore, the results need to be interpreted with caution.

For children under the age of eight, however, there is a lack of any suitable standardised assessment tools of this kind. There are also difficulties in applying the standard DSM-IV diagnostic criteria to very young children where the criteria for PTSD developed by Sheeringa et al (1995) are very useful. Special techniques are needed for working with very young children and children who are unable to communicate verbally, making use of non-verbal interactions and detailed observations of the child's behaviour, for example, their body language, moods, the way in which they interact with the people – and the furniture – in the room, the response to the available toys, and the number of times they ask to use the toilet during the assessment. Perry (1999) writes:

> 'the child's recall of a traumatic event involves not just the narrative shards as recalled using cognitive memory but also the intense fear of the emotional memory, the motor agitation of the motor memories and the physiological arousal, or dissociative response, of the state memory. Yet the syntax, semantics and grammar of these non-cognitive narrations do not yet have the standing in court that … verbal language does.'

How credible is the child's story?

There may be a number of factors that affect this. For example, discrepancies in the child's narrative may need to be accounted for. Could these be due to poor concentration associated with depression, and/or to the avoidance which is often seen with high levels of intrusive re-experiencing following torture or very shameful experiences such as rape? Perhaps repeated interviews have been a contributory factor – a particular hazard in cases where there have been *multiple* episodes of trauma that are similar (Herlihy et al, 2002). Perhaps the child's history is one where repeated traumatic disruptions of attachment give rise to a characteristically disjointed narrative. A child with no formal educational background may have difficulties in providing a clear narrative especially if they are anxious or traumatised. These questions can be checked out to some extent by exploring the child's capacity to provide a coherent detailed narrative around more neutral topics such as schooling or recreational interests.

Sometimes, we are asked to comment on the child's age and maturity. This is a question that often arises when a young person has arrived in this country alone, with no identifying papers. Such children may be assigned an age by the authorities on the basis of incomplete or incorrect information. One Somali adolescent said that he did not know how old he was. He had lost contact with his family when he was very young. He had been sent to the UK for safety much later by the family that had given him shelter. Many children give developmental histories whose schematic and fragmented qualities suggest multiple disruptions of attachment and location. Many have had very little formal education. The question of chronological age may be one that is best answered by a paediatrician. It may be possible to obtain some idea of such a child's mental age by assessing their cognitive functioning with the aid of psychological tests. However, the information obtained in this way will need cautious interpretation.

On the basis of our assessment, we hope to have a broad view of the child's mental health needs and the resources required to meet those needs. We present our general diagnostic conclusions within a framework where clinical data can be summarised and precipitating, predisposing and perpetuating factors can be pointed out. The child's treatment needs in relation to specific disorders can be described and information can be provided about the likely consequences of treatment not being provided. Finally, we go on to address the specific questions asked by the child's solicitor.

Treatment – what is effective?

Given what we now know about the importance of post-migration and post-trauma factors in the genesis of mental health problems, there are clearly important opportunities for preventive interventions with both children and families, as outlined above. The legal system, social services, education and housing have a crucial part to play. Assistance from the voluntary sector, refugee support groups, and befriending organisations can also play an important supportive role.

Children who suffer from psychiatric disorders such as adjustment disorders, PTSD or depression can benefit from help at a number of different levels. The first, most important requirement is a perception of physical safety and stability. When this is lacking, symptoms tend to recur or deteriorate. For example, the frequency of nightmares and flashbacks increase markedly when there is a threat of deportation.

We find that giving parents the support and treatment that they need can cause rapid improvement in the symptoms of their children. Many of the refugee children that we see at the clinic report that their symptoms are diminishing in intensity and frequency, especially when they feel settled into a routine at home and in their new school. School provides a particularly important island of normality for many children, who quickly learn the language, and are keen to grasp the opportunities for building a new life. Reports from teachers often speak of these children as being highly motivated and a pleasure to teach. However, we have found that these children remain very vulnerable to recurrence of their symptoms. For example, many children reported a deterioration of their nightmares and flashbacks in the wake of the disasters of September 11 (see also Kinzie et al, 1989 and Kinzie, Boehnlein et al, 2002) and in relation to the recent Iraq war.

Where traumatic experience has been severe and repeated, specialist help from mental health services is often needed in addition to the general measures outlined above. For example cognitive behaviour therapy can be very helpful with sleep problems, intrusive thoughts and other difficulties. Medication can help with hyperarousal, sleep problems and mood disorders. Family work may be needed to address the destructive effects of traumatic experience on the stability of family relationships. Often a package of care, combining a mixture of general and specific measures is required. Treatment can be very effective, but a child may not be able to benefit from specialist treatment if their basic need for safety and stability is not met.

Question 3. What is the likely effect on the child of being sent back to their country of origin?

This can be a difficult question to answer. As mental health professionals, we lack information and expertise about the country in question and are therefore in no position to venture an expert opinion. We can, however, use the reports of child or parent in forming our opinions. There are a number of issues on which we can usefully provide expert advice to the court.

(1) The likely effect of danger and further traumatic experience

For children who are suffering from PTSD, we emphasise that symptoms, particularly anxiety, may worsen if the environment does not meet the child's need for safety and security. There is now a considerable body of evidence to show that although many people with PTSD do recover, a proportion go on to develop the long term biological and psychological changes associated with chronic PTSD (for recent reviews, see Bremner et al, 1999; Perry 1999). Children are particularly vulnerable. In the case of children exposed to war, the long term effects can continue for many years (Elbedour et al, 1993). Studies of the effect of cumulative trauma (Follette et al, 1996; Turner & Lloyd, 1995) and the developmental impact of trauma (Cicchetti & Toth, 1995; Kendall-Tackett et al, 1993; Westen, Lohr, et al, 1990; Westen, Ludolph, et al, 1990) show that childhood trauma has lasting adverse impact and can cause serious and debilitating mental health problems. These include substance abuse and disorders of personality, attachment, adjustment and mood.

(2) The importance of exposure to triggers

Intrusive re-experiencing can be triggered by a wide variety of directly and indirectly related stimuli. If a traumatised child is exposed to stimuli which repeatedly trigger the symptoms of PTSD, there is a risk not only of repeated re-traumatisation but also of chronic PTSD having an adverse effect on normal functioning.

(3) The effects of disruption

It may be relevant to consider what effect an additional disruption could have on a child's psychosocial adjustment and education.

(4) The need for specialist treatment

How would removal impact on the child's ability to access any specialist treatment that they might need? For example, combination therapy for AIDS and specialist mental health resources unlikely to be available in their country of origin. It may therefore be appropriate for us to comment on how specific specialist treatment or the lack of it is likely to affect the child's adjustment and longer term prospects. Delayed treatment may increase their chances of long term psychiatric problems. In addition, in the absence of a safe environment, it may be impossible – even given adequate resources – for the child to make use of psychological treatment.

Conclusions

Refugee children and families have a high risk of developing mental health disorders. Mental health problems in a parent can dramatically affect the ability of the parent to provide the quality of care that a child needs. The refugee children and families that we have seen have not only experienced severe trauma in the past but often endure enormous continuing difficulties – not least the uncertainty of their status in this country, with all the attendant disadvantages that this brings. Environmental conditions as well as specialist treatment can help to alleviate many mental health difficulties.

Psychiatric assessments can help to identify the mental health needs of refugee children and the resources they require. Whilst it is obvious that these children and their families have many other need and that it can be unhelpful to pathologies (Summerfield, 2001) it seems important that the courts are as fully informed as possible when making difficult decisions about a family's right to remain in the UK. Psychiatric reports for the court have a small but crucial role to play here.

References

Bremner, JD, Southwick, SM & Charney, DS. 1999. The neurobiology of post-traumatic stress disorder: an integration of animal and human research. In *Post-traumatic Stress Disorder: A Comprehensive Text*, PA Saigh and JD Bremner. Needham Heights, MA: Allyn & Bacon.

Birleson, P. 1981. The validity of depressive disorder in childhood and the development of a self-rating scale: a research report. *Journal of Child Psychology and Psychiatry*, **22**, 73–88.

Cicchetti, D & Toth, S. 1995. A developmental perspective on child abuse and neglect. *Journal of the American Academy of Child & Adolescent Psychiatry*, **34**, 541–565.

Dyregrov, A, Gjestad, R, Raundalen, M. 2002. Children Exposed to Warfare: A Longitudinal Study. *Journal of Traumatic Stress*, **15.1**, 59–68.

Ekblad S. 1994. Viktigt folia upp asylsokande barn. Riskfaktorerna andres under krisfaserna. [Importance of follow-up of refugee children: Risk factors are changing during the different phases of the crisis]. *Lakartidningen*, 91:4012–4014, 4017.

Elbedour, S, ten Bensel, R & Bastien, DT. 1993. Ecological integrated model of children of war: Individual and social psychology. *Child Abuse & Neglect*, **17**, 805–819.

Espino. 1991. Trauma and adaptation: the case of Central American children. In *Refugee children. Theory, research and services*, ed. F Ahearn and JL Athey, pp 106–124.

Fazel, M & Stein, A. 2002. The mental health of refugee children. *Archives of Disease in Childhood*, **87**, 0–4.

Follette, V, Polusny, M, Bechtle, A & Naugle, A. 1996. Cumulative trauma. *Journal of Traumatic Stress*, **9**, 25–36.

Ford, JD & Kidd, P. 1998. Early childhood trauma and disorder of extreme stress as predictors of treatment outcome with chronic post-traumatic stress disorder. *Journal of Traumatic* Stress, **11(4)**:743–761.

Garbarino and Kostelny. 1996. The effects of political violence on Palestinian children's behaviour problems: a risk accumulation model. *Child Development*, **67**, 33 – 45.

Garmezy N, & Masten AS. 1994. Chronic adversities. In *Child and Adolescent Psychiatry: Modern Approaches*, ed. Rutter M, Taylor EA, Hersov LA. Oxford: Blackwell Scientific, pp 191–208.

Gorst-Unsworth, C & Goldenberg, E. 1998. Psychological sequaelae of torture and organised violence suffered by refugees in Iraq. *British Journal of Psychiatry*, **172**, 90–94.

Herlihy, J, P Scragg et al, 2002. Discrepancies in autobiographical memories implications for the assessment of asylum seekers: repeated interviews study. *British Medical Journal*, **324**: 324–327.

Hodes, M. 2000. Psychologically distressed refugee children in the United Kingdom. *Child Psychology and Psychiatry Review*, **5**, 57–68.

Hodes, M. 1998. Refugee children. *British Medical Journal*, **316**, 793–4.

Horowitz, MJ, Wilner, N and Alvarez W. 1979. Impact of event scale: A measure of subjective stress. *Psychosomatic Medicine*, **41**, 209–218.

Laor, N, Wolmer, R, Mayes, LC, Golomb, A, Silverberg, DS, Weizman, R & Cohen, DJ. 1996. Israeli pre-schoolers under Scud missile attack. *Archives of General Psychiatry*, **53**, 416–423.

Kendall-Tackett, K, Williams, L and Finkelhor, D. 1993. Impact of sexual abuse on children. *Psychological Bulletin*, **113**, 164–180.

Kinzie JD, Sack W, Angell R, *et al.*, 1989. A three-year follow-up of Cambodian young people traumatized as children. *Journal of the American Academy of Child and Adolescent Psychiatry*, **28**, 501–4.

Montgomery E. 1998. Refugee children from the Middle East. *Scandinavian Journal of Social Medicine. Supplementum*, **54**, 1–152.

McCloskey LA, Southwick, K. 1996. Psychosocial problems in refugee children exposed to war. *Pediatrics*, **97**, 394–397.

Mollica, RF, Poole, C, Son, L, Murray, CC & Tor, S. 1997. Effects of war trauma on Cambodian refugee adolescent's functional health and mental health status. *Journal of the American Academy of Child and Adolescent Psychiatry*, **36**, 1098–1106.

Nader, K, Pynoos, RS, Fairbanks, L, AI-Ajeel, M & Al-Asfour, A. 1993. A preliminary study of PTSD and grief among the children of Kuwait following the Gulf crisis. *British Journal of Clinical Psychology*, **32**, 407–416.

Pernice, R & Brook, J. 1996. Refugees' and immigrants' mental health: association of demographic and post migration factors. *Journal of Social Psychology*, **136**, 511–519.

Perry, B. 1999. The memories of states: How the brain stores and retrieves traumatic experience. In *Splintered reflections: Images of the body in trauma*, ed. Goodwin, Jean & Attias. Reina: Basic Books.

Pynoos, RS, and Eth, S. 1986. Witness to violence: the child interview. *Journal of the American Academy of Child & Adolescent* Psychiatry, **25**, 306–319.

Punamaki R. 1989. Factors affecting the mental health of Palestinian children exposed to political violence. *International Journal of Mental Health*, **18**, 63–79.

Realmuto GM, Masten, A, Carole F, et al, 1992. Adolescent survivors of massive childhood trauma in Cambodia: life events and current symptoms. *Journal of Traumatic Stress*, **5**, 589–599.

Rutter, M. 1999. Resilience concepts and findings: implications for family therapy. *Journal of Family Therapy*, **21**, 119–144.

Sack, WH, Seeley, JR & Clarke, GN. 1997. Does PTSD transcendent cultural barriers? A study from the Khmer adolescent refugee project. *Journal of the American Academy of Child & Adolescent Psychiatry*. **36**, 49–54.

Sack, WH, Clarke, GN & Seeley, JR. 1996. Multiple forms of stress in Cambodian adolescent refugees. *Child Development*, **67**, 107–116.

Sack W, Angell R, Kinzie JD, et al, 1986. The psychiatric effects of massive trauma on Cambodian children. *Journal of the American Academy of Child & Adolescent Psychiatry*. **25**, 370–375.

Scheeringa, MS, Zeanah, CH, Drell, MJ, Carrieu, JA. 1995. Two approaches to the diagnosis of post-traumatic stress disorder in infancy and early childhood. *Journal of the American Academy of Child & Adolescent Psychiatry*, **34**, 191–200.

Steel, Z, Silove, D, Bird, K, McGorry, P & Mohan, P 1999. Pathways from war to post-traumatic stress symptoms among Tamil Asylum seekers, refugees, and immigrants. *Journal of Traumatic Stress*, **12**, 421–435.

Smith P, Perrin, S, Yule W, Hacam B & Stuvland R. 2002. War exposure among children from Bosnia-Hercegovina: Psychological adjustment in a community sample. *Journal of Traumatic Stress*, **15.2**, 147–156.

Summerfield, D. 2001 The invention of post-traumatic stress disorder and the social usefulness of a psychiatric category. *British Medical Journal*, **322**, 95–98.

Turner, R & Lloyd, D. 1995. Lifetime traumas and mental health. *Journal of Health and Social Behaviour*, **36**, 360–376.

Turner S, Bowie C, Dunn G, Shapo L & Yule W. 2003. Mental Health of Kosovan Albanian refugees in the UK. *British Journal of Psychiatry*, **182**, 444–448.

Van Velsen C, Gorst Usworkth, C and Turner, S. 1996. Survivors of torture and organised violence – demography and diagnosis. *Journal of Traumatic Stress*, **9**, 181–193.

Westen D, Lohr, N, Silk, K, Gold L & Kerber, K. 1990. Object relations and social cognition in borderlines, major depressives, and normals. *Psychological Assessment*, **2**, 355–364.

Westen, D, Ludolph, P, Block, M, Wixom, J, Weiss, E. 1990. Developmental history and object to relations in psychiatrically disturbed adolescent girls. *American Journal of Psychiatry*, **147**, 1061–1068.

Westermeyer J. 1988. DSM-III psychiatric disorders among among refugees in the United States: a point prevalence study. *American Journal of Psychiatry*, **145**, 197–202.

Wood D, Halfon N, Scarlata D, et al, 1993. Impact of family relocation on children's growth, development, school function, and behavior. *Journal of the American Medical Association*, **270**, 1334–1338.

Yehuda, R, Schmeidler, J, Elkin, A, Houshmand, E, Seiver, L, Binder-Brynes, K. 1997. Phenomenology and psychobiology of the intergenerational response to trauma. In *Intergenerational handbook of multigenerational legacies of trauma*, ed. Y Danieli. Plenum Press: New York.

Zivcic I. 1993. Emotional reactions of children to war stress in Croatia. *Journal of the American Academy of Child & Adolescent Psychiatry*, **32**, 709–13.

HANDOUT – THE MENTAL HEALTH NEEDS OF REFUGEE CHILDREN AND THEIR FAMILIES

Guinevere Tufnell

Children at risk of developing PTSD – adapted from Smith et al 2002

Authors	Date	Subject	Rate of PTSD %
Vernon	1941	Effects of war on children	Low
Cairns	1996	Effects of war and political violence on children	Substantial minority
Saigh	1991	Effect of bombings and terror attacks on Lebanese children	27
Gupta, Dyregrov, Gjestad, & Mukanoheli	1996	Children exposed to genocide in Rwanda	79% at risk
Thabet &Vostanis	1999	Palestinian children from Gaza	41
Kuterovac, Dyregrov, & Stuvland	1994	Up to 74% of Croatian children were at risk for developing PTSD	74% at risk
Kinzie, Sack, Angell, & Clark	1989	Adolescents 5 years after exposure to war atrocities	Up to 50%
Kinzie, Sack, Angell, Manson & Rath	1986	Psychiatric effects of massive trauma on children in Cambodia	
Realmuto et al.	1992	Cambodia	
Arroyo & Eth	1985	Central America	
Smith, Perrin, Yule, Hacam & Stuvland	2002	Questionnaire study of 2976 Bosnian children aged 9–14. Community epidemiological study of children with high levels of exposure	52% likely cases
Giaconia et al	1995	Peacetime community prevalence of PTSD	6–7

Other reactions to war trauma (studied relatively little)

Author	Date	Topic	Rate
		Depression	
Saigh	1991	Depression among Lebanese children	Increased
Dyregrov & Raundalen	1992	Iraqi children	Increased
Kinzie et al.	1989	Cambodian children who survived war	Increased
Zivcic	1993	Croatian children	Increased
		Anxiety in children	
Saigh, 1991	1991		
Kinzie et al	1989		
Ziv and Israel	1973	Anxiety levels of Israeli kibbutzim children who had been exposed to recent shelling did not differ from those of children who had not been so exposed	
		Grief – little studied	
Dyregrov and Raundalen	1992	Following the Gulf War, Iraqi children who had witnessed the bombing of a shelter that resulted in the deaths of 750 people	Showed significant and lasting signs of grief.
Nader, Pynoos, Fairbanks, Al-Ajeel, & Al-Asfour	1993	Kuwaiti children and youth (aged 8–21 years) after the Gulf War, finding	98% of the sample reported at least one symptom of grief.
Smith, Perrin, Yule, Hacam & Stuvland	2002	Questionnaire study of 2,976 Bosnian children aged 9–14. Community epidemiological study with high levels of exposure	15% likely cases of depression (peacetime rates 10%) more related to PTSD than exposure. Anxiety scores elevated related to exposure. Grief scores elevated.

Risk factors for PTSD and other mental health disorders in children exposed to war (multiple, repeated, traumatic experience)

Author	Year	Topic	
Macksoud, Dyregrov, & Raundalen	1993	Multiple stressors: during war stressors are generally multiple, diverse, chronic, and repeated, including the violent death of a parent, witnessing the killing of close family members, separation and displacement, terror attacks, and bombardment and shelling.	Increases rates of disorder compared to peacetime disasters.
Chimienti, Nasr & Khalifehi	1989	Studies reporting a significant relationship between the amount of these kinds of war experiences and subsequent reactions.	
Gupta et al	1996		
Kuterovac et al	1994		
Mghir, Freed, Raskin, & Katon	1995		
Nader et al	1993		
Dyregrov and Raundalen	1992	Gulf War: children 6–18 years. Exposure to dead bodies and body parts was the best predictor of intrusion symptoms of PTSD.	Exposure to very strong sensory impressions (eg, smelling burning bodies and hearing screams for help) may result in more severe re-experiencing.
Dyregrov, Gjestad, & Raundalen	2002	Children exposed to warfare: 2-year follow up to 1992 study (above).	Many children still symptomatic.
Gupta et al	1996	In Rwanda found that the best exposure predictor of child outcome was a (perceived) direct life threat.	
Carlson & Rosser-Hogan	1994	Adult Pol Pot survivors suggesting that threat to survival may be related to post-traumatic stress symptoms across different cultures.	
Nader et al.	1993	Kuwaiti children, suggesting that threat to survival may be related to post-traumatic stress symptoms across different cultures.	

Smith, Perrin, Yule, Hacam & Stuvland	2002	Questionnaire study of 2976 Bosnian children aged 9–14. 2 years after end of worst fighting. Community epidemiological study with high levels of exposure.	Total exposure (explained most of variance) Gender (not clear why girls>boys); age; Coping facilitated when whole community affected?
Smith, Perrin, Yule & Rabe-Hesketh	2001	Children's coping and maternal mental health.	Maternal mental health is most significant predictor of children's coping.
Bryce, Walker, Ghorayeb & Kanj	1989	5–7 year old Lebanese children in Beirut war.	Most important predictor of child morbidity was mother's level of depression.
Dawes, Tredoux & Feinstein	1989	Crossroads Squatter's Camp in South Africa.	Children with multiple symptoms were more likely to have mothers with PTSD.
McFarlane	1987	Australian bush fires – family reactions and children's distress.	Parental adjustment more important than exposure for children's adjustment.
Flannery	1990	Social support enhances coping.	

References

Arroyo, W & Eth, S. 1985. Children traumatized in Central American warfare. In *Post-traumatic Stress Disorder in Children*, ed. Eth & RS Pynoos, pp 101–120. Washington, DC: American Psychiatric Press.

Bryce, J, Walker, N, Ghorayeb, F & Kanj, M. 1989. Life experiences, response styles, and mental health among mothers and children in Beirut, Lebanon. *Social Science and Medicine*, **28**, 685–695.

Cairns, E. 1996. *Children and Political Violence*, Oxford: Blackwell Publishers.

Carlson, EB & Rosser-Hogan, R. 1994. Cross-cultural responses to trauma: A study of traumatic experiences and post-traumatic symptoms in Cambodian refugees. *Journal of Traumatic Stress*, **7**, 43–58.

Chimienti, G, Nasr, J & Khalifehi, L. 1989. Children's reactions to war related stress II: The influence of gender, age, and mother's reaction. *International Journal of Mental Health*, **21**, 72–86.

Dawes, A, Tredoux, C & Feinstein, A. 1989. Political violence in South Africa: Some effects on children of the violent destruction of their community. *International Journal of Mental Health*, **18**, 16–43.

Dyregrov, A & Raundalen, M. 1992. *The impact of the Gulf war on the children of Iraq*. Paper presented at the International Society for Traumatic Stress Studies World Conference, Amsterdam, Netherlands.

Dyregrov, A, Gjestad, R & Raundalen, M. 2002. *Children exposed to warfare: a longitudinal study*. *Journal of Traumatic Stress*, **15**, 59–68.

Dyregrov, A, & Yule, W. May 1995. *Screening measures: The development of the UNICEF screening battery*. Paper presented at the Fourth European Conference on Traumatic Stress, Paris, France.

Flannery, R. 1990. Social support and psychological trauma: A methodological review. *Journal of Traumatic Stress*, **3**, 593–612.

Giaconia, RM, Reinherz, HZ, Silverman, AB, Pakiz, B, Frost, AK & Cohen, E. 1995. Traumas and post-traumatic stress in a community population of older adolescents. *Journal of the American Academy of Child and Adolescent Psychiatry*, **34**, 1369–1380.

Gupta, L, Dyregrov, A, Gjestad, R & Mukanoheli, X. 1996. *Trauma, exposure, and psychological reactions to genocide among Rwandan refugees*. Paper presented at the 12th annual convention of the International Society for Traumatic Stress Studies, San Francisco, CA.

Hacam, B, Smith, P, Yule, W & Perrin, S. November 1998. *Psychological services for children in war: experiences in Mostar*. Paper presented at the 14th International Congress of the International Association for Child and Adolescent Psychiatry and Allied Professions, Stockholm, Sweden.

Kinzie, JD, Sack, WH, Angell, RH & Clarke, G. 1989. A 3-year follow-up of Cambodian young people traumatized as children. *Journal of the American Academy of Child and Adolescent Psychiatry*, **28**, 501–504.

Kinzie, JD, Sack, WH, Angell, RH, Manson, S. & Rath, B. 1986. The psychiatric effects of massive trauma on Cambodian children: 1. The children. *Journal of the American Academy of Child and Adolescent Psychiatry*, **25**, 370–376.

Kuterovac, G, Dyregrov, A, & Stuvland, R. 1994. Children in war: A silent majority under stress. *British Journal of Medical Psychology*, **67**, 363–375.

Macksoud, MS. 1992. Assessing war trauma in children: A case study of Lebanese children. *Journal of Refugee Studies* **5**, 1–15.

Macksoud, MS, Dyregrov, A, & Raundalen, M. 1993. Traumatic war experiences and their effects on children. In *International Handbook of Traumatic Stress Syndromes*, ed. JP Wilson & B Raphael, pp 625–633. New York: Plenum.

McFarlane, AC. 1987a. Post-traumatic phenomena in a longitudinal study of children following a natural disaster. *Journal of the American Academy of Child and Adolescent Psychiatry*, **26**, 764–769.

McFarlane, AC. 1987b. Family functioning and overprotection following a natural disaster: The longitudinal effects of post-traumatic morbidity. *Australia and New Zealand Journal of Psychiatry*, **21**, 210–218.

Mghir, R, Freed, W, Raskin, A & Katon, W. 1995. Depression and post-traumatic stress disorder among a community sample of adolescent and young adult Afghan refugees. *Journal of Nervous and Mental Disease*, **183**, 24–30.

Nader, K, Pynoos, RS, Fairbanks, L, Al-Ajeel, M, & Al-Asfour, A. 1993. A preliminary study of PTSD and grief among the children of Kuwait following the Gulf crisis. *British Journal of Clinical Psychology*, **32**, 407–416.

Pynoos, RS, Frederick, C, Nader, K, Arroyo, W, Steinberg, A, Eth, S, Nunez, F & Fairbanks, L. 1987. Life threat and post-traumatic stress in school age children. *Archives of General Psychiatry*, **44**, 1057–1063.

Realmuto, GM, Masten, A, Carole, LF, Hubbard, J, Groteluschen, A & Chun, B. 1992. Adolescent survivors of massive childhood trauma in Cambodia: Life events and current symptoms. *Journal of Traumatic Stress,* **5**, 589–599.

Saigh, PA. 1991. The development of post-traumatic stress disorder following four different types of traumatisation. *Behavior Research and Therapy,* **29**, 213–216.

Smith P, Perrin S, Yule W, Hacam B, Stuvland R. 2002 War exposure among children from Bosnia-Hercegovina: Psychological adjustment in a community sample. *Journal of Traumatic Stress,* **15.2**, 147–156.

Smith, E, Perrin, S, Schwartz, D, & Yule, W. 1996. *Self-report of stress reactions: A cross-cultural validation study.* Paper presented at 12th annual meeting of the International Society for Traumatic Stress Studies, San Francisco.

Thabet, AM, & Vostanis, E. 1999. Post-traumatic stress reactions in children of war. *Journal of Child Psychology and Psychiatry,* **40**,385–391.

Vernon, PE. 1941. Psychological effects of air-raids. *Journal of Abnormal and Social Psychology,* **36**, 457–476.

Ziv, A, & Israel, R. 1973. Effects of bombardment on the manifest anxiety level of children living in kibbutzim. *Journal of Counselling and Clinical Psychology,* **40**, 487–291.

Zivcic, I. 1993. Emotional reactions of children to war stress in Croatia. *Journal of the American Academy of Child and Adolescent Psychiatry,* **32**, 709–713.

PLENARY DISCUSSIONS: LISTENING TO AND SAFEGUARDING CHILDREN WITH SPECIAL NEEDS

Panel: Beverley Prevatt-Goldstein, Ashok Chand, Dr Guinevere Tufnell

- The President commented that where you have a case in which a child of black or mixed ethnicity needs a long term permanent home, there has been a view amongst social workers that the child must go to a black family. It does not seem to matter that if a child is from the Caribbean you might find parents from West Africa. What is the right way to approach a placement where there are very few black families and more white families?

Beverley Prevatt-Goldstein said that was a very challenging question. She emphasised that each specific situation is different and only general guidelines are appropriate. You should look at what a black family can offer and what a family of the same culture can offer. She said that we are never going to get a repeat of the culture that the child left, but we need to place the child, if possible, with as close a cultural match as we can. Failing that, it is in the child's interests to be with a black family but of a particular quality. If there was one black parent and one white parent, we must find a black family who can value the white ethnicity within that child.

- The panel was asked to explain culture?

Ms Prevatt-Goldstein explained that each family has different take on 'culture'. She said that in her view we sometimes we look at culture very superficially, for example, just because we eat pasta it does not mean that we are familiar with Italian culture. We must look at the life of a culture, the routines and traditions, the vibrancy of a culture. Evidence suggests that children, particularly after the age of seven, get a tremendous amount from locality.

Ashok Chand said that his view has changed over time. Ultimately his preference would be for a child of Asian origin to be placed with a similar family, but if that opportunity does not exist then the child will suffer if he or she is being moved from one family to another anyway. He said that it was not just a matter of matching culture and language, it is important to look at how a white family are willing to look at culture, and respect and enhance it so that the child does not lose sight of it.

- Judge Peter Hunt said that judges are often faced with applications for permission to introduce experts with cultural dimensions. He said that he has generally taken the view that it behoves the guardian and the judge to be sensitive and attuned to ethnic and cultural specifics, and so there is no need for expert witness. He asked the members of the panel for their views.

Mr Chand said that it very much depends on the case as to whether you think there are indications that the family may need particular specialist intervention.

The other members of the panel agreed that an expert witness could be extremely helpful in certain cases.

PLENARY FIVE

Peter Clarke
Children's Commissioner for Wales

Peter Clarke did not present a paper, but instead presented a whistle-stop tour of his position as Children's Commissioner for Wales. His role is to promote and safeguard children's rights and welfare. His position is an independent one, he does not report to the National Assembly and is not answerable to it. The most important aspect of the relationship between the National Assembly and the Commissioner's Office is the mutual exchange of information. Mr Clarke recommended a paper by Catherine Hollingsworth and Gillian Douglas entitled, 'Creating a Children's Champion for Wales', which he said gave a very good account of his job.

The Commissioner has a budget of £1.5 million and 17 staff. The term of office is seven years only. In Mr Clarke's view, the reasons behind this are sensible: there is a danger of becoming stuck in one's ways after seven years, and after that period of time a Commissioner might get ideas above his station and lose contact with the children he represents.

He can be removed from his position in one of three circumstances: if he resigns; becomes too unwell to continue; or if he is 'guilty of serious misbehaviour'.

Mr Clarke was interviewed by a panel of young people. Twelve young people aged from 10 to 19 asked the candidates questions and scored the answers, then a second group of eight young people required the candidates to undertake role play, and put on plays themselves which the candidates were required to respond to. The short-listed candidates were then interviewed by a panel of 20, including two young people. It was the first time in the world that young people have participated in making this kind of political appointment. All of the Commissioner's staff went through a similar ordeal. Mr Clarke emphasised that the young people's involvement was a meaningful one, they were trained in interview technique, and their views genuinely canvassed.

The position comes with a number of powers and responsibilities. The Commissioner must be accessible to all young people, he must advocate on their behalf; have regard to United Nations Convention on Human Rights and have special regard to the rights and interests of young people who may be marginalised. His powers are primarily to obtain information, but he can also influence policy makers and make recommendations. He can conduct a review of local authorities and of the services they provide. He can also get contempts registered if he encounters obstruction when trying to gather information. The Commissioner's strongest power is to hold a public inquiry. He is currently engaged in an inquiry in relation to a teacher who committed suicide after it had been discovered that he had been abusing children. He also has the power to intervene in individual cases, not as first resort, but where a situation demands it. He said that he has found already that letting people know that the Commissioner's officer is aware of a situation tends to concentrate minds. Lastly, he can review systems for children to make complaints.

Mr Clarke went on to give some examples of his achievements since taking office. He explained the importance of gaining respect among the young people he acts for. He said that he was well aware of the time it takes to earn respect, and of how quickly it can be lost. He therefore spends a good deal of time trying to make real contact with children, particularly marginalised children so that he can represent their thoughts and concerns. This enables the young people themselves to set their Commissioner's work agenda. They have already brought up issues which have surprised him. He found that at least 50% of the children had complaints about school toilets. The effect of half of all school children in Wales refusing to use the toilets while at school is far reaching. This, Mr Clarke pointed out, was a small, but emblematic issue. He had not been aware of its importance, but the children persuaded him that it was, and through him their voice could be heard.

INVOLVING CHILDREN IN PLANNING AND REVIEW SERVICES

Professor June Thoburn
Social Work Academic, University of East Anglia

Summary of paper

The issue discussed in Professor June Thoburn's paper is how children can be involved in the planning and reviewing of the services which they and those who are important to them receive. She introduced her paper by saying that children can be involved in two ways; first in designing services used by everyone and secondly in designing their own services. Children who are too nervous to be involved in their own case can later become more assertive by becoming involved in general services.

She made three points about children's rights:

- *A child's right to decide is very limited, particularly in respect of major decisions, however it does increase with the child's age;*
- *The right to be consulted is relevant to children of all ages, including very young children and due consideration should be given to their wishes;*
- *The paramountcy principle sometimes does require a court to over-rule a child's wishes, but this should never be done unless evidence that this is unavoidable has been fully tested.*

Involvement means involving children, parents and carers; it can call for delicate negotiations between all parties. Professor Thoburn warned against going roughshod into children's lives and ignoring the caregiver or forgetting to tell parents and foster carers. She said that she has been alarmed at the number of guardians who have been stopped from talking to foster carers.

Professor Thoburn said that a major message in her paper was the importance of a trusting and consistent relationship between a young person and their social worker. She said that she is concerned about the shift in children's responses over the last ten years about their social workers. Children are angry because they know what they ought to be getting and they know they are not getting it. She was delighted at the Green Paper recommendation that there should be a key worker for each child.

The issue of confidentiality is difficult to get right. Most children loathe everyone knowing everything about them. Professor Thoburn recognised that information must be shared, but emphasised that thought must be given as to how it is shared, and the child should be involved in that process.

Professor Thoburn also highlighted the review process, and emphasised that it was a process rather than an event. She raised three major complaints:

- *That meetings have taken over casework, to the extent that young people, parents and carers rarely see their social worker in between;*
- *That the meeting itself is often attended by too many people, which raises the issue of confidentiality;*
- *That the review meeting which is designed to plan the next months or years of a young person's life, is often hijacked by other agendas, or expected to fulfil several other purposes.*

As far as court hearings are concerned, Professor Thoburn thought that some children feel cheated that they are not allowed to be involved in court process.

Professor Thoburn went on to discuss proposed improvements, in particular two 'solutions' which have been included in the Adoption and Children Act 2002, namely an increased role for advocates for young people looked after and a strengthening of the role of the independent reviewing officer. She stressed that the introduction of advocates will be very helpful but that it should not become routine.

In conclusion, Professor Thoburn raised two issues arising from the Adoption and Children Act 2002 which caused her some concern. The first was the issue of siblings; she said that she was concerned about situations in which a decision made in favour of one sibling may be at the expense of the other siblings. The second was the issue of placement orders. She said that her reading of the placement order is that the 'no order principle' will not apply to placement orders and contact.

Introduction

This paper draws on research interviews with looked after and adopted children; on two DH-funded studies of the involvement of children and parents in the safeguarding processes (Thoburn et al, 1995; Brandon et al, 2000); and on *Your Shout!* a recent NSPCC-funded survey of the views of over 700 looked after children (Timms and Thoburn, 2003). My reflections have also been influenced by involvement as an expert witness in complex care and adoption cases.

Children may, and indeed should, be involved in the planning and reviewing of the services which they and *those who are important to them* receive, and also in the services available generally to children in similar circumstances both nationally and locally. I shall concentrate on the first of these – how can children be more fully involved in the work of those who seek to help them and in the decisions made about *themselves*? However, it is through involvement in their own 'case' that some decide to move on to play a part in the design of services more generally; and it is through involvement in 'looked after children' and similar groups, that some children acquire the skills and confidence to become more assertive in making sure that they and those who are close to them are listened to when decisions are being made about them.

It is important to briefly un-pick the term 'involvement'. In our study of partnership-based practice (Thoburn et al, 1995) we concluded that whilst it was only possible in a minority of cases to work *in partnership* with children, from an early age, it is possible to keep them fully informed, in an age appropriate way, about planning and helping processes. For the younger children, this involves keeping those who have day-to-day care of them fully involved, so that they can reinforce the messages given by social workers and courts about what is happening. Consultation – finding out how they understand the situation and what they would like to happen – is possible for all children. Observation of the youngest children or those with severe disabilities, combined with a knowledge of child development, can lead to an informed opinion of what the child would be likely to say if he or she were able to communicate. I am always taken aback when, in the section on 'wishes and feelings of the child' a children's guardian writes 'child too young'. In a recent case when there was a plan to move an infant from a foster home where he had lived between the ages of 2 weeks and 15 months, and where it was clear from the reports that strong mutual attachments had developed, I would have expected to read, instead of 'child too young', 'from my observations of his behaviour and attachments I conclude that, if he were able to talk, he would want me to say that he does not wish to move from his present placement and will be very sad, at least for a time, if he has to do so'. The question of the different aspects of involvement is further explored in the Department of Health Guidance *The Challenge of Partnership in Child Protection*.

Rights, wishes and needs

It is impossible to discuss children's involvement in decision making without briefly considering the interaction between rights, wishes and needs, so I will first briefly stray onto the subject matter of the next session. Gillian Schofield and I explored this relationship in 1996 in a pamphlet for the Institute for Public Policy Research (*Child Protection: The Voice of the Child in Decision Making*, Schofield and Thoburn, 1996). The UN Convention on the Rights of the Child and UK Children and Adoption legislation and guidance unequivocally require that the child be consulted and that due consideration be given to his or her wishes and feelings. This right to influence decisions does not, except in limited circumstances, give to the child the right (and the onerous responsibility) of making life enhancing or life limiting decisions. However, the right to make decisions about aspects of daily living should be given to children as they demonstrate that they have the capacity to know what they want and weigh up the consequences. In response to the *Your Shout!* question about whether being in care made her feel safe, one child wrote:

> 'Sometimes I feel too safe and as though I can't do anything without someone watching me. Everything has to be planned out so much more and forms filled in. I hate having to leave phone numbers wherever I go and before I stay anywhere the police having to check my friends house. I may feel safe but not happy.' (Timms and Thoburn, 2003, p 33.)

This point is echoed in the studies by Thoburn et al (1995), Bell (2002) in respect of child protection work and by Thomas and O'Kane (1999) and Munro (2001) in respect of looked after children.

Children's wishes have to be set in the context of a full assessment of present and future needs in order to safeguard and promote their welfare throughout childhood and into adulthood. It is therefore possible that the duty of the court and agencies to hold the child's welfare as paramount will sometimes mean that the child's wishes, expressed through consultation, are overruled. The art of making decisions and judgements about children is firstly to make sure that one is as clear as possible about what the child's wishes are, and then never to disregard a child's wishes *unless* there is clear evidence that it is absolutely necessary to do so. That is why the children's guardian and the child's solicitor have such vitally important roles to play in ensuring that the child's wishes are fully put before the court, and that the evidence in support of alternative options, especially those that run counter to the child's wishes, is fully tested.

Involving children and involving parents

I shall concentrate in this paper on 'heavier end' cases when concerns are such that an element of coercion of parents and/or older children (whether through the formal child protection processes or the courts) is involved in the assessment and review processes. However, we must not forget that in the majority of cases in which social workers become involved, the parents retain full parental responsibility. In most s 17 family support cases, including most cases when children experience out-of-home care, children are not on any statutory order. The statutory services may, through the formal child protection procedures, make clear that they may seek to impose restrictions on parental behaviour, but the assessment and review process must involve close consultation with parents. Indeed, it is only when there are proceedings under children legislation or a local authority is considering whether to provide section 20 accommodation that the child's welfare becomes the paramount consideration. In other cases, children's involvement in planning and review of services provided to them has to be negotiated with their parents and carers. That point is particularly relevant when one is considering how best to involve children in child protection conferences and in family group conferences as well as in the multi-disciplinary family support meetings that are becoming more common. The question of how children's wishes and parents' wishes can fully inform welfare processes is particularly relevant in inter-parent disputes and in in-court and out of court mediation. The social worker and CAFCASS officer who is committed to involving children has to be skilled in putting across to parents and carers (including foster carers) why this is important. It is especially necessary to understand cultural differences in the way in which children's roles within the family are viewed.

Those working in the area of family group conferences have become skilled in understanding how to negotiate children's involvement in decision-making meetings (Marsh and Crow, 1998).

Even when there is an element of compulsion, as when proceedings are pending, a supervision order has been made, or a child in care is placed with parents, when children are living at home it is essential not to undermine parents by 'going over their heads' and reaching independent agreements with the child about how they should be involved. Our research on the involvement of parents and children in child protection processes (Schofield, Thoburn et al, 1996) indicated that children value social workers who can find ways of involving and consulting them without placing them in opposition to their parents. Though some older teenagers gain from being helped to assert their wishes in the presence of their parents, most children do not want to be in a meeting when they hear their parents' faults and inadequacies discussed by strangers. Shemmings (1999) was commissioned by the Department of Health to edit a Reader and put together training materials on ways of involving young children and young people still at home as well as in care in child protection and review meetings.

These two children had different views as to whether they were pleased that they had attended meetings the purpose of which, as they saw it, was to review the behaviour of their parents:

> 'They talk, they have witnesses and everything. There's coppers there. They talk about [younger brother]. They talk about how the people there, who are getting told off, how they are getting on.' (Shepherd, cited in Schofield and Thoburn, 1996, p 39.)

> 'They were talking about mum and me and everyone else so I wanted to hear what they were talking about – what they were saying and whether it was correct or not. It was the meeting that mum and I went to so they could decide whether or not she was good enough to keep me.' (Thoburn et al, 1995.)

There are similarities but also differences in the way in which parents and young people are consulted when relationships between them have broken down and they are placed out of the family on a long-term basis. Generally, the assumption should be made that, although parents' and children's wishes will sometimes differ, better decisions will be made if both are consulted and due consideration is given to the opinions of parents, carers and others who are important to the child. This is essentially because, from the perspective of both parents and children, the purpose of consultation is for them to be able to influence the nature, quality and quantity of services provided to meet their needs as parents and as children 'in need' or 'looked after'. Children have an interest in the needs of their parents being met and vice versa so differences between them in terms of their hoped for results from consultation occur less frequently than is sometimes implied when 'children's rights' are set in opposition to 'parents' rights'. This over-simplification of participation rights implies that an increase in the participation of one party will inevitably diminish the participation rights of another.

The assessment and review of the needs of looked after children and the consultation processes

What, then, are the stages of the decision-making and helping processes in which the child might be involved and who is responsible for ensuring that children are consulted and involved? Emphasis is often placed on children's involvement in meetings such as Child Protection Conferences and Review meetings for children looked after. However, to children and young people, day-to-day decisions made by their social workers and carers can be just as important. As noted above, whilst professionals may see consultation as a 'good' in its own right, for children and those who care for and about them, the purpose is to have a say in the decisions about what their needs are, and the way in which small as well as major needs are to be met. A survey of looked after children who phoned Childline (Morris and Wheatly, 1994, p 49) noted that children in foster care could feel particularly cut off and distant from the social workers but that those who are enabled to establish trust in their social worker greatly value it. They quote a 16 year old speaking of a former social worker:

> 'She was really good. She gave you good advice and I felt there was someone on my side that was willing to help me and, you know, show me the right direction.'

Sir William Utting, in his 'Safeguards Review' powerfully entitled *People Like Us,* drew particular attention to the importance placed by young people on their relationship (or lack of it) with their social worker (Utting, 1997). Although children interviewed by him and by the researchers already cited have good and bad things to say about reviews, it is for the work of their social workers that they reserve their strongest comments, whether positive or negative. Utting (paras 16.15–16.19) regretted what he saw as a deterioration in the service provided to young people by social workers and recommended that urgent steps be taken to find reasons and remedies. He saw this as an essential step in ensuring that the tasks of the 'corporate parent' are fulfilled in a way that includes and empower the child.

> 'The case for one official to be responsible for watching over the programme of care for each child seems unanswerable. It is plainly in the interest of the child to have one official committed to furthering his or her interests as a whole, to the extent of *acting as the child's advocate* within the welfare bureaucracy, so that the child is the subject of care rather than the object of unrelated caring processes.'

In response to Utting's recommendations, BASW commissioned Bilton (2003) to review recent publications involving interviews with looked after young people. Citing the research referred to above, this BASW publication sets out ways in which, despite the well-known problems of recruitment and retention of social workers, steps can be taken to respond to the wishes of young people for a reliable, trustworthy, relationship-based service that provides to young people greater continuity than is presently provided to many if not most of them. In his forward to this publication Sir William Utting updates his earlier conclusions in the light of recent proposals to strengthen independent representation for children.

> 'Developments in specialised roles such as advocacy, personal advice and leaving care are highly desirable in themselves. They leave unmet, however, and may merely illuminate, the fundamental need each child has for a single champion and companion through the changing needs and vicissitudes of a local authority childhood.'

For children looked after away from their parents, the first point at which legislation requires consultation is the decision as to whether or not the child should be looked after, and if so, whether this should be through voluntary arrangements or the seeking of a care order. The Children Act 1989 established that respite or short term accommodation should be viewed as a family support measure and not something to be avoided at all costs. This was influenced by Packman's (1986) research which, in a telling phrase, concluded that care was all too often 'unthinkable until it was too late to think at all' resulting in too many emergency admissions and consequent moves in care. Yet many of the parents had been asking for this form of help for some time. The post-Children Act research by the same author in the same authorities (Packman and Hall, 1998) indicated that planned accommodation, even when it was expected to happen, was rare. Some of the young people responding to the *Your Shout!* survey would have liked to have come into care sooner than they did. Others, though seeing its necessity, would have liked more say about how it was achieved, but could understand, sometimes with hindsight, why full responsibility should not be placed on their shoulders.

'I would have liked to have had a say about being put in care and who I was with. I was probably too young though.' (p 11.)

Asked what she would like to change, a 16 year old wrote:

'Nothing, although from the age of 12, I was reluctant to what S.S. wanted for my near future…I am now 16 and Semi-independent. And I am So So grateful for Social Services Support and Looking back they only wanted what was best for me and what would keep me safe. If it wasn't for their correct judgement .Id be dead, ive been on harsh drugs and been through a lot of pooh! But im now wririn a novel of my traumatic history.' (p 15)

Decisions about whether a young person should be accommodated are increasingly taken by 'panels' which, at best, combine advice to the social worker about the resources that may be used to help the family or young person without the necessity for accommodation. At worst, they serve only a rationing function. Since neither parents nor young people attend these meetings, they can be the cause of considerable frustration, especially if they overturn the recommendation of a planning meeting or family support meeting attended by the parents and young person which concluded that accommodation would be helpful. This point has particular relevance in view of the Adoption and Children Act amendment to s 7 of the Children Act which will allow children to be accommodated away from their parents but without the safeguards of becoming 'looked after' children. It will be important to monitor the way in which young people are informed and consulted as to whether being looked after would safeguard and promote their welfare, or, in the case of those aged 16, whether their welfare will be 'seriously prejudiced' (s 20(4)) if they are not 'looked after' rather than just provided with 'board and lodging'.

Your Shout! provides us with the views of young people looked after who had came into care through a care order, 152 of whom had been to court. Different decisions are made about children's participation in court hearings in respect of care and adoption hearings. The presumption is generally made that children will not want to, or should not, take part in care hearings and that their wishes will be made known via their guardian and solicitor, but that children of all ages will be present at the adoption hearing. However, the research by Thomas and Beckford (1999) indicates that some children worry about having to attend adoption hearings and would rather not do so, whilst *Your Shout!* suggests that some would like to attend care hearings. 88 of those who did not attend said they would have liked to, whilst 47 said they didn't attend and would not have wanted to. However only 11 of the 163 who said they had attended said they would have preferred not to. Twice as many of the girls as the boys said they would have liked to attend. When children were asked to tick a checklist of those who might have helped during court proceedings, only 7% of the whole sample and 6% of those who attended court ticked 'children's guardian' compared to 14% and 29% who mentioned solicitor and 30% and 28% who ticked 'social worker'. Over half of those who attended court said they did not have the chance to speak to the judge, including 19% of the court sample who said they wished that they had had the chance to speak to the judge. 34 of those who did not go to court said they would have liked the chance to speak to the judge.

When asked whether they were listened to and had their rights respected, 43% of the nearly 600 who responded said yes but 138 (39%) said no and 27% said they did not know.

'I would have wanted my opinion to be listened to rather than just my carers. But the social workers should have been listening to me instead of just the opinion of the carers.' (*Your Shout!*, p 13.)

'I would have liked to have more info and would of liked to have more say in the matter.'[1]

---

[1]   *Your Shout!* p 13

We have more knowledge about how children are consulted once they are looked after, whether through the accommodation or the care order route. The *Looking after Children* system provides a format for the consultation of children prior to their *Looked After Review*, and guidance urges social workers to discuss with the children how they would like their views to be taken on board. Three important publications, providing research-based guidance on ways of improving the involvement of young people, are those of Thomas and O'Kane (1999); Grimshaw and Sinclair (1997, summarised in Sinclair, 1998); and Monro (2001).

Grimshaw and Sinclair emphasise that the *Review* is a *process* and not an *event*. The review meeting comes at the end of the process of assessing the changing needs of the child and reviewing the range of decisions that need to be taken to ensure the success of corporate parenting. Around 80% of those who start to be looked after have left care by the end of two years, but for them, but for the most vulnerable short and long stayers, the court is heavily involved in setting the direction of the child's experience of corporate parenting through the care plan. The Children Act 1989 mandate is to seek to minimise the length of time that corporate parenting is needed by getting them back with their families or placing them with adoptive families as quickly as is consistent with the assessment of needs and finding the placement that best meets their needs. That is a period when there are many opportunities for children to be involved on a one-to-one basis with social workers, expert witnesses, children's guardians, independent advocates, solicitors, therapists, child contact services, and (possibly, as I have already noted, less often than some would like) judges. During this period, as well as child looked after reviews to which those 'of sufficient age and understanding' will be invited, there may be 'planning meetings' or 'permanence panels' or 'adoption panels' to which they will usually not be invited. For the minority who remain looked after, the pace settles down and the major way through which they can influence the decisions and the day-to-day corporate parenting is through the review process and the way in which the case-accountable social worker goes about his or her task.

Research indicates that parents and children value the greater care that is now taken to ensure that they and all those involved in ensuring that a child's welfare is promoted and safeguarded are now systematically involved in the review process. However, there are three major complaints. The first is that 'meetings' have taken over from casework to the extent that parents, carers and young people complain that they rarely see their social worker in between. One parent described it to me as a process of 'lurching from review to review' and nothing happening in between. The second and third complaints stem from this over-reliance on meetings. As demonstrated by Grimshaw and Sinclair's and Thomas and O'Kane's research, the review meeting itself is often attended by too many people (some of whom could have had a discussion with the social worker separately or sent in a written report). Young people complain that intimate details of their lives are discussed before people they do not know, or people who they do not want to hear this information. Echoing the wider tension between the importance of confidentiality of personal data on the one hand, and the need for co-operative working on the other, in the BASW policy document Bilton (2003) comments:

> 'There is a need for greater sensitivity in recording and more stringent control and limitation of access to records within the agency. Other people's access to their records is the process through which children lose control over the consequences of their conversations with their social workers.'

Writing of child protection processes more generally, Bell (2002), on the basis of her conversations with young people, comments on what she sees as the negative consequences of the increasing desire of government and social services agencies to standardise procedures and remove social work discretion and flexibility and thus their ability to respond to young people's wishes:

> 'The procedures in place for informing children, involving them in decision making forums, consulting them and offering choice, are not sufficiently child-centred and potentially model an unhelpful and

disempowering dominant/submissive pattern of relating which resonates with their previous experiences of abuse.'

Munro (2001) gives an example:

'The social worker may be willing and anxious to empower the child yet themselves feel restricted in the autonomy they have. Management will be out setting out objectives and priorities that they are under pressure to meet. If a 16-year-old says he thinks the action and assessment record is intrusive and unhelpful and he would prefer to spend the time talking to his social worker instead of completing it (as one young person in this study did), the social worker would face the dilemma of listening to the child or the manager.'

Whatever the explanations, it appears that in many cases children's wishes are either not clarified or not respected about how the review process should unfold, which combinations of people should hold pre-meetings or send in written reports and who should be at the review meeting that agrees the long and short term plans. A young person who is well settled in a foster family will understand that the review process will involve discussions between herself, her parents, grandparents and foster parents about the detail of contact, and whether she can stay overnight at her gran's. She will also understand that there will need to be a discussion about sexual health and possible involvement in the drugs scene and the reasons why she is at risk of being excluded from school. However, she will not want all these discussions to be held with the same people in the same room at a meeting which will also, she hopes, confirm that the plan is to give up attempts at restoration to her parents and agree that she will stay until adulthood with her foster parents.

Some of these issues of detail could have been resolved at an earlier stage of the review process, for example, at earlier meetings between parents, foster parents and the young person and social worker, or the foster parents, the school and the young person.

The third major problem with reviews, which leads some young people to refuse to go to the review meeting, and others to describe it as a highly stressful event, follows from the last point. A meeting that will plan how your life will unfold for the next months or even years is an important and inevitably stressful event. If it is expected to fulfil several other purposes, for example, if it is the only opportunity for a parent to get angry with the social worker because that is the only time she sees her, or for a foster parent to explain to a parent why a particular action has been taken because they otherwise never meet because contact takes place outside the foster home, these other agendas can all too easily hijack the meeting and greatly add to the stress on the young person.

The respondents to the *Your Shout!* survey give mixed messages, perhaps inevitably since some will have started to be looked after prior to the establishment of a more rigorous review process. The fact that only 55% of those who responded could name their care authority suggests weaknesses in the process of keeping young people informed. 69% responded that they knew what their care plan was but 28% said that they did not. There was evidence that some were bewildered by their 'in care' status:

'Being in care made me feel uncumfertable, insacur and made me feel like I wasn't there, like I didn't exist.'

Some seemed aware of and satisfied with the arrangements for their care. When asked if they knew how to get changes made, a young man said:

'I wouldn't because I'm happy as I am & hAppy with the day to day agreements.'

However, this young person said:

'It makes me feel difficult and scared some times know one talks to me so I'm puzzled.'

There were particular issues around contact with people whom they cared about and wanted to see and separation from siblings. Of the people they wanted to see, 39% said they did not have enough contact with their mothers,; 60% with their fathers, 37% with siblings; 49% with other relatives; 28% with friends and 57% with previous carers. It may be that the 'no order' principle in the Children Act is working *against* the presumption of contact. The question needs to be asked as to whether the wishes of these children are being made known to courts and review meetings and due consideration given to them. The only s 34 order that is regularly made is a 34 (4) order to allow a local authority to restrict contact. In the light of the evidence in *Your Shout!* and other research that the wishes of so many children in respect of contact are either not known or not adhered to, it may be that more defined s 34 contact orders should be made to ensure that children's wishes are given sufficient weight when care plans are implemented and reviewed. This question will arise when placement orders are made as the first stage in the adoption process under the Adoption and Children Act 2002, especially as it is rare for children or their advocates to attend permanency planning meetings and adoption panels. It does not appear that the 'no order' principle is to be applied when s 26 contact orders are being considered at the time that placement orders are made. This may be helpful to children wishing to stay in contact with siblings placed elsewhere and to their parents and relatives as it should ensure that any proposed changes in contact arrangements agreed in the care plan are properly scrutinised and children's wishes sought and given due consideration.

Discussion of proposed improvements

So, whilst the research concludes that strides have been made in the involvement of young people, many problems remain. Two 'solutions' will be discussed which have been included in the Adoption and Children Act 2002: an increased role for advocates for young people looked after; and a strengthening of the role of the independent reviewing officer. Both potentially involve an increased role for the courts and children's guardians in monitoring care plans to ensure that assessed needs are being met, but will they also ensure that children's wishes are not being unnecessarily overruled when decisions are taken about what their needs are and how best to meet them? Section 118 of the Adoption and Children Act potentially strengthens the children looked after reviewing process. It is now established practice for the reviewing officer to be a local authority manager who does not have accountability for the child's case, and increasingly those who chair reviews specialise in that area of practice. Although some have called for the reviewing officer to be more clearly independent by being employed by a different agency, my own view is that this would be unhelpful as the reviewing officer has to be in a position to argue for the resources needed to follow the recommendations of the care plan.

However, once the care order is made and the child no longer has a children's guardian and very rarely retains contact with his or her solicitor, systems are needed to ensure that the child's voice is heard. In most cases a combination of the child's field or residential social worker, the foster carers and parents or relatives should ensure that the child's wishes are obtained and listened to, and that any needs identified at the care order stage, or agreed if the child is accommodated, are met as the plans evolve. I have already referred to the debate outlined in the Utting Report and subsequent publications about the relationship between the advocacy role of the social worker and the role of a specialist advocate. However, social work recruitment is problematic and, as evidenced yet again by the *Your Shout!* respondents, changes of social worker are frequent. Also, there are occasions when a social worker concludes that what the child wants is contrary to what he or she needs. For these reasons it is essential that all children for whom care is being considered, or who are looked after, should be made aware that they can be introduced to someone independent of the care authority who will listen to their views and help them to put them across, irrespective of what they themselves think is good for the child. A young person interviewed by Scutt (1995) clearly got the point:

'My advocate was there to put my views across … she only knew my story, and not Mum and step-Dad's and therefore was able to say what I felt and not get in-between it all. If she knew their story maybe she would get muddled up and not want to say something because it may upset them.'

Another stressed confidentiality:

'Different from my social worker because he (advocate) offers me a totally confidential role. I can say what I want and it won't go any further unless I want it to.'

The importance of the s 118 amendments to the Children Act is that they leave the way open for the children's guardian and the courts to be brought back into the case if it becomes clear that the care plan is being changed in such a way that important identified needs of the child are not being met. This will provide a way forward for the child or young person to protest if wishes and needs recognised by the Court are being overruled. The Department of Health, in 2002 published *the National Standards for the Provision of Children's Advocacy Services*, and the advocacy service to help children looked after to complain or make representations has, in theory at least, been strengthened by s 119 of the Adoption and Children Act. It remains to be seen whether guidance and regulations will ensure that more children will be helped by their family or professional circle playing an informal advocacy role or through access to an independent advocacy service as encouraged by these provisions. Little has been said to date as to how these provisions are to be resources.

In conclusion, I want to point to some as yet unresolved issues in the implementation of the Adoption and Children Act that will have a profound impact on the way in which children are helped to ensure that wishes expressed and accepted as valid at the time that a placement order is made are not forgotten or overruled for pragmatic reasons. The combination of government targets, whether on time-scales, keeping children out of care, or proportions of children placed for adoption, combined with the scarcity of resources in terms of children's guardians, social workers, advocates, foster parents and adopters, can make children particularly vulnerable to the consequences of making pragmatic decisions. This is all too obvious in the research findings and in some of the cases I have been involved in. In particular, it probably explains why so many of the children responding to the *Your Shout!* survey were seeing too little of or had been cut off, against their wishes, from parents and siblings. If it is not acceptable for a parent to put their needs and wishes before those of the child, why is it acceptable for an adopter to refuse contact between the three year old recently placed with them and the older siblings who are acutely distressed at the lack of contact and believe that they had been promised that they would remain in touch? Even children well settled in care or in their adoptive families talk to researchers about the distress they still feel at loss of contact with siblings.

'If I had a choice I would of liked to had met the people who have looked after me but still be living with my mum step dad new sister and brother [name] because I can't see [name] at all.'

'Second of all [of things that should have been done differently] separating us from our loved and cherished brothers.'

Will an advocate assist more children in this position to take up one of the more radical provisions in the Children Act 1989 and seek leave to make an application for contact under s 26, or a s 8 order at the time of the adoption hearing? Will the independent reviewing officer be aware that the care plan anticipated that the three year old would be placed with siblings or, if that were not possible, have regular contact with them? If it seems likely that needs and wishes recorded in the care plan are unlikely to be fulfilled when detailed long term plans are being arrived at, will the reviewing officer 'consider it appropriate' to refer to CAFCASS? Will the provisions of s 118 apply equally when children are looked after but a placement order has been made and therefore they are no longer 'in care' but merely 'looked after'? And will these provisions apply after the child has been placed with prospective adopters?

Finally, it is still not clear whether children will be able to have their say as parties, or to be represented by a children's guardian, in the adoption hearing. Section 122 b of the Adoption and Children Act (amending s 41 of the Children Act) leaves the way open for the adoption hearing as well as the placement order hearing to be 'specified proceedings' at which the child may have party status.

In a Reader accompanying training materials prepared by Family Rights Group when the Children Act 1989 was introduced, the definition of partnership concludes:

'In short, each partner is seen as having something to contribute, power is shared, decisions are made jointly, roles are not only respected but also backed by legal and moral rights.' (Family Rights Group, 1991.)

However skilled the social worker or advocate are in helping a child to work out what she would like to happen, if the aspiration towards involvement is not backed by robust legal and administrative provisions, the promise of partnership will often turn out to be another empty promise. Once more her inability to make an impact on the things that are upsetting her will be reinforced and a further dent placed in her ability to trust adults to do what they say they will do.

References

Bell, M. 2002. Promoting children's rights through the use of relationship. *Child and Family Social Work*, **7.1**

Brandon, M, Lewis, A, Thoburn, J and Way, A. 1999. *Safeguarding Children with the Children Act 1989*, London: The Stationery Office

British Association of Social Worker and Bilton, K. 2003. *Be My Social Worker: The Role of the Child's Social Worker*, Birmingham: Venture Press.

Family Rights Group. 1991. *The Children Act 1989: Working in Partnership with Families*, London: FRG.

Grimshaw, R and Sinclair, R. 1997. *Planning to Care: Regulation, Procedure and Practice under the Children Act 1989,* London: National Children's Bureau.

Morris, S and Wheatley, H. 1994. *Time to Listen: The Experiences of Young People in Foster and Residential Care*, London: Childline.

Munro, E. 2001. Empowering looked-after children. *Child and Family Social Work*, **6.2**.

Packman, J. 1986. *Who Needs Care?* Oxford: Blackwell Science.

Packman, J and Hall, C. 1998. *From Ccare to Accommodation: Support, Protection and Care in Child Care Services*, London: HMSO.

Schofield, G and Thoburn, J. 1996. *The Voice of the Child in Child Protection*, London: Institute for Public Policy Research.

Scutt, N. 1995. Child Advocacy. In *Participation and Empowerment in Child Protection*, ed. C Cloke and M Davies. London: Pitman.

Shemmings, D (ed.). 1999. *Involving Children in Family Support and Child Protection*, London: The Stationery Office.

Sinclair, R. 1998. Involving children in planning their care. *Child and Family Social Work*, **3 (2)**.

Thoburn, J, Lewis, A and Shemmings, D. 1995. *Paternalism or Partnership? Family Involvement in the Child Protection Process*, London: HMSO

Thomas, C and Beckford, V. (1999) *Adopted Children Speaking*, London: BAAF.

Thomas, N and O'Kane, C. 1999. Children's participation in reviews and planning meetings when they are 'looked after' in middle childhood. *Child and Family Social Work*, **4 (3)**.

Timms, J and Thoburn, J. 2003. *Your Shout! A Survey of the Views of 706 Children and Young People in Public Care*, London: NSPCC.

Utting, W. 1997. *People Like Us: The Report of the Review of Safeguards for Children Living Away from Home*, London: The Stationery Office.

THE CHILDREN'S TASKFORCE AND THE NATIONAL SERVICE FRAMEWORK – WHAT DO THEY MEAN FOR CHILDREN, YOUNG PEOPLE AND FAMILIES?

'Do ye hear the children weeping, o my brothers, ere the sorrow comes with years?'

Professor Al Aynsley-Green
*National Clinical Director for Children, Department of Health
Nuffield Professor of Child Health, Institute of Child Health,
University College London
Director of Clinical Research and Development, Institute of Child Health
and Great Ormond Street Hospital for Children NHS Trust
Honorary Consultant Paediatrician, Great Ormond Street Hospital
for Children, NHS Trust*

Summary of paper

Professor Al Aynsley-Green introduced his paper by posing three questions to the conference:

- *Why are children important?*
- *Do they get a good deal?*
- *Is all well with the services provided for them?*

In relation to the first question he said that it was not a self-evident truth that children are important, and that there was a serious lack of capacity in the minds of people who matter to understand the importance of children and children's issues. Children make up 25% of our population and they are vital for personal and national survival. Professor Aynsley-Green's paper argues that children are important for emotional, demographic, economic and service-related reasons.

Professor Aynsley-Green said that in every country he visits he asks his second question: Do children get a good deal? In every Anglo-Saxon country he visits the answer he receives to that question is no. In Professor Aynsley-Green's view there is something very peculiar about English society's ambivalence to children and young people. He accepted that many children are doing very well but many are not with widening inequalities between rich and poor families. He was particularly concerned about the near invisibility of the disabled children in our society and the ignoring of their requirements.

The third question posed by Professor Aynsley-Green was whether all is well with our services for children. There are many dedicated staff working in all aspects of children's services, but he said that any complacency should be blown out of the water by the Laming Report and Kennedy Inquiry. In particular, the reports highlight the absence of any responsibility for children, the failure of communication and an absence of leadership.

His paper compares Victorian times with today. Then, intellectual outrage was caused by the social turmoil arising from massive industrialisation and urbanisation. This led to the formation of voluntary organisations which put pressure on Parliament. Eventually a raft of legislation intended to improve the lives of children was put into place. Professor Aynsley-Green argued that we are going through equally turbulent times today. He pointed to the dramatic changes that have taken place and asks 'Who cares?'

He called for debate about these fundamental questions, and said that there was a remarkable lack of willingness to look at the construct of children in contemporary society.

However, Professor Aynsley-Green did offer some light at the end of the tunnel. He said that in his view this Government is doing more for children than any other government for the last fifty years and went on to examine the Government's agenda. He said that the initiative that he is leading is looking at the creation of integrated evidence based and needs-led services, which position the child at the centre of the services. This includes thinking about all aspects of the life of the child not just the disease and developing a needs-based approach.

Professor Aynsley-Green concluded by calling for real change at the front line. He said that this would mean training, particularly interdisciplinary training, so the different agencies understand each other, and a common competency programme. He also identified a need for people who will advocate for the needs of children. Finally, he emphasised the importance of individual responsibility for improving the lives and health of children and young people.

'This lecture is dedicated to children everywhere, particularly to those who are disadvantaged or disabled through no fault of their own.'

Madame President, Lord Justice Thorpe, distinguished participants, it is a real privilege and a genuine pleasure to contribute to this important conference today. I begin by asking three 'exam' questions that underpin the thought train of this lecture. I ask you to think about them as my presentation unfolds because the questions are highly relevant to the theme of the conference, namely, 'the Voice of the Child'. I hope that they may offer some 'pegs' upon which to hang aspects of the discussion that follows both here and subsequently outside Dartington. They are:

- Why are children important?
- Do children get a 'good deal' at present?
- Is all well with the services provided for them?

Now to the title of my presentation. It is taken, as the literary cognoscenti amongst you will recognise immediately, from one of the verses of the poem entitled *The Cry of the Children* by Elizabeth Barrett Browning in 1843. The relevance of this sombre title will become clear as I progress through the lecture.

We are all here today because we love children and care deeply for them, being concerned particularly for those who have profound disadvantage, inequalities, impairments, handicaps and disabilities through no fault of their own. The vulnerability of the human child and the instinct for care and for protecting our vulnerable young is a powerful emotion that has sustained the human race through millennia of evolution.

We are, however, entering a new and most unexpected era in Western society, with more and more couples choosing not to have children. This is different from the heartbreak of infertility, and it has been the subject of a fascinating book, recently published, by a father and son, Laurie and Matthew Taylor. It raises some profound questions over why so many young women are deciding not to have children. It highlights the emergence of a new species, particularly in the United States of America, namely the TINKERs – two incomes, no kids and early retirement! Such people are in high positions of authority, determining policy, budgets and responsibilities. Many of these people appear not to be concerned about children and do not see the relevance of children to their existence. So, we have to marshal some arguments to persuade the agnostics that children really are important. The arguments I offer to answer the first 'exam' question, namely why are children important, are emotional, demographic, economic and service-related. Thus:

- Nothing matters more to families than the health, welfare and success of their children. There is an immediate paradox between the emotional commitment we give to children in our own families and the lack of commitment and concern demonstrated by recent successive governments to their welfare. A view of children is also encapsulated by this quotation from Postman, 1982:

'children are the living message we send to a time we will not see.'

- Children are the lifeblood of the nation, and they are vital for personal and national survival. However, for the first time in our history, we are currently producing fewer children per couple then the number required to sustain our population at an even level. It can be guaranteed only by immigration, but as the Taylors argue in their book, this is a source that cannot be sustained forever. In some parts of the world, particularly in Japan, governments are approaching near panic as they realise the demographic implications of the skewing of the population distribution. There, for the first time, there are now more people over the age of 70 than there are under the age of 10. Children are vital for the future economic success of our nation.

- Healthy children become healthy adults, and poverty is the single most pernicious adverse influence on the life and the health of the child. Sir Donald Acheson's report, *Reducing Health Inequalties*, in 1998 was triggered by the current Government and its findings are very important in highlighting the growing inequalities of health, wealth and educational attainment in our society. The influences of poverty are pernicious and include:

  - Difficulty in accessing mainstream services.
  - We have one of the highest rates of teenage pregnancy in Europe, and this is profoundly linked to inequalities.
  - Low birth weight, increased infant mortality and admission to hospital.
  - Breast feeding – unheard of in some communities, coupled with obesity in later childhood.
  - A failure to ensure appropriate immunisation and dental health.
  - The physical environment of housing, smoking, pollution, accidents and crime. Accidents are still the most important cause of death and handicap in children and a child in a poor environment is ten times more likely to suffer a severe head injury than a child living in an affluent locality. Imagine the impact on a poor family living in a tower block when a previously normal eight year old suddenly becomes severely disabled as a result of a head injury caused by deficiencies in the safe play environment for young children.
  - Child protection – the experiences of Victoria Climbié as graphically portrayed in Lord Laming's report should justify outrage in society on the impact of inadequate child protection.
  - Educational attainment is poor in children who have been looked after. Quite bluntly, society is failing to give these children the necessary skills to be competent and responsible adults.
  - Finally, the impact of poverty on life expectancy is unacceptable. On a recent visit to Portsmouth I was told that in some wards of the city a child born today will live ten years less than an equivalent child also born today ten miles up the road in affluent Hampshire.

We are the fourth richest nation in the world – does anyone care about child poverty?

- Of particular significance is the fact that so many adult diseases have their roots in childhood. Some fourteen years ago Sir David Barker in Southampton first proposed his hypothesis now known as the 'Barker Hypothesis'. He argued from carefully kept records of birth weight and early infant growth that adult diseases including high blood pressure, stroke and heart disease in 60–80 year olds had their roots in how the infant was nourished before birth and fed immediately after birth. There is now hard scientific evidence to support the concept. Thus, the baby's body and organs are 'plastic' and are subjected to a wide range of external influences, including nutrition and emotional support that 'programme' subsequent development. Emotional programming is especially important. An example of the difficulties arising when babies are deprived of the crucial short window of opportunity when they should be receiving and experiencing love, affection and bonding from a caring adult, is seen in the Romanian orphan children who are adopted into Western families. Many of these families have considerable difficulties in these children relating emotionally to their new families.

- The best (or worst!) example of a childhood antecedent of adult disease is the current pandemic of obesity in children currently sweeping Western countries. Health economists are now predicting that health services soon will be groaning under the impact of the consequences of the health problems caused by adult obesity in children who are now developing obesity in early years.

Thus, there are emotional, demographic, economic and health service reasons why children really should be a focus for Government action through giving them appropriate priority and resources. Sadly, there has been, until now, a mismatch between the emotional care we express for our children in our families and the lack of concern for children by successive governments.

The origins of this curious lack of focus on children has prompted me to engage in personal research into the history of children and childhood, and this can be summarised in the following quotation from Lloyd de Mause in his book '*The History of Childhood*', 1973:

'The history of childhood is a nightmare from which we have only recently begun to awake. The further back in history one goes the lower the level of childcare and the more likely children are to be killed, abandoned, beaten, terrorised and sexually abused.'

This is a stark and bleak overview of the history of childhood.

Looking back into the foundation of our Western civilisation, it is noteworthy that there is almost no portrayal of the child in sculpture or in works of art from ancient Greek society. What does that say about how Greeks regarded their children? There was certainly an emphasis through Plato and others on education, but this was not our concept of childhood education. Abortion, infanticide, sacrifice and abandonment; the sale of children into slavery and child labour; castration and sexual exploitation; punishment and control – this was the norm for much of childhood. In Western Europe it is only in the last three hundred years or so that castration was outlawed to prevent boys being mutilated to produce the castrati voices that were so beloved of Renaissance and Baroque music.

Quinitilian, a wealthy Roman author at the turn of the Christian era, was the first to document that perhaps there are some things that children should not be exposed to. He says:

'... they hear us use such words; every dinner party is loud with foul songs, and things are presented to their eyes of which we should blush to speak.'

This infers that children should be protected from some aspects of adult life and be allowed to be innocent.

We like to think that Christianity is a child-friendly religion and this quotation from the New Testament is often used to illustrate this:

'Then there were brought unto him little children that he should put his hands on them and pray ... he laid his hand on them, and departed thence.'

However, there may be a more sinister interpretation of this. A theme recurring throughout history is that children are born evil. Here, Christ was exorcising that inherent evil from those children.

When we move into the medieval period we get onto a firmer basis of fact with respect to society's views on children. I commend to you a wonderful book by Nicholas Orme on the life of the medieval child in which he argues that children were valued. They had separate lives, certainly in wealthy families who were concerned about their well-being. The Breughel painting on the front cover of the book shows the lives of children in everyday society, with children everywhere - a point I am going to come back to repeatedly.

Of particular significance is the proposal that our current construct of childhood is the result of the invention of printing press during that era. The explosion of the availability of the printed word transformed society; it created a social division between those who were literate and those illiterate. For the first time, 'childhood' appears, being the time to learn to read and write to become God-fearing adults.

An explosion in schooling followed, and it is interesting that in the later Middle Ages, England was thought to be the most educated country in Europe.

We get from Shakespeare:

'... the whining schoolboy, with his satchel, and shining morning face, creeping like snail, unwillingly to school.'

School, education, childhood were well known to Shakespeare and to his audiences at the Globe Theatre.

The two philosophers whose key influences built on this concept of childhood were John Locke and Jean Jacques Rousseau. Locke created the concept that the child's mind, far from being evil, was a 'blank slate', and it was the responsibility of adults for what was written on it. Jean Jacques Rousseau identified three key aspects of childhood. The first was that the child is important in its own right. This focus on the rights of man in general was the foundation of the French Revolution, but Rousseau argued specifically for the rights of the child. Second, he highlighted the 'joie de vivre' of childhood; the enthusiasm, the excitement, the intensity of childhood. Third, he argued that children should learn through experience, this concept being built on by Froebel, Montessori and others into their approaches to teaching.

So, Locke and Rousseau were highly influential, building on the concept of the critical period of 'childhood'. At the same time, the importance of parents and parenting emerged. Here is a contemporary quotation:

'that parents are the guardians, custodians, protectors, nurturers, punishers, arbiters of taste and rectitude.'

Parents were identified to be responsible for making children God-fearing, literate adults.

So, my overview of what I call the 'cauldron' of childhood' up to 1800 highlights the extreme brutality and exploitation of children, softened by the impact of the 'Age of Enlightenment'. The emergence of the Foundling Hospital in Corams Field in 1741, was one of the first examples of society's concern for children who would otherwise be abandoned.

The impact on children of the cultural and societal transformations that occurred in Victorian society during the nineteenth century was cataclysmic. This was the most turbulent period of British history, with industrialisation and urbanisation. It was accompanied by a massive population explosion coupled with the development of extremes of wealth and poverty. Increasing concern began to be expressed by leading intellectuals over the social pressures caused by children in the midst of this turmoil. The pressures were of illness, death, and poverty. A famous painting that I am drawn to repeatedly whenever I visit the Tate Gallery in London is by Sir Luke Fildes and entitled '*The Doctor*'. It is a vivid and emotional tableau portraying the wise doctor in a humble abode facing an unconscious dying child on a makeshift bed. In the background the child's mother is collapsed on the table, and the distraught father is trying to comfort her with a hand on her shoulder. The picture draws the viewer into a powerful sense of seeing not only the reality of the approaching death of the child, but we can almost hear the hiss of the paraffin lantern, the sobbing of the mother and touch and feel the foetid atmosphere in this child's last hours. A very powerful and highly charged emotional painting emphasising the Victorian's concern for the ill and dying child.

This was reflected in the popular poem of the era:

> 'Never more would he awaken,
> Those sweet little eyes were closed for aye;
> And the little lips were silent,
> Loving words no more to say.
> Brief and bright his life and sinless;
> Spared perhaps long years of pain;
> Would he thank them could they call him
> Back from Heaven to earth again?'

Powerful and moving words, drawing attention to the comfort of the strong religious belief in a happy afterlife.

By far the greatest consequence of Victorian industrialisation was the impact of poverty. In city centres such as London, Leicester, Manchester, Newcastle and Glasgow, half of all infants died. This was due to dirt, poor water, diet, neglect and ignorance coupled with diseases we seldom see in the twenty-first century. Such diseases included diarrhoea, measles, whooping cough, diphtheria, smallpox and TB. In older children, accidents were (and remain to this day) the single and most important cause of death and handicap. During this period, young children worked in the mines as trappers, holding open the doors to allow coal wagons to pass through thereby maintaining the airflow through the colliery. Children as young as four years, worked for up to 14 hours per day in darkness in unspeakable conditions, often lost for days in the labyrinths; beaten, abused, prone to accidents, disability and usually condemned to early death. These circumstances are described movingly in Alan Gallop's recent book *'Children of the Dark'*. By our standards, an outrageous exploitation of the most vulnerable in society.

It was not just in the mines, but also in the cotton mills. Young children were employed as 'scavengers' to crawl beneath the whirling looms and machinery to rescue lint, pieces of cloth and yarn. It is hardly surprising that many children were fatally injured or suffered permanent disability as a consequence of these dreadful conditions. The social circumstances of the slum properties in central London were appalling; children lived in poverty and in overcrowded conditions.

These circumstances led to increasing child destitution and this was the impetus for a relentless social conscience in the minds of leading intellectuals of the day. Such children were orphaned, deserted, neglected and left to fend for themselves by working parents. Street children, marauding gangs, theft, scavenging and prostitution were the norm in poor communities coupled with poor health, disease and starvation. Crime flourished, as documented in Jeanne Duckworth's *'Fagin's Children – Criminal Children in Victorian England'*. Photographs from this time illustrate destitute children scavenging for food.

These circumstances led Elizabeth Barrett Browning to write her moving poem, from which the title of my lecture is taken. Here is one of the most heartrending of the 14 verses:

> 'Now tell the poor young children, O my Brothers
> Look up to Him and pray;
> So the blessed One who blesseth all the others,
> Will bless them another day.
> They answer, 'Who is God that He should hear us
> While the rushing of iron wheels is stirred?

When we sob aloud, the human creatures near us
Pass by, hearing not, or answer not a word.
And we hear not (for the wheels in their sounding)
Strangers speaking at the door;
It is likely God, with angels singing round Him,
Hears our weeping any more?'

The impact of Victorian society on the life and the health of children outraged key intellectuals. They became the social reformers and triggered the age of philanthropy. Famous names, including Bramwell Booth, Dr Barnardo, Joseph Rowntree and Charles Dickens. I select Mary Carpenter for particular prominence as she was one of the first to argue that children should be treated as a child by the criminal justice system and not as a man. In those days children could be transported for stealing apples to relieve hunger.

Important institutions were founded, many of which still exist today. These include the National Children's Homes, and the Waifs and Strays Society, now the Church of England Children's Society. In 1884 the Liverpool Society for the Protection of Children was formed and subsequently transformed into the National Society for the Prevention of Cruelty to Children. It is, of course, noteworthy that the Royal Society for the Prevention of Cruelty to Animals had been founded some 60 years earlier in 1824. What does this say about the importance given to children over animals in nineteenth-century England?

The outrage of Charles Dickens and Charles West led to the founding of Great Ormond Street Hospital for Children on 14 February 1852 to address the needs of the sick children of the poor.

Eventually, pressure from the intellectuals led to action through Parliament with the state intervening, particularly under the instigation of Lord Shaftesbury, to introduce a raft of legislation including the Mining Act 1842, the Education Act of 1870, and the Protection of Infants Act 1872. These transformed the lives of children, particularly by pulling them out of the atrocious working circumstances and to give them statutory education.

Let us now scroll forward to 2003 and consider the social construct for children and childhood today, and ask my second 'exam' question, namely, do children get a good deal?

I argue that our current society is experiencing turbulence equivalent to that of the Victorian era but for very different reasons. It is certainly true that in the 150 years or so since the founding of Great Ormond Street Hospital there has been a massive improvement in the health and survival of children. Parents expect their children to survive and do not expect them to be handicapped or to die. Health, nutrition and material benefit have improved beyond recognition. There have been undoubted successes in the lives of the majority of young children becoming competent and productive adults in society. However, there are dramatic changes including:

- The emergence of our multicultural society.
- The changing requirement for the workforce away from traditional heavy industry to the need for articulate, intelligent and literate workers.
- The collapse of traditional family values with the emergence of many children who do not have any experience of two parents portraying appropriate role models.
- The falling birth rate is only now being recognised by politicians to be an important issue for the future.
- Evidence for widening inequalities of wealth, health and education, with the gap between the richest and poorest children in society widening year on year.
- An explosion of vulnerable children, including those who require protection and care by statutory intervention.
- An influx of refugee children and more young offenders locked away in penal institutions in this country than in any other equivalent Western society.

- Sexual exploitation of children continues with child prostitution and, as Operation Ore has so sadly shown, profound exploitation of children for international pornography.

Coupled with all of these changes is my argument that there is something very peculiar about English society's ambivalence to children and young people, this being evident in a number of ways.

First, the dichotomy between the need to protect and rescue innocent children, yet, on the other hand the demonisation of children, especially adolescents. Lurid press headlines from the dreadful events that followed the murder of two children in Soham, Cambridgeshire in 2001 illustrated the outpouring of national grief, in which large numbers of bouquets of flowers were laid in the churchyard and a local cathedral service was held.

Yet, there is a double standard, because where were the bouquets of flowers and the cathedral service for Victoria Climbié, a child who was murdered after dreadful and longstanding torture at the hands of her malevolent carers? She was a black child from a deprived population – does society have a double standard in how it looks after, regards and wishes to protect its young children?

Furthermore, we all remember the crowds baying for the blood of two other ten year old children; Venables and Thompson, who murdered James Bulger ten years ago. This equally disturbing national outpouring lends credence to the view that many in our society regard children to be born evil.

The demonisation of children extends to the adolescent age group in particular. Evidence collected in collaboration with colleagues in the National Children's Bureau shows that the media portrayal of adolescents is almost entirely in a negative stereotype. The invisibility of adolescents in health care is revealed by the fact that there is only one full time physician in the whole of the UK who is trained in the medical needs of adolescents.

An issue of the *Sunday Times* magazine in 2001 documented the experiences of a young girl in a young offender's institution – she is quoted as saying:

> 'I used to look at the birds outside my cell window and wish I was them. At night you hear the girls screaming…but I got used to it!'

Why do we have so many young offenders incarcerated behind bars, and who cares about their emotional, psychiatric, health and educational needs?

A further example of the ambivalence of our society to children and young people is the near invisibility of the disabled child and the ignoring of its requirements. A further *Sunday Times* magazine article commented on the plight of children with learning disabilities. The article said that two million British children have special educational needs. The law says the authorities must provide for them. But all they get is a wall of silence. Who cares about children with special educational needs?

A recently published report from the Joseph Rowntree Foundation discussed the housing needs of families who have disabled children. It makes harrowing reading – particularly in the context of disabled children living in poor circumstances. Who cares about disabled children in our current society?

The final example of our ambivalence to children and young people is the fact that there is, by and large, a wish to ignore the effects of poverty on children's lives and health, the consequences of which have been described above.

All of these facts have led some commentators to express serious concern over contemporary childhood. They argue that it is bleak and under threat. Such authors include Neil Postman in his book *'The Disappearance of Childhood'*, and Phil Scraton in his book *'Childhood in Crisis'*. By far the most powerful comments come from our own recently appointed Archbishop of Canterbury. Rowan Williams in his book *'Lost Icons'* proposes that childhood as we have known it is rapidly disappearing under the pressures of relentless commercialisation of children, early sexualisation and the disappearance of time for children to be children.

Growing support for this concern over the commercialisation of children is to be found in Greg Critser's book entitled *'Fat Land'*. This documents how Americans have become the fattest people in the world, due largely, he argues, to the relentless commercialisation of children through the fast food industry. How is it that a leading fast food manufacturer has been allowed the franchise of one of the most popular British children's television series each weekend? It is not for me to say whether it is good or bad. However, there has been an astonishing silence in society on this development. That is but one of the many issues that we should be concerned about and debating.

All of this leads me to propose Al's thesis! Namely, that the current difficulties confronting children and children's services reflect the low standing and value of children, young people and parenting in contemporary society.

Central to this is the inability of our nation to recognise that children have human rights. Is it not thoroughly unacceptable that England is one of few European countries that has not taken the courageous step to appoint a parliamentary ombudsman or commissioner to be responsible for protecting the rights of children?

On a recent visit to Sweden I was given three key milestones to explain how Sweden has developed, over a period of twenty years, the best indicators for child life and health in the world. These are:

- The introduction of legislation in the 1960s to ban corporal punishment in children. It is salutary to recall the violently antagonistic media coverage in the last few weeks when a key House of Commons Committee proposed that such legislation was necessary in England.
- The incorporation of the UN convention on the rights of the child into every aspect of emerging legislation.
- The creation of the post of the children's ombudsman, supported by a network of local ombudsmen in their individual communities across Sweden.

The best example of the concern for children in Sweden is the creation of an office that reports to Parliament. The function of this office is to vet every aspect of emerging legislation and every budget from the Government from the child's perspective. In talking to Swedish colleagues they look with incredulity at the failure of society in England to take a more responsible attitude to the welfare of children, our most precious resource.

To be really provocative, I ask where is there now the intellectual debate, the effective advocacy for children that characterised the Victorian era? Who cares about children?

This leads, finally, to my third 'exam' question – is all well with our services for children?

It is certainly true that there are many dedicated staff working in all aspects of children's services leading to thousands of children's lives being saved and many children being effectively protected. Stunning technological advances are curing diseases thought untreatable only 10 years ago. Nonetheless that all is not well nationwide was vividly exposed by Sir Ian Kennedy's National Inquiry following the events concerning children's heart surgery in Bristol, and the recently published report by Lord Laming into the murder of Victoria Climbié. The reports highlighted the subordination of children's services to the demands of adults, the absence of any responsibility at any level for children, fragmentation of services, lack of strategy, failure of a partnership with parents and children, failure of communication and an absence of organisational and professional leadership. Kennedy described children's services to be the 'Cinderella' of the NHS.

Is all gloom and despondency? No. I can offer some light at the end of the tunnel. I genuinely believe that our current Government under the premiership of Tony Blair is doing more for children than any other Government for the last fifty years. His personal commitment is encapsulated by a quotation of the 18th of September 2002, namely:

'Our objectives are...to make sure that every child of the next generation has the opportunity to flourish, regardless of where they are born, where they grow up, where they are educated.'

These are powerful words, the like of which have not been uttered by any previous Prime Minister for many years in giving such an explicit commitment to children.

In fact, examining the totality of the Government's commitment to children demonstrates a most impressive and commendable agenda. This includes:

- The macroeconomic policies of the Chancellor focusing on unemployment, inequalities and family tax credits.
- Neighbourhood renewal both urban and rural.
- Specific programmes across Government including:
  - Investment in education.
  - The Children and Young People's Unit charged with defining a cross-government strategy for children and young people.
  - The Children's Fund, bringing a closer interaction with the voluntary sector.
  - Sure Start and focus on early years, this being the most exciting social experiment for some considerable time through the deliberate targeting of services to the most vulnerable 0-4 year old children in our most deprived localities both urban and rural.
  - Quality Protects, Connexions and the Adoption Bill focused on disabled and vulnerable children.
  - The Youth Justice Board focusing on young offenders and the responsibilities of parents.
  - The cross cutting review on inequalities and the current Green Paper on prevention of children at risk.
  - The Children's Taskforce and the remit to deliver the National Service Framework for Children.
  - Finally, the very recent creation of a new Minister for Children and Families, with a focus in the DfES for all government strategy and policy for children.

The question that must be asked of Ministers is why until now, has there, seemingly, been an unwillingness to package this totality and celebrate the extent of its commitment to children. Although children themselves cannot vote, I argue that parents and especially grandparents (the power of the grey vote!) empathise readily with the cause of childhood and any Government portraying the totality of its commitment must surely find a resonance in the voters. Why is Government not packaging and portraying the excellence of its achievements to date?

The Children's Taskforce was established in November 2000 and I was given the privilege of chairing it from January 2001. It meets regularly and currently has 34 members from health, social care, education, management, voluntary and non-Government organisations together with a cohort of highly talented cross-government officials.

It is charged with defining a strategy for engaging children and young people and carers as partners in developing health-related services; providing a vision for children's services through the construction of a National Service Framework for Children, and finally, actively engaging with frontline staff to challenge and improve our current practices.

National Service Frameworks ('NSFs') are new instruments of Government policy introduced some four years ago and designed to effect rapid change in key services. The difference between NSFs and a report is that the latter can sit on a shelf and gather dust, whilst NSFs define standards that must be implemented.

The Children's NSF is currently being crafted by a team of colleagues working in eight external working groups with seven areas of work underpinning the development. The first standard has been published, and full details can be found on the Children's Taskforce and NSF website at:

www.doh.gov.uk/childrenstaskforce
www.doh.gov.uk/nsf/children/gettingtherightstart.htm

What do we want to achieve through the Children's NSF?

We wish to improve the lives and health of children and young people through the delivery of appropriate, integrated, effective and needs led services and to improve the experiences and satisfaction of children and young people and their carers from the services provided for them. We introduced the second part of this mission statement in the light of listening to the families of children with disability. Most of them are incandescent over the difficulties they experience in obtaining information on their children's problems and accessing services that are delivered in a coherent, integrated and needs led fashion.

How are we going to improve service delivery through the National Service Framework?

By three key principles:

- Making the child the centre of services.
- Always considering 'the whole child' (the interweaving of health, social care, and education – the child's life).
- A needs-based approach.

These simple concepts are easy to say, but difficult to implement in practice, since all of them require partnerships, communication and getting out of the current silos and bunkers that delineate and constrain individual professions and agencies.

We offer as a practical instrument the concept of the child's journey. In other words we encourage staff in their daily activities to consider the circumstances which has brought a child into their services whether they be health, social care or education. We ask the staff to identify the milestones that a child will pass through as she or he experiences the journey. Having identified the milestones it is then important to list the needs of the child and of the carer at each of these milestones after discussing those needs with them and drawing them into a full partnership.

Having identified the needs it is then possible to consider the competencies (please note, not immediately the professional bunkers). Once the needs and competencies have been identified it is then possible to consider the information and the evidence upon which to base appropriate services and only then to consider their configuration. Central to the delivery of services must, of course, be the workforce considerations and the budget that is necessary.

Can we extend to this the Vancouver model of a 'patch-based' approach to the life of the child? I have just returned from that city to see for myself their Early Human Learning Partnership that has evolved from their mapping of children's lives and health in the city. In Vancouver they have post-coded everything to do with children. The initiative was driven by the need for the City Council to know where children were living. This was driven by Chinese immigration. Where they thought children were living turned out to be not where they were living. A child population density map of Vancouver illustrates that the largest concentrations of children are in the deprived, run-down, downtown parts of Vancouver. Against the map and the domicile, they applied health indicators: birth weight, growth, immunisation uptake. They post-coded education outcomes in relation to resource allocation and the use of local resources, including library usage and safe play areas. So this kind of model, post-coding on a patch basis, is, I propose, a very powerful service and research tool. Much of the information that is in Vancouver is already available here – noone is charged with collating it and making it a tool to improve service delivery.

I acknowledge that all of my colleagues in the field of children's services take substantial pride in their dedication to their patients and charges. Many of my colleagues have driven themselves, literally, to an early grave through their extreme hard work and commitment to children. However, dedication is not enough! *Advocacy* is also needed.

Real success depends not only on dedication but also having the best facilities and resources for our services. To do this we have to speak effectively for the needs of children and families and this, bluntly, means understanding politics. None of us as professional members of staff has trained to be a politician, yet politics is the means of influencing change and policy is the engine for so doing.

I argue that for too long we have had our heads buried in the sand, but, reassuringly, many of us are now lifting our heads out of the sand. So my challenge is what are you going to do? Which actions will each of you take tomorrow to speak more effectively for children in order to improve their lives and health? The fine words of Government policy and the emerging NSF will, by themselves, effect no change. Improvement will occur only if everyone at the *local* level is active in demanding and delivering change.

The means of delivering change will be proposed in the NSF, but in essence, all of the following levers need to be pulled, remembering that the NSF is not the end – it is a means to an end:

- Greater understanding and rigour in the commissioning of children's services.
- Formal inspection to generate a culture of continuous improvement
- Listening to the voice of the child, young person and family.
- Clear accountability and responsibility for managing services.
- Investing in strategic, leadership and organisational capacity.

These in turn need to be linked to Al's 'operational triad'. *Information* on local children (epidemiology, demography, current service provision, workforce and spend), *strategy*, including the creation of local strategic partnerships, and *integrated service development* through managed networks of care overseen by local children's teams that encompass the key agencies, professional and voluntary organisations and consumers. The just-announced creation of 35 Children's Trust Pathfinders is an exciting opportunity to evaluate new ways of service delivery.

In conclusion, I have rehearsed briefly some insights into the history of children and childhood, emphasising and supporting the commentary by Lloyd de Mause. I argue that the current turmoil in contemporary society is generating new and pernicious influences on children. Yet, where is the intellectual debate about these influences?

Despite this the current focus by Government on children is not only refreshing but extremely important. Time will tell whether the new Minister for Children and Families and her directorate will be able to influence government policy and direct the appropriate allocation of resources for children's services to be given fair focus. It is up to us to translate the fine words of policy into real action to improve the services with which children, young people and families can best be supported. Is it not time to recreate the 'movement for children' that characterised the Victorian era?

Acknowledgements

I acknowledge the contributions to this lecture from the writings of many authorities listed in the bibliography below. I have collated them and then given my own interpretation. I note with special pleasure the key books by James Walvin, Jules Kosky, Peter Ackroyd, Rowan Williams, Berry Mayall, Neil Postman, Phil Scraton, Alan Gallop and Jeannie Duckworth.

I also acknowledge the substantial help given by my Personal Assistant, Ruth Johnston, in her indefatigable pursuit for me of original sources of information.

Selected Bibliography

Ackroyd, P. 2002. *Dickens: Public Life & Private Passion*, London: BBC Worldwide Ltd.

Ariès, P. 1986. *Centuries of Childhood*, Middlesex: Peregrine Books.

Camden & Islington Health Authority. 1999. *The Health of Children & Young People: Public Health Report 1999*, London: Camden & Islington Health Authority.

Cleverley J & Phillips DC. 1986. *Visions of Childhood – Influential Models from Locke to Spock*, New York: Teachers College Press

Colón, AR & Colón, PA. 1999. *Nurturing Children: A History of Pediatrics*, USA: Greenwood Press.

Critser, G. 2003. *Fat Land: How Americans Became the Fattest People in the World*, Boston: Houghton Mifflin Company.

de Mause, L. 1980. *The History of Childhood: The Evolution of Parent-Child Relationships as a Factor in History*, London: Souvenir Press (Educational & Academic) Ltd.

Duckworth, J. 2002. *Fagin's Children; Criminal Children in Victorian England*, London: Hambledon and London.

Gallop, A. 2003. *Children of the Dark*, Stroud: Sutton Publishing.

Getting the Right Start – The National Service Framework for Children, Mothers and Families: the Hospital Standard and Emerging Findings. 2003. London: Her Majesty's Stationary Office.

Hardyment, C. 1984. *Dream Babies*, Oxford University Press.

Kennedy, I. 2001. *The Bristol Royal Infirmary Inquiry*, presented to Parliament by the Secretary of State for Health by Command of Her Majesty, Queen Elizabeth II.

Kosky, J. 1989. *Mutual Friends: Charles Dickens & Great Ormond Street Children's Hospital*, London: George Weidenfeld & Nicholson Ltd.

Laming, Lord H. 2003. *The Victoria Climbie Inquiry*, presented to Parliament by the Secretary of State for Health and the Secretary of State for the Home Department by Command of Her Majesty, Queen Elizabeth II.

Mayall, B. 2002. *Towards a Sociology for Childhood: Thinking from Children's Lives*, Buckingham: Open University Press.

McCleary, GF. 1933. *The Early History of the Infant Welfare Movement*, London: HK Lewis & Co Ltd.

Mitchels, B & Prince, A. 1992. *The Children Act & Medical Practice*, Bristol: Jordan & Sons Ltd.

Newell, P. 2000. *Taking Children Seriously: A Proposal for a Children's Rights Commissioner*, London: Calouste Gulbenkian Foundation.

Nichols, BL, Ballabriga, A & Kretchmer, N. 1991. *History of Pediatrics 1850-1950*, New York: Raven Press.

Orme, N. 2001. *Medieval Children*, New Haven & London: Yale University Press.

Phaire, T. 1955. *The Boke of Chyldren*, Edinburgh & London: E & S Livingstone Ltd.

Postman, N.1994. *The Disappearance of Childhood*, USA: Vintage Books.

Scraton, P. 1997. *Childhood in 'Crisis'?* London: UCL Press.

Still, GF. 1996. *The History of Paediatrics*, England: College of Paediatrics & Child Health, The Lavenham Press Ltd.

Stoate, H & Jones, B. 2002. *All's Well that Starts Well*, London: The Fabian Society.

Taylor, L & Taylor, M. 2003. *What are Children For?* London: Short Books.

The Hospital for Sick Children. 1854. *How to Nurse Sick Children: Intended as a help to the Nurses at The Hospital for Sick Children*, London: Longman, Brown, Green & Longmans.

von Rosenstein, NR. 1977. *The Diseases of Children & their Remedies*, London: The Nutrition Foundations' Reprints, Johnson Reprint Company Ltd.

Walvin, J. 1982. *A Child's World: A Social History of English Childhood 1800 –1914*, Middlesex: Penguin Books.

Williams, R. 2000. *Lost Icons: Reflections on Cultural Bereavement*, Edinburgh: T & T Clark Ltd.

Winnicott, DW. 1969. *The Child, the Family, and the Outside World*, Middlesex: Penguin Books Ltd.

Woodroffe, C, Glickman, M, Barker, M & Power, C. 1995. *Children, Teenagers & Health: The Key Data*, Buckingham: Open University Press.

PLENARY SIX

LISTENING TO YOUNG CHILDREN: PROMOTING THE 'VOICES' OF CHILDREN UNDER THE AGE OF EIGHT[1]

Y Penny Lancaster
Coram Family's Listening to Young Children Project

Summary of paper

Penny Lancaster said that if we are serious about listening to the voices of children, we need to revisit taken for granted concepts and rethink how we relate to young children.

One of the findings of the Listening to Young Children project is that the starting point for listening is in developing socially inclusive relationships. These are relationships which balance the tension of protection and participation through mutual respect and practically by sharing power. She stressed the importance of hearing, observing and responding seriously to what we have heard and seen.

One of the concepts which she believes needs to be revisited is that of childhood. How we view children needs to change because that will impact how we relate to them – it is important that children are viewed as people already. They are not learning to exist for the future, they are accomplishing for the present. For children to be key players they need to be recognised as people in their own right with different skills, experiences and evolving capacities. They are competent to partner with adults in decision making. Competence grows through experience rather than along some continuum based on age and ability.

Ms Lancaster said that everyone has a story to tell, even babies. Socially inclusive relationships promote the idea that the telling of stories young children have is not dependent on the age of the teller, but rather on the sensitivity of the listener.

The second concept is around language, the concept of children's voices and in particular the influences that limit or empower their voices. For them to be heard, one of issues we need to look at is how we make generalisations. Children speak from multiple, combined and intersecting positions. Different children have different needs, experiences and preferences, all generalisations do is disadvantage those who do not fit them. Listening to different children individually challenges generalisations, but to hear the different realities of children time and space are required.

A further area is the context within which a child's voice is heard. The physical space in which children find themselves will influence what they say or do not say. The reason for the interaction also has a powerful influence. Children learn through the implicit messages that we give through words and body language what their status is and the role they are expected to play.

The concept of interpretation is another important area. We all have a social and cultural grid which we use to make sense of the world – children included. Our perception of experiences is mediated through our assumptions, values and beliefs and we must be careful we do not construct meanings for children and to give children time to express their views.

---

[1] This paper is based on Lancaster, YP (2003). *Promoting Listening to Young Children: The Reader*, in *Listening to Young Children*, YP Lancaster and V Broadbent (Maidenhead: Open University Press).

In rethinking practice Ms Lancaster went on to discuss the notion of RAMPS which is a framework that helps professionals translate the rhetoric of 'listening to young children' into practice. It involves adults:

Recognising children's many visual and verbal languages;
Assigning space for documentation and feedback;
Making time for children to make informed decisions;
Providing genuine choices;
Subscribing to a reflective practice.

Ms Lancaster felt that if one of the benefits of human rights legislation is the opportunity to revisit taken for granted concepts and rethink our practice, we need to make certain this includes consideration of how to ensure that the voices of the youngest children in society are not overlooked. We can do this by developing socially inclusive relationships, using the notion of power sharing RAMPS.

Background

The Waterhouse report (2000) suggested that if children in the care of local authorities had been listened to, the abuse they suffered at the hand of their carers could have been limited, if not prevented. Although children had attempted to voice what was happening to them, adults had failed to hear them. Many had to wait until they were adults before their experiences were taken seriously. Why did adults fail to listen to these children? Perhaps the old adage that children should be seen and not heard had ensured that their voices fell on deaf ears. The more recent Laming Report has revealed just how tragic consequences can be when a child is not heard. Victoria Climbié needed someone to listen to her life experiences, her concerns, her feelings and her perspective of her situation, but noone did. Victoria was known to three housing departments, four social services departments, two GPs, two hospitals, an agency-run family centre and two police child protection teams – 'the extent of the failure to protect Victoria was lamentable', (Lord Laming, Coram Family Annual Lecture, 2003.)

The UN Convention on the Rights of the Child (UNCRC) and UK legislation (primarily the 1989 Children Act) have played a significant role in promoting the notion that children's views must be taken seriously. They are intended to ensure that listening to children, enabling children to express their views, feelings and concerns is paid more than lip service. Together they are a laudable endeavour to promote the voice of the child in decision-making processes that have traditionally been the domain of adults.

Article 12 of the UNCRC declares that:

'1. States Parties shall assure to the child who is capable of forming his or her own views the right to express those views freely in all matters affecting the child, the views of the child being given due weight in accordance with the age and maturity of the child.

2. For this purpose, the child shall in particular be provided the opportunity to be heard in any judicial and administrative proceedings affecting the child, either directly, or through a representative or an appropriate body, in a manner consistent with the procedural rules of national law.'

Article 12 details an important step change in promoting children's participation: it does not undermine the responsibility of adults to ensure the best interests of the children they care for or work with (Lansdown and Lancaster, 2001), and yet it tends to evoke a sense of threat to parents and professionals alike who work with and/or care for children.

Article 5 declares:

'States Parties shall respect the responsibilities, rights and duties of parents or, where applicable, the members of the extended family or community as provided for by local custom, legal guardians or other persons legally responsible for the child, to provide, in a manner consistent with the evolving capacities of the child, appropriate direction and guidance in the exercise by the child of the rights recognised in the present Convention.'

Once a child is deemed competent the responsibility rests on the parents to provide guidance for their evolving competencies. While the framework of the UNCRC includes both an emancipatory and developmental concept in promoting children's participation, it also includes a protective concept. To the extent children have an entitlement to participate in all matters that affect their lives and to have their views taken seriously there is likewise provision for children to be protected from their unevolved capacities (Lansdown, The Open University *Childhood Reconsidered* Conference, 2003). Engaging with children within a rights based approach requires balancing children's best interests and their right to participate in matters that affect their lives.

Nevertheless, despite children's participation being on the social, health and educational agendas there are still too many children who are not accessing decision-making processes in matters that affect their lives (HM Treasury Document, 2001). One group of children that tends to be overlooked are those who are under the age of eight. There appears to be still an assumption that children under the age of eight are too young to meaningfully participate in matters that affect their lives. And yet in response to Lord Laming's report on Victoria Climbié, who was eight years old when she died, it is important that a step change is achieved so that young children are no longer excluded from decision-making processes on account of their age. Making this step change however, is fraught with difficulties whether we are thinking of child-focused contexts such as nurseries and schools or contexts such as the courts, which are designed primarily for adults. Translating the rhetoric of listening to children under the age of eight into practice often raises more questions than answers, and in particular when we are thinking about family law proceedings.

The Listening to Young Children project

Coram Family, with the support of the Esmée Fairbairn Foundation and Bernard van Leer Foundation, has recently completed a three-year research and development project (2000–2003) which sought to understand 'when listening works' for children under the age of eight, within the education, social care and health sectors. This work culminated in the development of *Listening to Young Children*,[2] which is an integrated resource that supports parents and professionals alike to relate more effectively to young children. The project particularly focused on the role of the arts, both visual and performing, in enabling young children to express their views, concerns and feelings about matters that affected their lives. This paper draws on this project, which was undertaken initially with approximately 170 children aged between 0 and 8 who attended services (a parent's centre, a local authority and a parent-run nursery, a child contact centre and a homelessness centre for families) on Coram Community Campus in addition to a neighbouring primary school. This investigation informed a prototype resource that was piloted UK wide with 300 children under the age of eight in 26 diverse educational, health, social care and voluntary sector settings.

The theoretical framework that informed the project was interdisciplinary in nature (education, international development, psychology, childhood studies, health and sociology) and was influenced by social and rights based literature that argues for respecting the views of people who have little or no voice in society, children, young people and minority cultures. The

---

[2]   YP Lancaster and V Broadbent (2003) *Listening to Young Children*, Open University Press, Maidenhead.

project contributes to the social inclusion debate by promoting respectful adult-child relationships in which young children are enabled to express their views, concerns and feelings about their learning, social care and health circumstances. Listening to children helps parents and professionals to be more effective in responding to the changes in children's lives, meeting their diverse needs, and improving care and services. When listening is the subtle thread of adult/child relationships young children's views are heard.

This paper suggests that developing socially inclusive relationships is the starting point for listening to become the 'subtle thread' of all our work with and care for children under the age of eight, to become the listeners they need. These are relationships, which balance the tension of protection and participation through mutual respect and practically by sharing power. The remainder of this paper draws on the findings of the *Listening to Young Children* project to explore some of the thinking that needs to be addressed in developing socially inclusive relationships and how the notion of participation provides a quality assurance framework from which to translate the rhetoric of children's voices into practice.

Developing socially inclusive relationships

Considering childhood

Prout (2001) suggests that for children's voices to be actually heard, even when a notional space has been created, the way children are viewed needs to be changed. Quortrup, et al (1987) argue that we should view children as social actors who are 'beings', rather than 'in the process of becoming', in transition to becoming mature. It is a fact that children are at different stages of developing socially, physically, spiritually and cognitively, but how we understand this development is a matter of culture; child development is social construction (James and Prout, 1990). Young children, like all of us, are making sense of their lives, and in doing so are developing preferences, views, aspirations, concerns and interests (Delfos, 2001). Children are not simply learning and practising to exist for the future, but rather they are already living and accomplishing in the present. As active participants, they not only have something worthwhile to say about their lives, but they are also able to communicate their views about matters that concern them (Alderson, 2000).

Our view of childhood impacts on our understanding of young children's evolving capacities, on whether children's voices are heard or silenced. An adult/child dichotomy in which adults are seen as more reliable to express the child's view than the child directly overlooks children as experts of their own experiences, as meaning makers and as being competent to partner with adults in decision-making processes. Woodhead (The Open University *Childhood Reconsidered* Conference, 2003) argues that one way we can break down this kind of dichotomy is to puncture the myth about maturity. Defining competence as social, physical or cognitive development does not take into account the way that young children cope with their experiences and the understanding that they have about their social world (Alderson, 2000). Competence grows through experience, rather than with age or ability.

Recognising young children as social people in their own right, as meaning makers, and experts in their daily lives, but with different skills, experiences and capacities helps to break down traditional views of children that exclude. This requires a step change towards a view of childhood that promotes reciprocity of perspectives, within socially inclusive relationships so that children are key players in matters that affect their lives. Everyone has their story to tell, even babies (Riihelda 1996). For instance at a baby massage class a first time mother arrived with her six month-old baby boy. The class had been recommended to her because she was finding it difficult to build a relationship with her child, 'he is so fractious and will not settle. I feel such a failure – I don't think he likes me '. She was returning to work within the next three months and was not happy that she had not built a loving relationship with him. With her consent I videoed their 'baby massage' experience which included time in which she gave her son his bottle. Afterwards the mother and I viewed the footage at slightly slower than normal speed. It was only at this speed that we saw that while she held him close to her he was calm and for the most part intently gazing at her. For the first time this mother, to her delight, 'heard' her son interacting with her, communicating that he wanted to build a relationship with her. As Riihelda (1996) argues, the telling of the stories young children have is not dependent on the age of the teller, but rather on the sensitivity of the listener

The voices of children

Young children belong to a category of people that is inherently diverse, not only because of their differences in age and capacities, but also in terms of the mix of ethnicity, race, gender, and ability that they each represent. There is no single concept of childhood (James and Prout, 1990) as any one child sees and speaks from multiple, combined and intersecting positions: gender, ethnicity, class and disability influence all children's lives (Prout, 2001). Different children are interested in different things (Dunn, 1996) and have different experiences, wishes and expectations (Davis, 1998). Describing children in homogeneous terms, in 'common-sense' generalisations overlooks the different realities of children's lives resulting in disadvantaging children who do not fit these simplified descriptions. Developing socially inclusive relationships involve promoting children's different and diverse perspectives, taking into account the difference and diversity amongst and between children. Listening to 'the voices of children' demonstrates that children's perspectives in decision-making processes are valued in that their inclusion helps to avoid the silences and distortions that otherwise would exist. Focusing on children's different realities through listening to each of them directly helps to counter stereotyping, challenges homogeneity, and empowers them (Siraj-Blatchford, 1996).

Ritala-Koskinen (1994) and Davis (1998) amongst others argue that in order to make visible the different realties of children it is essential to gather their perspectives in a range of different social contexts. While children are making sense of the different social relationships that they encounter in their daily lives, they are learning what is appropriate in different domains (James, 1996). On one hand this involves learning a set of behaviours, the culturally bounded values and judgements that constitute each of the social contexts that they experience (Vygotsky, 1978). Embedded in the explicit messages that are communicated in social interactions young children are learning implicit messages about the ground rules that define their status in that setting, and the role they are expected to play. Subsequently young children learn quickly the degree to which their concerns, views, aspirations and experiences will be respected and to what extent their views will be taken seriously, for instance at home, in school or in family law proceedings.

On the other hand children are also learning what is and is not appropriate to express through the language (verbal and body language) that different participants in the interaction employ. The same child can demonstrate different social understanding within different relationships (Tizard and Hughes, 1984). For instance at one school where the *Listening to Young Children* project worked, younger children could choose to whom they expressed their views about the playground. Assisting in this was a group of girls aged from 9 to 11. However, even with considerable training in which they demonstrated skilful understanding of listening principles the girls adopted, 'on the day', an authoritarian role with the younger children through the tone of their voice, the gestures that they used, the closed questions they asked and the projection of their interpretation on their experience of the situations they heard. They took control of the conversations resulting in the younger children responding in short responses. This was in contrast to the lengthy and often enthusiastic stories that these same children expressed to the adult members of the project team. What the children expressed and likewise did not express was influenced by who was participating in the interaction.

Language, whether communicated verbally or through gestures, encodes social relationship between participants (Halliday, 1978). As a result interactions are potentially peppered with a mix of liberated and constrained talk. The *nature* of the interaction mediates what is learnt, the quality of the talk and the relationship that prevails (Vygotsky, 1962). Playing a facilitative role, supporting children to express the meanings that they are searching for in different social contexts, encouraging them to ask questions, giving them undivided attention and valuing their perspectives helps children make sense of their experiences while supporting the listener, whether child or adult, to gain an understanding of children's views (Bruner, 1975; Tizard and Hughes, 1984). This kind of interaction empowers children (Wells, 1978), giving rise to socially inclusive relationships.

Interpretation

We all try to make sense of the world using the particular social and cultural frameworks (Guba and Lincoln, 1989; Sparkes, 1992) that we have learnt from our experiences at home, our social networks, in education and the workplace, and from our faith community. Our perception of our daily life experiences is mediated through the assumptions, values and beliefs that this multiple interpretative framework has given rise to. Subsequently our insights into experiences and situations, even those that we experience together, are not necessarily going to be the same or even similar to another person's perception. The particular set of assumptions and beliefs that shapes how we make sense of social experiences can only ever provide us with an interpretation, a partial and tentative insight giving rise to socially constructed realities rather then captured objectively. For instance one nursery that worked with the *Listening to Young Children* project now gives each new child a camera to record their views on this transitional experience from home to school. One of the children took a photo that for the most part illustrated the sensory garden. The nursery teacher, on seeing this responded by saying how delighted she was that he liked the sensory garden, but the child said 'it's not a picture of the sensory garden, I took a picture of the mud, I don't like it, I don't like the mud'. The mud could be clearly seen, but to have his meaning count, for it to be significant the child had to first challenge the nursery teacher's interpretation. Without neutral procedures 'seeing and telling it like it is' (Eisner, 1992), is problematic.

Acknowledging that all realities are socially constructed potentially engenders the time and space for children's voices to be heard. There is no doubt that decision-making processes tend to be at their best when the views of all those involved in a matter are tabled and where the process of gathering perspectives is inclusive rather than exclusive (Lansdown, 2001). It helps to establish which plans, problems, and values are agreed in any matter, and which are shared and where they differ or need to work towards some agreement (Alderson, 2000). However, having said this, young children tend to be dependent upon the willingness of adults to provide the time, space and provision of appropriate media so that they can participate in voicing their perspectives.

Recognising that our interpretations are open to debate fits a rights-based approach in relating to children. Promoting young children's rights to participate in decision-making processes does not mean that the views of the significant adults in their lives should not likewise be supported and upheld. Young children are viewed as experts in their own lives, but they are not ascribed the status of having the sole expertise. Taking what young children say seriously, either within decision-making processes or as participants within their community need not be at the expense of others. Rather what is advocated is that 'another chair' be pulled up, alongside those already present around the decision-making tables: parents, carers, practitioners and policy makers. A rights-based approach promotes moving away from viewing young children as passive recipients of adult's decisions, where choices are made on their behalf and moving towards viewing young children as active participants in their surroundings (Lansdown and Lancaster, 2001), where their perspectives of experiences and situations are likewise actively sought.

Participation

This paper suggests that for the voices of children to be heard then listening needs to become the subtle thread in all our relations with them. This is the starting point in making a step change attitudinally in how we relate to children under the age of eight. Listening works for young children when they are experiencing inclusive relationships in which they are perceived as social actors, people who are competent to make a meaningful contribution. These are also relationships in which children are given access to processes in which they are enabled to express their views, feelings and concerns and so have a real influence in, for instance family law proceedings, education, health and social service planning and delivery. To examine this practical aspect further the following section focuses on the nature of participation and how together with the notion of 'ramps', a power-sharing framework, the rhetoric of listening to young children is translated into practice.

An important contribution to understanding what constitutes participation, across a range of disciplines, has been made by Robert Chambers (1994a, 1994b, 1994c). He suggests that the hallmark of participation is that it values and highlights the voices of those who would otherwise be silent. An essential component is that the practices employed are inclusive: respectful, flexible, creative, non-threatening and context-appropriate. Participation empowers children under the age of eight to take part in decision-making and problem-solving processes about matters that affect their lives and to have those views taken seriously.

Promoting participation for young children actively counters the power relations that are inherent in child-adult relations. Subsequently any promotion of 'young children's voices' in matters that affect their lives is not a neutral concern. Different groups within society hold differing degrees of power and privilege and those with more power tend to seek ways of maintaining this imbalance. Fairclough (1989) argues that ascribing people social identities (such as ethnicity, social class, gender, age, and disability) supports the distribution of power. Language plays a role in determining who is ascribed a restrictive or unrestricted status. The idea for instance that young children are somehow lacking in maturity linguistically and in understanding their daily lives tends to ascribe the perspectives of adults with more weight (Delfos, 2001) often resulting in children's realities being silenced or judged as wrong (Alderson, 2000).

Participation is a power-sharing framework that has quality assurance at its core. First, participation challenges those who facilitate participatory processes to be reflective in their practice (Chambers, 1994c). This involves being critically self-aware of our behaviour and attitudes in relating to young children, of prejudices, assumptions, cultural voices and values that have shaped our particular view of childhood; checking that young children's voices are taken seriously, that they do count and are tabled alongside the other significant people; being confident that children are competent to share their feelings, concerns, experiences, interests, views and aspirations; being willing to listen and learn from them: to be willing to hear a different and perhaps unexpected perspective to those of the adults involved. Secondly, participation empowers children rather than dominates them. This involves taking into account that listening works best when young children can be 'heard' over different times, spaces and by using a range of visual or verbal media which are accessible, appropriate, authentic, non-threatening, flexible, exploratory and interactive and in which children's direct voices are taken as meaningful contributions, after checking that their intended meaning is understood, to be tabled alongside those who are also contributing. Power-sharing also involves children being given choice to participate or not, to change their mind so that they can either withdraw or be included throughout the process.

Participation legitimises children's use of visual languages. It challenges the deficit construct that tends to be ascribed to children's language repertoire, their nominal use of talk to express their views feelings and concerns. Legitimising children's body language and the use of the visual and performing arts counters the view that children lack the maturation to participate in decision-making processes and challenges the practice of replacing children's direct voices for those deemed more reliable. Freire (1974) argues that those who speak on behalf of others first need to '*normalise*' what has been said to make it fit within their own social and cultural lens. This '*act of extension*' results in children's voices being mediated by an adult's view of reality. In contrast participation promotes children's direct voices. It promotes the value of the language resources that children are able to tap into, and which we as adults have lost through socialisation (Delfos, 2001; Children's hundred languages, Malaguzzi, 1993) such as music, movement, dance, story telling, role play, drawing, painting, sculpturing and photography enable children to express their views directly, on their terms (Chambers 1994b; Petrie, 1999). Participation challenges the myth that children's perspectives are going to be the same as those who know them best and that adults can always be relied upon to act in the child's best interest (Alderson, 2000; Lansdown and Lancaster, 2001).

Listening to Young Children: translating the rhetoric of children's voices into practice

Listening to Young Children is a resource that respects and treats young children as reasonable people (Alderson, 2000); as people whose views are valued. It supports parents and professionals to share power with children under the age of eight, encouraging the positive use of power so that young children can access decision-making processes that affect their lives. However, because children's direct voices have often been excluded from domains such as family law proceedings it is likely that they will need initial support (Franklin, 1995). This paper suggests that given the absence of experience and evidence of young children's participation, parents and professionals also need support in working towards a social inclusion agenda that includes children under the age of eight.

Listening to Young Children contributes towards the support needed by children, parents and professionals alike through the notion of 'RAMPS'. 'RAMPS' is analogous with the ramps that have been constructed so that people who use wheelchairs can gain access to spaces that had been previously denied to them. RAMPS is a framework that helps professionals to translate the rhetoric of 'listening to young children' into practice, to develop strategic policy and practice so that young children can access traditionally adult domains and have their direct voices taken seriously.

RAMPS involves adults: **R**ecognising the many visual and verbal languages that children use to express themselves (Rinaldi, 1993). These include their use of fantasy, play, and visual and performing arts (Drummond, Rouse, and Pugh, 1992; Delfos, 2001), which helps children to explore and represent their perspectives in their own terms (Chambers, 1994b). Children being heard are largely dependent on the adults 'hearing' (David, 1996); **A**ssigning space for documentation and feedback so that young children have tangible proof that their views, feelings and concerns have been valued (Scott, 1996; Prout, 2001). Documenting spontaneous and honest accounts of the moment helps to change power relations (Tizard and Hughes, 1984; Wells 1987; Wood 1988; Cooper, 1993); **M**aking time to give children information that is relevant, makes sense to them and focuses on what they want to know (Burke 1999) so that they can make informed decisions, and ensure that the context is one in which children can ask questions and negotiate understanding (DoH, 2000); **P**roviding choice to children to participate or not and then offering a range of visual and verbal media to express their interests, experiences, concerns, feelings and aspirations. This helps children in often-powerless positions to unlock their emotions (Tolfee, 1996) and to communicate without having to use words (Drummond, Rouse, and Pugh, 1992; Delfos, 2001); and **S**ubscribing to a reflective practice to ensure that interpretations gathered are immediately checked so that 'hearing' becomes only the first step towards gaining understanding, rather than signalling what is 'understood'. This also promotes the different realities that exist not only amongst children, but also between adults and children (Mayall, 1994).

The notion of RAMPS is also embedded in the set of eleven creative, flexible and non-prescriptive *shared experiences* or activities that are included in the resource *Listening to Young Children*. They provide a range of different opportunities based on the arts that enable young children to express their views, concerns and feelings. The *shared experiences* are a springboard from which to work *with* children rather than doing things *to* them (Smith and Barker, 1999). Some of these have been informed directly by children. For instance the 'Wish Catcher' was developed with the help of a young boy who came to my 'Have your say' stall during a 'fun day' that I helped organise at a supervised Child Contact Centre. He said with much emotion and conviction, 'I don't ever want to see my dad again'. He then took some paper, wrote some of his thoughts and attached it to one of the 'have your say' signs. I did not know how to respond so I asked him how I could show him I was listening, even though I could not initiate any change in his circumstances. He said 'just listen, let me say it, I know you can't do anything, just listen to me'. Even though he knew he had to see his dad again, he needed to be heard and to have space so that he could express his view and feelings about the court order that imposed the visits he did not want. A few weeks later, I met with him and two other children, who also experience supervised visits with a non-resident family member, and together we brainstormed about ways in which their voices and the voices of much younger children could be heard in the midst of problems and difficulties. The most important message was not the creative medium that could be offered, but how we as adults would give them time and space to express their feelings and their views, no matter how uncomfortable it made us – we know you cannot always change things for us; we want you to know how we feel and what we think about things, we want you to hear us!

The *shared experiences* draw on the understanding that children have more control when they are engaged in mutual experiences such as taking photos and using the performing and visual arts. They provide an environment for children to work in ways that are familiar to them for instance through their talk, play, creativity and actions, and all the subtle ways in which very young children can represent their views, feelings and concerns (Pugh and Selleck, 1996). Although the *shared experiences* are largely mediated and centred on an adult-driven agenda (James, Jenks, and Prout, 1998) they are linked inextricably with making a cultural shift in relating to children under the age of eight. Offering children real opportunities for their voices to be heard is not about employing tools and techniques that have been found to overcome previously held difficulties and challenges, or supporting adults to connect with current legislation and demands. The *shared experiences* are part of a holistic approach in relating to young children, which involves problematising attitudes, challenging assumptions about childhood and raising awareness of the role, that language and the social context plays in limiting or empowering children's voices. By locating power-sharing centrally to participation parents and professionals are supported in gaining understanding of the world through the eyes of young children, and in evaluating practices through their eyes (Siraj-Blatchford, 1996).

When thinking about including children under the age of eight in traditionally adult domains such as family law proceedings participation is not without its challenges. However, the benefits that can be obtained for children, adults and society far outweigh these. For instance at one Family Centre three brothers aged from 3–5, one of whom is hearing-impaired, used cameras to record their contact experiences with non-resident family members, their father, grandfather and grandmother. Initially they took photos of themselves, with the use of a mirror, each other and then different members of their family. Photographs were taken in between playing with games and toys and being involved in art activities with their family. At the next contact visit they organised the photographs according to whom they most wanted to be with and felt closest to. This helped the boys to express their aspirations that as a family they would *'live together again'*. Some of the benefits that have been identified when children *routinely* participate in decision-making processes include children's ability to clarify their needs and communicate them; to develop confidence and skill to take on new responsibilities; to develop their self-esteem and resilience; and their capacity to think, choose, plan, and challenge evolves. Children feel valued (Pugh and Selleck, 1996). Children's voices, when documented, directly revealed their attitudes about their role in their surroundings, showing often how different their perspective is to others and children who perhaps would not normally have been included in decision-making processes are heard. Adult awareness is raised about issues of which they had previously no understanding resulting in services being effectively improved so that they are more relevant; and the non-prescriptive nature and flexible nature of the arts supports adults to respond to children's interests, concerns and preferences.

Conclusion

If one of the particular benefits of human rights legislation is the opportunity for *judges and lawyers to revisit concepts* that have been taken for granted and *to rethink the way things* are accomplished (Butler-Sloss, 2003) then endeavours to ensure that the voice of the child is heard need to make certain that voices of children under the age of eight are not overlooked. For the voices of the youngest members of society to be heard then the more powerful members of society need to make a step change in relating to them. Developing socially inclusive relationships that balance the tension of protection and participation support making a cultural shift, from viewing children's communication and understanding from a deficit model towards embracing their contribution to family law proceedings as legitimate. But for a change in attitude to be translated into practice young children need our commitment to help them access previously denied domains. Rethinking the way things are accomplished[3] requires us to build power-sharing ramps that enable young children to actively participate in matters that affect their lives, in having their direct voices taken seriously, in allowing us to see the world through their eyes.

Acknowledgments

I would like to thank Dr Gillian Pugh, CEO Coram family, for her helpful comments on this paper.

---

[3] The *Listening to Young Children* project is now offering a training and consultancy service to support professionals take this next step.

References

Alderson, P. 2000. *Young Children's Rights: Exploring Beliefs, Principles and Practice*, London: Jessica Kingsley/Save the Children.

Bruner, JS.1975. From communication to language: a psychological perspective. *Cognition*, **3**, 255–87.

Butler–Sloss, E. 2003. 'Are we failing the family? Human rights, children and the meaning of family in the 21st century', The Paul Sieghart Memorial Lecture, British Institute of Human Rights, King's College London.

Burke, A. 1999. *Communications and Development: A Practical Guide*, London: Department for International Development, Social Development Division.

Chambers, R. 1994a. The Origins and Practice of Participatory Rural Appraisal. In *World Development*, vol. 22, no 7, pp 953–969.

Chambers, R. 1994b. Participatory Rural Appraisal (PRA): Analysis of Experience. In *World Development*, vol 22, no 9, pp 1253–1268.

Chambers, R. 1994c. Participatory Rural Appraisal (PRA): Challenges, Potentials and Paradigm. In *World Development*, vol 22, no 10, pp 1–17.

Cooper, P. 1993. Learning from pupil's perspectives. *British Journal of Special Education*, **20 (4)**: 129–133.

David, T. 1996. Their Right to Play. *In Respectful Educators – Capable Learners: Children's Rights and Early Education*, ed. C. Nutbrown. London: Paul Chapman.

Davis, JM. 1998. Understanding The Meanings Of Children: A Reflexive Process. In *Children & Society*, **12**: 325–335.

Delfos, MF. 2001. *Are you listening to me? Communicating with children from four to twelve years old*, Amsterdam: SWP.

Department of Health (DOH). 2000. *Make it happen! Report on six children and young people's participation events*.

Drummond MJ, Rouse, D and Pugh, G. 1992. *Making Assessment Work*, London: NCB/NES Arnold.

Dunn, J. 1996. Family Conversations and the Development of Social Understandings. In *Children, Research and Policy*, ed. B Bernstein and J Brannen. London: Taylor & Francis.

Eisner, E. 1992. Objectivity in educational research. *Curriculum Inquiry*, **22 (1)**:9–15

Fairclough, N. 1989. *Language and Power*, Harlow: Longman Group Ltd.

Franklin, B (ed.). 1995. *A Handbook of Children's Rights*, London: Routledge.

Freire, P. 1974. *Education for Critical Consciousness*, London: Sheed and Ward.

Guba, E. and Lincoln, Y. 1989. *Fourth Generation Evaluation*, London: Sage.

Halliday, MAK. 1978. *Language as a Social Semiotic*, London: Edward Arnold.

HM Treasury. December 2001. 'Tackling child poverty: giving every child the best possible start in life'. A pre-budget report document.

James, A and Prout, A. 1990. Contemporary issues in the sociological study of childhood. In *Constructing and Reconstructing Childhood*, ed. A James and A Prout. London:Falmer Press.

James, A. 1996. Learning To Be Friends: Methodological Lessons From Participant Observation Among English Schoolchildren. *Childhood*, **3**: 313–330.

James, A, Jenks, C and Prout, A. 1998. *Theorising Childhood*, London: Polity Press.

Lansdown, G. 2001. *Promoting Children's Participation in Democratic Decision-making*, Florence: UNICEF.

Lansdown, G and Lancaster YP. 2001. Promoting Children's Welfare by Respecting their Rights. In *Contemporary Issues in the Early Years*, ed. G. Pugh. London: Paul Chapman Sage.

Malaguzzi, L. 1993. History, ideas and basic philosophy. In *The Hundred Languages of Children – the Reggio Emilia Approach to Early Childhood Education*, ed. E Edwards, L Gandini and G Forman. Norwood: Ablex.

Mayall, B. 1994. Children and childhood. In *Critical issues in social research: Power and prejudice*, ed. S Hood, B Mayall, and S Oliver, Buckingham: Open University Press.

Petrie, P. 1999. Satisfaction with out of School Services: Children and Parents of African and African Caribbean Background, *Research brief No. 8*. Thomas Coram Research Unit: London.

Prout, A. 2001. Representing children: reflections on the Children 5–16 programme. *Children & Society*, **15**, 193–201.

Pugh, G and Selleck, DR. 1996. Listening To And Communicating With Young Children. In *The Voice Of The Child: A Handbook for Professionals*, ed. R Davie, G Upton and V Varma. London: Falmer Press.

Quortrup, J, Bardy, M, Sgritta, S and Wintersberger, H. (eds). 1987. *Childhood Matters: Social Theory,*

Practice and Politics, Aldershot: Avebury.

Riihelda, M. 1996. *How Do We Deal with Children's Questions? Semantic aspects of encounters between children and professionals in child institutions*. Helsinki: University of Helsinki.

Rinaldi, C. 1993. The emergent curriculum and social constructivism. In *The Hundred Languages of Children – the Reggio Emilia Approach to Early Childhood Education*, ed. E Edwards, L Gandini and G Forman. Norwood: Ablex.

Ritala-Koskinen, A. 1994. Children and the construction of close relationships: how to find out the children's point of view. In *Children in Families*, ed. J Brannen and M O'Brien. London: Falmer Press.

Scott, W. 1996. Choices in Learning. In *Respectful Educators – Capable Learners: Children's Rights and Early Education*, ed. C Nutbrown. London: Paul Chapman.

Siraj-Blatchford, I. 1996. Language, Culture And Difference: Challenging Inequality and Promoting Respect. In *Respectful Educators – Capable Learners: Children's Rights and Early Education*, ed. C Nutbrown. London: Paul Chapman.

Smith, F and Barker, J. 1999. Learning To Listen: Involving Children In The Development of out of School Care. *Youth and Policy*, **63**:38–46.

Sparkes, A. 1992. Validity and the Research Process: An Exploration of Meanings. *Physical Education Review,* **15 (1)**:29–45.

Tizard, B and Hughes, M. 1984. *Young Children Learning*, London: Fontana.

Tolfree, D. 1996. *Restoring Playfulness*. Stockholm, Radda Bannen.

Vygotsky, LS. 1962. *Thought and Language,* Cambridge: MIT Press and Wiley.

Vygotsky, LS.1978. *Mind in Society: the Development of Higher Level Psychological Processes,* Cambridge: Harvard University Press.

Waterhouse Report, *Lost in Care,* June 2000.

Wells, G. 1978. Talking with children: the complimentary roles of parents and teachers. *English in Education* **12 (2)**:15–38.

Wells, G. 1987. *The Meaning Makers: Children Learning language and Using Language to Learn,* London: Hodder and Stoughton.

Wood, D. 1988. *How Young Children Think and Learn,* Oxford: Blackwell.

'THE VOICE OF THE CHILD': CHILDREN'S RIGHTS ARE HUMAN RIGHTS

Peter Newell

Former Chair, Children's Rights Alliance for England

Summary of paper

Peter Newell said that the purpose of his paper was to emphasise how far our society and government has to go to recognise children as people who are holders of human rights.

He pointed out that in the government Green Paper, the word 'rights' does not occur at all. Institutions for children have been set up in each of the four countries of the United Kingdom, but Mr Newell argued that it is significant, symptomatic and pathetic that word rights has been left out of the title of each of them. He said that despite the obligation in the United Nations Convention on the Rights of Child (Art 12) ('CRC'), that children have the right to express their views freely on all matters that concern them and that due weight must be given to their views, we still do not have a consistent reflection of that right in our laws. Mr Newell accepted that excellent progress has been made in respect of building listening to children into government, but stressed that listening is not an end in itself, but merely part of a strategy of respecting them as people. His message to the conference was that the acknowledgement of rights is about the recognition of human dignity and about recognising even little people as people.

His paper details the many respects in which the UK's record of achievement on children's rights has been found to be wanting. It dwells particularly on one issue: the right of parents to hit, hurt or humiliate, and the 'reasonable chastisement' defence. Mr Newell saw this issue as being symbolic of adult hypocrisy. He pointed out that in days gone by a man thought it was his right to beat his wife, but it now accepted that domestic violence is wrong and it is against the law. However, the government's definition of domestic violence is constructed to exclude the violence of adults towards children. The accepted target of 'zero tolerance' does not cover children. The monitoring body for the CRC has reported that the reasonable chastisement defence is not compatible with the Convention.

Mr Newell said he was confident that within a few years the human rights mechanisms of the Council of Europe will have effectively forced the governments of all member states to afford all children their right not to be hit or humiliated. He called for the government to ensure that the UK was not the last country to act. He stressed that the issue is one of human rights, and that if we are serious about building a culture of human rights, we cannot pick and choose the rights we decide to protect. He said that it is not enough simply to listen to children, we have to stop hitting them as well.

Introduction

Children's rights are human rights. The international and European human rights instruments guarantee rights for 'everyone'; for 'all members of the human family'. 'All human beings are born free and equal in dignity and rights', states the Universal Declaration of Human Rights, adopted in 1948.

Most of the rights accorded to children in the UN Convention on the Rights of the Child (CRC), adopted in 1989, were already included in the Universal Declaration and the two International Covenants (on civil and political rights and economic, social and cultural rights). But the distinctive task of the CRC is to emphasise that 'everyone' does include children; that children too are holders of and subjects of rights; not possessions of parents or of the state, not simply objects of concern or protection.

The right to be heard

In one important respect, the CRC goes beyond the other instruments. Everyone has the right to freedom of expression, to express their views freely on all matters that affect or concern them. But for children, the CRC asserts an additional right and a matching governmental, adult obligation: states must ensure that children like the rest of us have the right to express their views freely on all matters that concern them – and in addition, the views of the child must be given 'due weight' in accordance with age and maturity (Art 12). This is fair enough, given that children have no vote and no significant power to influence adult decision-making.

The Dartington seminar is focused on 'The Voice of the Child'. And there has been very positive progress in the last few years towards building the habit of listening to children into administrative and judicial procedures. It is not a novel principle – our law has been asserting the principle for some children and some sorts of court processes since the 1975 Children Act, even before the drafting of the Convention on the Rights of the Child began in 1979. Application of the principle was extended in the Children Act 1989.

Government departments now have policies for engaging directly with and consulting children. We have a Minister for Children (no longer having to fit the portfolio in with prisons, the police and community safety, as her predecessor did), a Children and Young People's Unit and independent Children's Commissioners in Wales, Northern Ireland and Scotland. England, which has 11.3 million children under 18, compared with a total of 1.2 million in the other three countries of the UK, has been promised one too, belatedly, but there is as yet no clarity as to what the Government means by a Commissioner.

It is significant, and symptomatic and pathetic, that in each of the three countries it has been decided to leave the word 'rights' out of the title of these human rights institutions, despite strong advocacy from non-governmental organisations and children to include it. If the real purpose is to try to increase respect for the child as a subject of rights, then surely one uses the title of the office as a powerful free promotional message.

All this progress towards developing governmental and independent structures which are sensitive to children and building listening to children into government is excellent, and in time it could encourage consistent respect for children's rights within government and across our society. But we have a long way to go. Sometimes it seems as if people believe that the only right children need is the right to be listened to, that listening to children is an end in itself, rather than a necessary but not at all sufficient strategy for respecting them as people. And even in relation to this particular right for children, we lag behind other countries in not consistently reflecting the right in all relevant legislation – in particular in family law and education. The most recent (2002) Education Act allows the Secretary of State to issue guidance – which local authorities, governing bodies and schools are required 'to have regard to' – on pupil participation.[1] But guidance is not an adequate way of implementing a clear obligation under the Convention on the Rights of the Child; it is ironic that the education system has been particularly resistant to the idea of consulting children.

Accountability to international human rights standards

While some ministers and officials do use the term children's rights with growing confidence, there is clearly a distaste for or terror of it in some quarters in government. But states cannot pick and choose which human rights to respect and who should enjoy them; this Government

---

[1]   Section 176, Education Act 2002.

has been very ready to accuse other countries which are selective in their respect for international human rights standards.

Outside the US and Somalia, all states have accepted the principles and standards of the Convention on the Rights of the Child for their children; the UK did so, with all party support, back in 1991. But when the Committee on the Rights of the Child (monitoring Treaty Body for the CRC) examined the UK's first report under the Convention in 1995, and issued its conclusions and recommendations, MPs asked relevant Ministers what action they proposed to take in response.[2] The common reply, recorded in Hansard, was 'None', and there was no serious parliamentary debate.[3]

By the time the Committee examined the UK's second report, in September 2002, things had changed for the better. The Children and Young People's Unit coordinated the reporting and led the team of senior officials who met the Committee in Geneva. There was a candid admission that the UK's second report was a 'chaotic' mess whose sections did not relate clearly to our obligations under the Convention. The Committee's conclusions on the report, issued in October, were again very critical.[4] The response from Government, while still defensive, was much more serious and detailed. There was a full parliamentary debate in October 2002.[5] Subsequently, the Parliamentary Joint Committee on Human Rights carried out an inquiry and published a lengthy report in June 2003, analysing the concluding observations.[6] This was the Committee's first review of the UK's implementation of an international human rights instrument. It concludes by acknowledging that the Government has given serious attention to issues affecting children's rights, 'but the evidence suggests that its record of achievement is uneven and, in criminal justice and penal matters at least, questionable'.

The significance of the reporting process under the UN Convention on the Rights of the Child is that it is the only external accountability most countries face on how far they respect children's human rights. The UK has been examined twice by the Committee on the Rights of the Child, and has been found seriously wanting. The Government has made much of its commitment to building a culture of human rights. But building that culture for the future must depend hugely on children. If children do not enjoy human rights, experience what it means to be a holder of rights and see adults and government taking children's rights seriously, what hope is there of that culture developing?

The UK's children's rights record

The Committee's 2002 concluding observations on the Government's second report do acknowledge progress, in particular the development of child-focused government structures across the UK and the commitment to end child poverty in a generation. But there are many detailed concerns, among them:

- The lack of a rights-based approach to policy development for children;
- Unequal enjoyment of rights through discrimination against various groups of children, including disabled children, poor children, Irish and Roma travellers, asylum-seeking and refugee children and others from minority ethnic communities, children in the care system,

---

[2] Committee on the Rights of the Child, concluding observations issued following examination of UK's initial report under the Convention on the Rights of the Child, CRC/C/15/Add.34, 1995 (all the Committee's documents are available at www.unhchr.ch).

[3] See, for example, *Hansard*, HC Deb, col 370 (9 February 1995); *Hansard*, Lords Debates, col 1577 (2 March 1995).

[4] Committee on the Rights of the Child concluding observations issued following examination of UK's second report under the Convention on the Rights of the Child, CRC/C/15/Add.188, October 2002.

[5] Westminster Hall debate, Hansard, HC Deb, col 139–182WH (24 October 2002).

[6] Parliamentary Joint Committee on Human Rights, tenth report of session 2002–03 *The UN Convention on the Rights of the Child*, HL Paper 117; HC 81.

locked up children and adolescents;

- Basic principles of the Convention, including respect for children's views and the best interests principle not consistently reflected in legislation and policies;
- High numbers of child deaths through abuse or neglect, the lack of statutory child death reviews and no coordinated national strategy to reduce child deaths;
- The high proportion of children living in poverty;
- Inequalities in health and access to health services;
- High rates of temporary and permanent exclusions from school and lack of any statutory right to education for children in detention;
- Retention of the 'reasonable chastisement' defence;
- Use of physical restraint on children in detention and residential institutions;
- Lack of rights for children of unmarried parents, adopted children and children born as a result of assisted conception to know the identity of their biological parents 'as far as possible';
- Detention of asylum-seeking and refugee children and many aspects of their treatment;
- 'Deep concern' that about one third of the annual intake into the armed forces are below 18, at the arrangements for recruiting under 18s and at widespread allegations of bullying of young recruits;
- Minimum wage not applied to young workers;
- Worsening of the situation of children in the juvenile justice system since the UK's first report; very low age of criminal responsibility; higher numbers of children in custody, at earlier ages for lesser offences; many aspects of treatment of children in detention.

It is a long and detailed 15-page indictment of many aspects of the UK's treatment of its children. When States ratify the Convention or other international human rights instruments, they are taking on obligations under international law to respect and implement them. The Vienna Convention on the Law of Treaties of 1969 states: 'Every Treaty in force is binding upon the parties to it and must be performed by them in good faith'. But the problem, for children and others, is that, aside from international embarrassment, there is no real enforcement procedure. Some of the international instruments – not the Convention on the Rights of the Child – have Optional Protocols allowing individual applications alleging breaches of rights, but the UK has not accepted any of these procedures.[7]

European human rights mechanisms

Europe's children are lucky to have other, regional human rights instruments which protect their and all other citizens' rights: the European Convention on Human Rights and the European Social Charter – developed within the Council of Europe (not the European Union). These instruments, unlike the UN ones, do have strong enforcement mechanisms. The Council, now with 45 member states, is founded on human rights and the rule of law and based in Strasbourg, France. The European Court of Human Rights allows applications from individuals alleging breaches of their rights under the European Convention, and the Court delivers judgments which are binding on the state concerned. The European Committee of Social Rights monitors compliance with the Social Charter, covering economic, social and cultural rights, through a complex reporting procedure – a process which can end in binding recommendations to non-complying states. There is also a procedure for collective complaints under the Charter – but the UK is not among the 13 member states that have so far accepted the procedure.

---

[7] There are Optional Protocols allowing individual communications to the International Covenant on Civil and Political Rights, the Convention against Torture and Other Cruel, Inhuman or Degrading Treatment or Punishment and the Convention on the Elimination of All Forms of Discrimination against Women; none has been accepted by the UK.

Over the last three decades, these human rights mechanisms have had a substantial impact on respect for human rights, including children's rights, in the UK. European Court judgments have led to changes in legislation affecting, for example, children in care, the method of trial and sentencing of young offenders, access to social work and other records, child protection procedures and the age of consent.

The human rights challenge to corporal punishment of children

One particular issue on which the European Court has been highly influential is corporal punishment of children. A series of applications against the UK from children and young people and in some cases their parents has led the Court progressively to condemn corporal punishment of children, first in the penal system, then in schools including private schools and most recently in the home, as set out below.[8] These applications forced the UK to end corporal punishment in all schools (although we were by many years the last country in Europe to do so, with the process only completed in 2003 when abolition was extended to cover all private schools in Northern Ireland).

But this still leaves parents and other informal carers in the home with the freedom to use 'reasonable chastisement'. There is no more symbolic demonstration of the lack of respect for children's rights than the persisting and much used freedom of adults to hit and humiliate them with impunity. Hitting people breaches their fundamental rights to respect for their physical integrity and human dignity. Children are people too – simply smaller and more fragile people. The existence of the 'reasonable chastisement' defence breaches children's equally fundamental right to equal protection under the law.

This common law defence has lingered on, long after removal of the rights of husbands to beat wives and masters to beat their servants. In the still-quoted leading case which dates back to 1860, Chief Justice Cockburn stated: 'By the law of England, a parent ... may for the purpose of correcting what is evil in the child, inflict moderate and reasonable corporal punishment, always, however, with this condition, that it is moderate and reasonable'.[9] It is left to the judge or jury to decide what is meant by 'moderate and reasonable' in any particular case. If the defence is used, it is up to the prosecution to prove beyond reasonable doubt that the punishment was not moderate and reasonable.

As documented below as a detailed case study, the UK is now under unprecedented external human rights pressure to discard this archaic defence. The Government's persisting resistance contradicts and obstructs its positive aspirations for children, its child protection targets and above all its commitment to respect for human rights. There is no way we can expect children to take human rights seriously while as a society we support through the law and through public and political attitudes the right of adults to hit them.

The illogicality of the government's current position is demonstrated with particular clarity in a recent (June 2003) White Paper on domestic violence, entitled 'Safety and Justice':

'Attitudes towards domestic violence have changed in recent years. For example, it used to be the case that society thought a man was entitled to beat his wife – that it was his responsibility and right to control her, and using violence was an accepted way of doing so. Few considered it a crime. ... Over time, the law developed to make it clear that the violence was not legal, but prosecution remained rare and there was still a prevailing attitude that the violence was acceptable. ... Now, it is generally accepted that domestic violence is wrong and against the law. The remaining challenge is to make sure

---

[8]   See, for example, European Court of Human Rights, *Tyrer v UK* (A/26), (1979–80) 2 EHRR 1; *Campbell and Cosans v UK* (No 2), (A/48), (1982) 4 EHRR 293; *Costello-Roberts v UK* (Case No 89/1991/341/414) [1994] ELR 1, ECHR, and *A v UK* (Human Rights: Punishment of Child) [1998] 2 FLR 959, sub nom *A v UK* (1999) 27 EHRR 611. All judgments of the European Court are at *www.echr.coe.int.*

[9]   *Hopley* (1860) 2 F & F 202; 175 ER 1024.

that the attitude no longer remains, anywhere, that violence is acceptable or justifiable.'[10]

Strong words ... but the governmental definition of domestic violence has been constructed to exclude direct violence by adults to children in the domestic context. The effect on children of witnessing violence between adults is included – but the accepted target of 'zero tolerance' of violence is not extended to cover hitting children.

Documenting the pressure that the Government is now under to remove the 'reasonable chastisement' defence and thus give children equal protection under the law on assault, illustrates just how far the UK is from treating with appropriate respect the international human rights standards and the mechanisms which it has played a prominent part in developing.

The Committee on the Rights of the Child first recommended removal of the 'reasonable chastisement' defence when it examined the UK's first report under the CRC in 1995. The Committee was disturbed by reports it had received on the physical and sexual abuse of children, and it recommended:

'... that physical punishment of children in families be prohibited in the light of the provisions set out in articles 3 and 19 of the Convention. In connection with the child's right to physical integrity, as recognized by the Convention, namely in its articles 19, 28, 29 and 37, and in the light of the best interests of the child, the Committee suggests that the State party consider the possibility of undertaking additional education campaigns. Such measures would help to change societal attitudes towards the use of physical punishment in the family and foster the acceptance of the legal prohibition of the physical punishment of children.'[11]

The Committee has consistently condemned all corporal punishment and recommended abolition to at least 120 states in all continents.[12] So it was not surprising that the Committee returned to the issue when it examined the UK's second report in October 2002, stating that it:

'... deeply regrets that the UK persists in retaining the defence of 'reasonable chastisement' and has taken no significant action towards prohibiting all corporal punishment of children in the family. ...The Committee is of the opinion that governmental proposals to limit rather than to remove the 'reasonable chastisement' defence do not comply with the principles and provisions of the Convention and the aforementioned recommendations, particularly since they constitute a serious violation of the dignity of the child. Moreover, they suggest that some forms of corporal punishment are acceptable and therefore undermine educational measures to promote positive and non-violent discipline. ...The Committee recommends that the State party: with urgency adopt legislation throughout the State party to remove the 'reasonable chastisement' defence and prohibit all corporal punishment in the family and in any other contexts not covered by existing legislation; promote positive, participatory and non-violent forms of discipline and respect for children's equal right to human dignity and physical integrity, engaging with children and parents and all those who work with and for them, and carry out public education programmes on the negative consequences of corporal punishment.'[13]

---

[10] Home Office, *Safety and Justice – The Government's proposals for domestic violence*, June 2003, p 8.

[11] See 1: Committee on the Rights of the Child, concluding observations issued following examination of UK's initial report under the Convention on the Rights of the Child, CRC/C/15/Add.34, 1995.

[12] For an analysis of the Committee's jurisprudence in relation to corporal punishment, see UNICEF, *Implementation Handbook for the Convention on the Rights of the Child*, fully revised edition 2002, page 265 et seq.

[13] Committee on the Rights of the Child concluding observations issued following examination of UK's second report under the Convention on the Rights of the Child, CRC/C/15/Add.188, October 2002.

In May 2002, another UN human rights Treaty Body, the Committee on Economic, Social and Cultural Rights, following examination of a report from the UK, concluded:

> 'Given the principle of the dignity of the individual that provides the foundation for international human rights law (see paragraph 41 of the Committee's General Comment No. 13) and in light of article 10(1) and (3) of the Covenant, the Committee recommends that the physical punishment of children in families be prohibited, in line with the recommendation of the Committee on the Rights of the Child...'[14]

But the heavier pressure on the UK is coming from the Council of Europe's human rights mechanisms. In 1998, the European Court of Human Rights found unanimously that UK law – the 'reasonable chastisement' defence – failed to give children 'adequate protection' including 'effective deterrence'.[15] It found that the beating of a young English boy by his stepfather amounted to inhuman or degrading punishment. The stepfather had been prosecuted in an English court, used the defence of 'reasonable chastisement' and been acquitted. This acquittal led to an application by the boy to the European Commission of Human Rights and to the European Court's landmark judgment in September 1998, *A v UK*.[16]

Five years on, the UK Government has done nothing to remedy the situation. In fact, in November 2001 it announced that it would not change the 'reasonable chastisement' defence, although it would keep use of it under review.[17] This followed consultations on law reform; in England and Wales the consultation paper rejected complete abolition and proposed instead various ways of limiting the 'reasonable chastisement' defence. Following devolution, there were separate consultations in Scotland and Northern Ireland. In Scotland, unlike England, respondents were at least asked their views on complete abolition.[18] In 2002, the Scottish Executive announced proposals to ban all corporal punishment of children up to their third birthday, and to ban use of implements, shaking and blows to the head for all children. But during the passage of these proposals through the Scottish Parliament, they came under criticism from the Parliament's Justice Committee, and with elections to the Parliament looming, the Executive dropped the proposal for a complete ban for babies and toddlers.

The Criminal Justice (Scotland) Act 2003 introduces the concept of 'justifiable assault' of children to Scottish law, defining use of implements, shaking and blows to the head as unjustifiable. (It was these proposals to try and define how children can be hit that were specifically criticised in the Committee on the Rights of the Child's observations in 2002, see above, page xx). These changes have not as yet been implemented – the Executive has suggested it will develop an education campaign first.

Northern Ireland carried out a much more thorough consultation, including pro-actively consulting with children.[19] Because of the suspension of devolution, the results of the consultation and proposals for change have yet to be announced by the Office for Law Reform (July 2003).

---

[14] Committee on Economic, Social and Cultural Rights, concluding observations on UK's fourth periodic report under the International Covenant on Economic, Social and Cultural Rights, E/C.12/1/Add.79, 17 May 2002.

[15] European Court of Human Rights, judgment *A v UK*, see fn 8 above.

[16] Originally, there was a two-tier process for consideration of individual applications, first by the European Commission on Human Rights and then by the European Court. This was replaced by a single, unified Court process in 1998/9; see *www.echr.coe.int* for details.

[17] Department of Health, *Protecting Children, Supporting Parents – a Consultation Document on the Physical Punishment of Children*, January 2000; Department of Health Press release, 8 November 2001, 'Protecting children, supporting parents: no smacking ban'.

[18] Scottish Executive, *The Physical Punishment of Children in Scotland – a consultation*, Scottish Executive Justice Department, February 2000 (see *www.scotland.gov.uk*).

[19] Office of Law Reform, Department of Finance and Personnel Northern Ireland, *Physical punishment in the home – thinking about the issues, looking at the evidence: a consultation paper for Northern Ireland*, Office of Law Reform September 2001 (see *www.olrni.gov.uk*).

It is the Committee of Ministers of the Council of Europe which is responsible for ensuring that governments 'execute' European Court of Human Rights judgments. It has had a succession of discussions on *A v UK*. During the most recent consideration of the case, in February and June 2003, delegations from other European states expressed serious concern at the UK's lack of action in response to the five-year-old judgment. In particular, the deputies were concerned that the UK Government had given an undertaking to the Court that it would reform the law allowing 'reasonable chastisement'. There will be further discussion of the case later this year (2003), and the Committee is likely to pass an interim resolution seeking proper execution of the judgment.

There have been other relevant and important Strasbourg decisions about corporal punishment, emphasising that prohibiting all corporal punishment does not breach other Convention rights to family or private life or religious freedom. In 1982, the European Commission on Human Rights rejected an application by Swedish parents alleging that Sweden's 1979 ban on parental corporal punishment breached their right to respect for family life and religious freedom.[20] In 2000, the Court rejected an application challenging the abolition of corporal punishment in private schools in the UK on grounds that it breached rights to family life and religious freedom.[21]

Yet more human rights pressure for complete abolition of all corporal punishment is building up under the European Social Charter. In 2001, the Charter's monitoring Committee, the European Committee of Social Rights, issued an interpretative 'General Observation' on corporal punishment, concluding that compliance with Art 17 of the Social Charter requires abolition of all corporal punishment:

> '... the Committee considers that Article 17 requires a prohibition in legislation against any form of violence against children, whether at school, in other institutions, in their home or elsewhere. It furthermore considers that any other form of degrading punishment or treatment of children must be prohibited in legislation and combined with adequate sanctions in penal or civil law.'[22]

Since issuing the Observation, the Committee has been systematically reviewing the legal status of corporal punishment in the 45 member-states of the Council of Europe. In February 2003, in its conclusions published following examination of Poland's report on compliance with Art 17, it issued a finding of non-conformity – the first on the grounds that corporal punishment in the home is not prohibited. In July it issued a similar conclusion on the Slovak Republic.[23]

In its conclusions on the UK's most recent report on implementation of Art 17, the Committee states:

> '... As regards corporal punishment, the Committee notes that it was prohibited in private schools by the School Standards and Framework Act 1998, with the result that corporal punishment is now prohibited in all schools. The Committee wishes to be informed whether legislation prohibits corporal punishment in other institutions caring for children. It notes that not all forms of corporal punishment are prohibited within the family. The Committee refers to its general observations on Article 17 in the General Introduction and decides to defer its conclusion on this point pending more information from the British Government on the situation and on its intentions in this regard. It also wishes to receive information on the situation in Northern Ireland and Scotland.'[24]

The UK's next report under Art 17 is due by March 2004. The conclusions of the European Committee of Social Rights will be issued between March and December 2004. The Committee

---

[20] *Seven Individuals v Sweden*, European Commission of Human Rights, Admissibility Decision 13 May 1982.

[21] *Philip Williamson and Others v UK*, admissibility decision, 7 September 2000.

[22] European Committee of Social Rights, Conclusions XV 2 – Volume 1, General Introduction, 2001.

[23] European Committee of Social Rights, Conclusions XVI–2, Volume 2, Chapter 14.

[24] European Committee of Social Rights, Conclusions XV–2, Volume 2, Chapter 15.

will undoubtedly find UK law, allowing 'reasonable chastisement', not in conformity with Art 17. The Committee's conclusion goes to a Governmental Committee and then to the Committee of Ministers. If the UK does not remedy the situation, the Committee of Ministers is likely to issue a resolution at the latest by December 2005, setting out the action required to comply.

The European Social Rights Committee states in its Observation that it has been influenced by the European Court judgment, *A v UK*, by the consistent recommendations from the United Nations Committee on the Rights of the Child that States must ban all corporal punishment, and by developing law reform across Council of Europe states: a quarter have introduced explicit laws to prohibit corporal punishment and a number of others have removed existing defences similar to the 'reasonable chastisement' defence. The Committee's position, like that of the Committee on the Rights of the Child, does not allow for any compromises: there must be explicit and effective prohibition of all corporal punishment.

So there is now a strong process systematically reviewing children's protection from all corporal punishment across Europe. At a Council of Europe seminar in Strasbourg in November 2002, the Deputy Secretary General concluded:

'It is of vital importance that everybody concerned with children work collectively as well as individually towards ending corporal punishment of children ... I would therefore like to take this opportunity to challenge the governments of the member states of the Council of Europe to stop defending – or disguising as discipline – deliberate violence against children and to accept that children, like adults, have the fundamental human right not to be assaulted. In the face of such a fundamental right states cannot remain indifferent – it is their duty to interfere: hitting children is no more acceptable than hitting anyone else. There can be no divide in the respect of human rights.'[25]

It seems not over-optimistic to suggest that within a few years the human rights mechanisms of the Council of Europe will have effectively forced the governments of all member states – including the UK – to respect children's fundamental and equal right not to be assaulted. Of course, that is a positive outcome. But it is a very sad indictment of adults' and governments' attitudes to children that they have had to wait so long to be the last people to be accorded this fundamental protection. There is still time for our Government to choose not to be the last state in Europe to give up this disrespectful and dangerous habit.

Taking human rights seriously

The 2003 report of the Parliamentary Joint Committee on Human Rights shows a new determination by Parliament to encourage Government to take its human rights, including children's rights, obligations seriously. Amongst many detailed recommendations, the Committee confirms that retaining the 'reasonable chastisement' defence is incompatible with the UK's obligations under the UN Convention on the Rights of the Child. A report published by the Health Select Committee on the same day came to the same conclusion from the perspective of child protection.[26] Other specific recommendations relate to remedying many of the concerns of the Committee on the Rights of the Child, in particular in relation to criminal justice and custody, children and armed conflict and asylum-seeking children.

More generally, the Joint Committee proposes that Government should:

- Develop a five-year plan of strategic action in relation to children's rights;
- Demonstrate more conspicuously a recognition of its obligation to implement the rights under the Convention;

---

[25] Council of Europe Forum on Children and Families, Seminar on corporal punishment of children within the family, 21 November 2002: Opening address by Ms Maud de Boer-Buquicchio, Deputy Secretary General.

[26] Health Committee, sixth report of the 2002–2003 session on 'The Victoria Climbié Inquiry Report'.

- Consider incorporating child impact assessments in the explanatory notes to Government Bills.
- Involve children and young people much more fully in preparation of the next report under the Convention.
- Ensure that the forthcoming overarching strategy for children should include specific reference to the rights, principles and provisions of the Convention and explain how these underpin its goals.

If the Government takes these recommendations and those of the Committee on the Rights of the Child to heart and begins to build respect for children's rights systematically into policy development from the earliest stages, the process of building a culture of human rights for the future will really begin.

YOUNG PEOPLE'S EXPERIENCES OF CARE

Dr Maureen Winn-Oakley
NSPCC Senior Research Fellow, University of Warwick

Tom Oakley
Nikki Cox
Nirupana Uthaykumar
Ammanda Walsh
Alison Price
Rights of Children (Birmingham)

The five young people from Rights of Children ('ROC') in Birmingham shared with the conference their experiences of being in care and spoke about their work for ROC. Their message to the conference was that young people can and should be involved in improving and shaping the services provided for them. They called for professionals to consult with young people and to be inventive in thinking of ways to allow young people to engage more.

Dr Winn-Oakley said that they were not saying that young people should be the decision makers, but that they may, for example, like to go to court and meet some of the people involved in their case. She stressed the importance of being flexible. One of the initiatives suggested was a court user group that deals specifically with children's issues. She recognised that many courts had already taken steps, but said that more needs to be done and that it was simply a matter of facilitating young people going to court and getting them more involved in their own cases.

PLENARY SEVEN

CHILDREN'S PARTICIPATION IN PROCEEDINGS –
THE VIEW FROM EUROPE

Andrew Moylan QC
Queen Elizabeth Building

Summary of paper

Andrew Moylan QC introduced his paper by outlining its central issue, namely, in respect of the participation of children in court proceedings, what are the standards which domestic courts must adopt if they are not to be at risk of breaching the obligations imposed by the European Convention on Human Rights (ECHR)? He emphasised that these obligations represent the floor of the rights which should be afforded to children and not the ceiling to them.

Mr Moylan gave an overview of the approach taken by the ECtHR when determining the nature of these obligations and identified two important factors:

- *the existence of a generally accepted view amongst member states; and*
- *the rights contained in other international conventions.*

Examples of this are contained in the paper. In particular, he referred to two very recent appellate decisions from Strasbourg, Sahin v Germany *and* Sommerfeld v Germany *in which the ECtHR (Grand Chamber) had emphasised that the United Nations Convention on the Rights of the Child 1989 (UNCRC) sets the standards to which all governments must aspire.*

As a result of this approach, Mr Moylan noted that the obligations imposed by the ECHR will encompass the obligations contained within other international conventions. In his view the United Kingdom could not escape the effect of these latter obligations even if the United Kingdom had not signed or ratified the relevant convention. If the European Court will determine our obligations by reference to these conventions (and generally accepted standards), Mr Moylan considered that domestic courts must likewise determine our obligations by reference to them.

In relation to the Conventions themselves, Mr Moylan highlighted the following:

- *Article 12 of the UNCRC which provides that children have the right to express their views and to be heard. Although limited to children who are capable of forming their own views, Mr Moylan did not consider that this should be viewed restrictively. The guiding principle is that children have the right to participate in the decision making process.*
- *Article 9.2 of the UNCRC states that all interested parties are to be given the opportunity to participate in proceedings and make their views known. The UNICEF website makes it clear that the child is an interested party who must have the opportunity to participate.*
- *The European Convention on the Exercise of Children's Rights 1996 ('ECECR') which has not been ratified or signed by the UK. It contains more detailed provisions on the issue of children's participation in proceedings under three key areas - (a) the provision of information; (b) consultation and expression of views; and (c) representation. The rights granted are limited generally to children of 'sufficient understanding'. Again, Mr Moylan did not consider that this should be viewed restrictively, particularly in the light of the message from other speakers on the capacity and*

understanding of very young children.

Mr Moylan stated that, whilst there could be debate about the extent of the obligations, the broad thrust is clear: there is an obligation to ensure that all children have genuinely participated and been heard.

Mr Moylan next emphasised that the means by which our obligations are implemented must be effective. For example, in Glaser v United Kingdom *the ECtHR examined whether there was an accessible and coherent mechanism for the enforcement of the applicant's contact rights under an order. One way of testing what was required was by looking by way of analogy at parental participation. Strasbourg jurisprudence has established that parents must be involved in the decision making process to a degree sufficient to ensure adequate protection of their interests. If this is necessary for parents, why, Mr Moylan asked, should it not be true for children?*

The appellate decisions in Sahin *and* Sommerfeld *had clarified that it was not necessary in every case for the child to be seen by the judge or for expert evidence to be obtained. However, decisions must be supported by sufficient material, including about the child's views, which might involve additional expert evidence.*

Mr Moylan concluded by saying that if the UK is not to be at risk of being in breach of its ECHR obligations, it must have mechanisms in place which provide for the effective participation of children in proceedings so that their voices are properly heard. At para 42 of his paper he sets out a summary of what might be required of the UK's family justice system. He acknowledged that these are broad themes and reiterated the guiding principle, that children have the right to participate.

Introduction

(1) I start with the immediate catalyst for this paper, the domestic case of *Re T (Contact: Alienation: Permission to Appeal),*[1] in which a father[2] relied on Strasbourg jurisprudence[3] to support his argument that the judge at first instance had not sufficiently investigated his child's true wishes and feelings when deciding a contact dispute. The Court of Appeal allowed the appeal, without specifically answering the question at the heart of the case: had the father's rights under Arts 6 and 8 of the European Convention on Human Rights ('ECHR') been breached because of a failure to involve him in the contact proceedings, by failing properly to investigate and make findings about the cause of his child's alienation? Thorpe LJ, however, highlighted the Strasbourg cases as raising issues requiring further consideration:

> 'Those cases as they stand suggest that the methods and levels of investigation that our courts have conventionally adopted when trying out issues of alienation may not meet the standards that Arts 6 and 8 of the European Convention for the Protection of Human Rights and Fundamental Freedoms 1950 (the Convention) require. There are policy issues here that the Government and the judiciary may need to consider collaboratively. Should judges see children to ascertain their wishes and feelings? If that is to become the norm, what training should judges receive? To what extent should separate representation be made available to the child at the heart of the case in private law proceedings? What services can the Children and Family Court Advisory and Support Service be expected to provide in order to assist the forensic process to satisfy Convention standards? These European cases were not cited to the judge below. I do not in the present appeal found my conclusion upon them.'[4]

(2) Although *Re T* focuses on the judge's failure sufficiently to address the issue of alienation, it

---

[1]   [2003] 1 FLR 531.

[2]   For ease of reference, it is assumed throughout this paper that any dispute is between parents in private family law proceedings.

[3]   *Elsholz v Germany* [2000] 2 FLR 486; *Sahin v Germany; Sommerfeld v Germany; Hoffmann v Germany* [2002] 1 FLR 119.

[4]   [2003] 1 FLR 531 at para 25.

puts the spotlight on the role of the child in private family law proceedings.[5] If we look at the scope of a child's participation in such proceedings, the general view is usually, at most, involvement pre-hearing: providing the child with some information and ascertaining the child's *'wishes and feelings'*. Participation, in this sense, rarely involves participation in the hearing itself and could be viewed as being simply part of the evidence gathering process in the determination of the dispute between the child's parents. What if there is no dispute, either because there are no proceedings or because there is agreement after the commencement of proceedings? In the former situation, there will be no child participation at all in the separation/divorce process; in the latter it may be very limited. Do our domestic standards meet the standards of the ECHR? What are the wider European and international standards concerning the participation of children?

(3) The title of this paper refers only to *the view from Europe*. However, in order properly to survey this view, this paper cannot be confined simply to an examination of the ECHR and the jurisprudence of the Strasbourg Court. The ECHR and the Court seek to identify and apply the standards and obligations which are necessary for human rights to be effectively implemented. In this endeavour other conventions are not only relevant aides to interpretation, they are also important guides to identifying the proper extent of these standards and obligations. Shared views or generally accepted standards will at least inform, and possibly determine, the manner in which a state should act.

(4) In *Odievre v France*[6] it was made clear that the discretionary margin afforded to states under the ECHR does not entitle a state to act in a manner which does not accord with the shared views held by the other member states of the Council of Europe. In *Ignaccolo-Zenide v Romania*[7] the Strasbourg court interpreted the positive obligations implicit in Art 8 of the ECHR in the light of the requirements of the Hague Convention on International Child Abduction. In *Sahin v Germany* (see below) the Grand Chamber stated:

> 'The human rights of children and the standards to which all governments must aspire in realising rights for all children, are set out in the Convention on the Rights of the Child.'

Our domestic jurisprudence also, independently,[8] recognises the need to take account of these rights and standards. Accordingly, in addition to the ECHR and the jurisprudence of the European Court, this paper will look at the provisions of a number of other European and International Conventions.

(5) The essential message that comes from these instruments is that children have the right to participate in the process through which decisions affecting them are made. The focus of Unicef's 2003 Report on the state of the world's children is 'Child Participation'. In the foreword, Kofi Annan, Secretary-General of the United Nations, states that this focus was:

> 'intended to remind adults of their obligation to elicit and consider the views of children and young people when decisions are being made that affect their lives.'

One of the goals of the Report is to encourage States to promote children's *'authentic involvement'*

---

[5] This paper does not directly address public law proceedings, in which the child is always represented, and which raise very different issues.

[6] 13 February 2003: Application no. 42326/98: para 47, where this point is made in reverse and para 16 of the joint (7) dissenting opinion which speaks powerfully of: 'permitting the rights guaranteed by the Convention to evolve, taking accepted practice in the vast majority of countries as the starting point'.

[7] (2001) 31 EHRR 7, para 95.

[8] Eg *Re H (Paternity: Blood Test)* [1996] 2 FLR 65, 80, referring to Art 7 UNCRC; *Shields v Shields* 2002 SLT 579, applying Article 12 UNCRC.

in such decisions. This theme, of authentic and meaningful participation, is extremely broad and applies to all aspects of a child's life, including judicial and other proceedings.

(6) Another reason for broadening the scope of this paper is that the view from Europe, on the participation of children in proceedings, changed on 8 July 2003. In the two key decisions referred to in *Re T*, namely those of *Sahin* and *Sommerfeld*, the German Government appealed the Chamber's judgments to the Grand Chamber. The appeals in both cases were successful and the Grand Chamber found that there was no breach of Art 8 (by 12 votes to 5 and 14 votes to 3 respectively).[9]

(7) This paper will deal firstly with conventions other than the ECHR; then with the ECHR and Strasbourg jurisprudence; and, finally, a few points on our domestic family justice system.

International Conventions

(8) **(i) United Nations Convention on the Rights of the Child 1989**
The Convention on the Rights of the Child ('UNCRC') is said to be the most universally accepted human rights instrument in history – it has been ratified by every country in the world save three.[10] It contains an agreed set of non-negotiable standards and obligations intended not only to protect children but also to provide them with their own rights as individuals. By Art 4, State Parties are required to undertake all appropriate legislative, administrative and other measures for the implementation of the rights recognized in the Convention.

(9) Unicef's website proclaims the impact of the Convention:

'The most powerful change wrought by the Convention is the way in which children have become visible. Politicians, media, NGOs and broader civil society feel a clear obligation to include children in their respective public domains, interventions, dialogues, debates, mandates. You can't ignore children any longer and get away with it. The Convention has raised consciousness in dramatic fashion.'[11]

(10) The right to participate, contained in Art 12, has been identified as one of the guiding principles of the Convention by the Committee on the Rights of the Child.[12] It provides:

1. States Parties shall assure to the child who is capable of forming his or her own views the right to express those views freely in all matters affecting the child, the views of the child being given due weight in accordance with the age and maturity of the child.

2. For this purpose, the child shall in particular be provided the opportunity to be heard in any judicial and administrative proceedings affecting the child, either directly, or through a representative or an appropriate body, in a manner consistent with the procedural rules of national law.

How the right to participate is to be effected – the practical meaning of the right – has to be considered in each matter concerning children. The UNCRC sets no minimum age at which children can begin expressing their views freely, nor does it limit the contexts in which children can express their views. It acknowledges that children can and do form views from a very early age and refers to children's 'evolving capacity' for decision-making.

---

[9]   Judgments given by the Grand Chamber on 8 July 2003.
[10]   USA and Somalia, which have signalled their intention to ratify by formally signing the Convention, and Timor-Leste, which became independent in May 2002.
[11]   Stephen Lewis, Deputy Executive Director, UNICEF, at the Commission on Human Rights, 1999: *www.unicef.org/crc*.
[12]   An internationally elected body of independent experts that monitors the UNCRC's implementation.

(11) To take another quote from Unicef's website which appears under the title *Genuine participation versus tokenism*:

'Tokenism is a particularly difficult issue to deal with, because it is often carried out by adults who are strongly concerned with giving children a voice but have not begun to think carefully and self-critically about doing so. The result is that they design projects in which children seem to have a voice but in fact have little or no choice about the subject or the style of communicating it, or no time to formulate their own opinions.'[13]

(12) Under Art 12, the opportunity to be heard does not have to be direct, but clearly the procedure by which a child is '*heard*' must be effective. Are children heard in the separation/divorce process? In private family law proceedings do children have little or no choice about the subject or the style of communicating? Do they have time to formulate their own opinions? Are they provided with sufficient information to enable their views to be informed and their participation to be relevant and meaningful?

(13) Other articles in the UNCRC also deal with the participation of children.

- **Article 9**

  This Article is concerned with the separation of a child from his or her parent(s). It stipulates that a child has the right to maintain personal relations and direct contact with both parents on a regular basis, except when this is contrary to the child's best interests. In addition, under 9(2), all '*interested parties*' must be given an opportunity to participate in the proceedings and make their views known. The wording of the Article does not make it clear whether this includes children. However, the Unicef website refers specifically to a child as being an interested party.

- **Article 21**

  This Article deals with adoption. The child is one of the persons concerned who should be heard and whose informed consent should be obtained (although 21(a) stipulates that consent should be obtained only '*if required*').

(14) In its Concluding Observations (9 October 2002) on the report submitted by the UK, the Committee on the Rights of the Child referred to concerns about the participation of children:

'29 … the Committee is concerned that the obligations of article 12 have not been consistently incorporated in legislation, for example in private law procedures concerning divorce, in adoption, in education and in protection throughout the State party. In addition, the Committee is concerned that the right of the child to independent representation in legal proceedings, as laid down in the Children Act 1989, is not systematically exercised…

30 …Furthermore, it recommends that the State party take further steps to consistently reflect the obligations of both paragraphs of article 12 in legislation, and that legislation governing court procedures and administrative proceedings (including divorce and separation proceedings) ensure that a child capable of forming his/her own views has the right to express those views and that they are given due weight. The Committee further recommends that procedures be established that would allow the views expressed by children to be taken into account in and to have an impact on developing programmes and policies affecting them.'

In the Committee's assessment, our domestic practice does not pay sufficient attention to the

---

[13] Roger Hart, 'Children's Participation: The Theory and Practice of Involving Young Citizens in Community Development and Environmental Care': *www.unicef.org/crc*.

right of children to participate in matters and proceedings affecting them. It highlights in particular divorce, adoption and the right of the child to independent representation in proceedings under the Children Act.

(15) To digress briefly: the Committee's Observations also draw attention to the absence of an independent human rights institution for children in England.[14] England is unusual in Europe in having no such institution. Such institutions exist in 18 European countries and a number of other countries outside Europe.[15] The devolutionary process has enabled Wales to appoint a Children's Commissioner; the Northern Ireland Assembly has published a Bill to establish one; and the process is underway in Scotland. The need for a children's commissioner has also been recommended by the Parliamentary Joint Committee on Human Rights. The establishment of a commissioner for England could not but assist in the task of ensuring that children have a proper voice which results in authentic participation.

(16) **(ii) European Convention on the Exercise of Children's Rights 1996**
The European Convention on the Exercise of Children's Rights ('ECECR') came into force in July 2000. It has been signed by 24 countries, of which nine have ratified it.[16] The United Kingdom has neither signed nor ratified the ECECR. However, the Convention provides a European perspective on how the issue of children's participation in judicial proceedings should being dealt with.

(17) The Convention defines its scope and object as being to promote children's rights, and specifically:

> 'to grant them procedural rights and to facilitate the exercise of these rights by ensuring that children are, themselves or through other persons or bodies, informed and allowed to participate in proceedings affecting them before a judicial authority.'[17]

The procedural rights of interest are as follows:

- **Article 3 – Right to be informed and to express his or her views in proceedings**
A child has the right to receive all relevant information[18]; to be consulted and express his or her views; and, to be informed of the possible consequences of compliance with these views and the possible consequences of any decision.
- **Article 4 – Right to apply for the appointment of a special representative**
The child has the right to apply for a special representative[19] in proceedings affecting the child where internal law precludes the holders of parental responsibilities from representing the child as a result of a conflict of interest.

---

[14]   Para 16.
[15]   See the European Network of Ombudsmen for Children: *http://www.ombudsnet.org/*.
        There has been much lobbying for the establishment of a Children's Commissioner in England: see *http://www.ombudsnet.org/ThematicProfiles/Legislation/luk.htm*, for a draft Bill to establish a Children's Rights Commissioner for the UK. The campaign for children's rights commissioners in the UK began nearly a decade ago. Over 120 organisations formally support their establishment across the UK.
[16]   See: *http://conventions.coe.int/Treaty/EN/cadreprincipal.htm* for the full list of countries which have signed and ratified the Convention.
[17]   Article 1.
[18]   Defined in Art 2 as: 'information which is appropriate to the age and understanding of the child, and which will be given to enable the child to exercise his or her rights fully unless the provision of such information were contrary to the welfare of the child.'
[19]   Representative is defined in Art 2 as: 'a person, such as a lawyer, or a body appointed to act before a judicial authority on behalf of a child'.

- **Article 5 – Other possible procedural rights**

Parties to the Convention shall consider granting children additional procedural rights, in particular, the right to apply to be assisted by an appropriate person of their choice in order to help them express their views; the right to apply for the appointment of a separate representative, in appropriate cases a lawyer; the right to appoint their own representative; and the right to exercise some or all of the rights of parties to such proceedings.

B. Role of judicial authorities

- **Article 6 – Decision-making process**

In proceedings affecting the child, the judicial authority, before taking a decision,

- – shall ensure that the child has received all relevant information;
- – consult the child in person in appropriate cases, if necessary privately, itself or through other persons or bodies, in a manner appropriate to his or her understanding, unless this would be manifestly contrary to the best interests of the child;
- – allow the child to express his or her views;
- – give due weight to the views expressed by the child.

- **Article 9 – Appointment of a representative**

  (1) Where the holders of parental responsibilities are precluded from representing the child as a result of a conflict of interest between them and the child, the judicial authority shall have the power to appoint a special representative for the child in those proceedings.

  (2) States shall consider providing that, in proceedings affecting a child, the judicial authority shall have the power to appoint a separate representative, in appropriate cases a lawyer, to represent the child.

(19) The ECECR is the most explicit of the European Conventions in terms of the procedural rights given to children in judicial proceedings.

(a) Provision of Information

A child of sufficient understanding has the right to receive all relevant information (Arts 3, 6 and 10). A decision would have to be made in each case, based perhaps on general presumptions, about what information should be made available to enable children fully to exercise their rights. It expressly includes information about the consequences of any decision and of compliance with the child's views (Art 3). The court is also specifically directed under Art 6 to ensure that the child has received all relevant information before taking a decision.

(b) Consultation and Expression of Views

The child has the right to be consulted and to express his or her views (Art 3 and 6). The words *'consulted'* and *'views'* carry with them, in my view, a stronger emphasis than the current wording in s 1 of the Children Act 1989 which requires a court, simply, to have *'regard'* to *'the ascertainable wishes and feelings'* of a child. It is clear that the right of the child to express his views is equally as important as the right of the parents to express their views. Further, the court is specifically directed under Art 6 to consult the child and allow the child to express his or her views.

(c) Representation

There is considerable weight given to the importance of a child having a special representative. Under Art 4, the child is provided with the right to apply for such a representative. The only limitation, apart from the child having sufficient understanding, is that the holders of parental responsibility are precluded from representing the child as a result of a conflict of interest. Under Art 9, the judicial authority is also empowered to appoint a representative for the child. Additionally, under 9(2), parties to the Convention are required to consider providing courts with the power to appoint someone to represent the child. This last provision highlights the potential difference under the Convention between a '*special representative*' and representation in proceedings.

(20) The ECECR contains measures which aim to promote the rights of children, in particular in family proceedings before judicial authorities. The judicial authority and any person appointed to be the child's representative have a number of duties designed to facilitate the exercise of rights by children. Children should be allowed to exercise their rights (for example, the right to be informed and the right to express their views) either themselves or through other persons or bodies. The judicial authority performs a review function: ensuring that the child has sufficiently participated in the proceedings according to his or her understanding, including if considered appropriate, by consulting the child directly.

(21) (iii) European Convention on Contact Concerning Children 2003
The European Convention on Contact Concerning Children 2003 ('ECCCC') was opened for signature on 15 May 2003 and has been signed by 13 Member States of the Council of Europe.[20] Again, the United Kingdom has not signed the ECCCC.

(22) The preamble to the Convention identifies, as two of its objectives, the 'desirability of recognising not only parents but also children as holders of rights' and 'of promoting measures to assist children in matters concerning contact with parents and other persons having family ties with children'. On a simple level this involves replacing the notion of 'access to children' with 'contact concerning children'. Its broader aim is to reinforce the basic right of children and their parents to maintain contact on a regular basis.[21] As part of this it contains provisions dealing with the participation of children in proceedings, reiterating, to a very limited extent, those contained in the ECECR.

(23) Art 6 of the ECCCC provides:
The right of a child to be informed, consulted and to express his or her views

1. A child considered by internal law as having sufficient understanding shall have the right, unless this would be manifestly contrary to his or her best interests:

– to receive all relevant information;
– to be consulted;
– to express his or her views.

2. Due weight shall be given to those views and to the ascertainable wishes and feelings of the child.

(24) (iv) Charter of Fundamental Rights in the European Union
The Charter of Fundamental Rights also gives rights to children. Art 24(3) provides:

---

[20]   Austria, Belgium, Bulgaria, Croatia, Cyprus, Czech Republic, Italy, Malta, Moldova, Portugal, San Marino, Turkey and Ukraine.

[21]   Article 4 - Contact between a child and his or her parents:
'A child and his or her parents shall have the right to obtain and maintain regular contact with each other.'

'Every child shall have the right to maintain on a regular basis a personal relationship and direct contact with both his or her parents, unless that is contrary to his or her interests.'

The Charter also requires the child's views to be taken into consideration (Art 24(1)). There are no specific procedural requirements. However, in the same way that the ECHR imposes positive obligations on the state, it can be expected that the broad right contained in 24(3) will form a similar foundation for measures to be implied in order to make the right effective.

(25) (v) Brussels IIB

The proposed Brussels IIB yet again confirms two key elements of international child conventions. First, the right of the child to maintain, on a regular basis, a personal relationship and to have direct contact with both parents unless this is contrary to his or her interests (Art 3). Secondly, the right of the child to be *'heard'* on matters relating to parental responsibility over him or her in accordance with his or her age and maturity (Art 4).

(26) European Convention on Human Rights

The terms of arts 6 (fair hearing) and 8 (private and family life) of the ECHR are so well-known as not to require repeating. However, I summarise some of the important rights and obligations arising from these Articles.

(27) The right to respect for family life under Art 8 applies to individual members of a given family unit rather than to the unit itself.[22] The child is therefore one of the individual members of the family and falls independently within the scope of the Article. The mutual enjoyment by parent and child of each other's company constitutes a fundamental element of family life, even if the relationship between the parents has broken down, and domestic measures hindering such enjoyment amount to an interference with the right protected by Art 8.[23] More specifically:

'"respect" for family life (...) implies an obligation for the State to act in a manner calculated to allow these ties to develop normally'[24] and 'to take measures that will enable a parent and child to be reunited.'[25]

As we know, the ECtHR is not an additional court of appeal. In cases concerning parental disputes over children, it tests the measures taken against the standards required by the Convention and does not substitute itself for the domestic authorities. It reviews, in the light of the Convention, the decisions taken by those authorities in the exercise of their discretionary power.[26] In practice, however, it can be difficult to see the distinction between substitution and review and the Court has held that:

'stricter scrutiny is called for in respect of any further limitations, such as restrictions placed by those authorities on parental rights of access, and of any legal safeguards designed to secure an effective protection of the right of parents and children to respect for their family life.'[27]

(29) The imposition of positive obligations is one of the most dynamic and effective means by which the Convention remains a 'living instrument'. The positive obligations, under Art 8, include not only 'a parent's right to the taking of measures with a view to his or her being reunited with his or her child' but also a separate obligation 'on the national authorities to take

---

[22] *Law and Practice of the European Convention on Human Rights and the European Social Charter*, Donna Gomien, David Harris, Leo Zwaak, Council of Europe, 1996.

[23] *Johansen v Norway* (1996) 23 EHRR 33, para 52; *Elsholz v Germany*, para 43.

[24] *Scozzari and Giunta v Italy* [2000] 2 FLR 771 para 221.

[25] *Kutzner v Germany* (2002) 35 EHRR 256, para 61.

[26] *Hokkanen v Finland* (1995) 19 EHRR 139, para 55.

[27] *Elsholz v Germany*, para 49.

such action.'[28] In identifying their extent, the ECtHR has certainly not shied away from stating that a states' positive obligations can involve the implementation of *'specific steps'.*[29] It is for each state to equip itself with adequate and effective means to ensure compliance with its positive obligations under Art 8.[30] As an example, in *Glaser v United Kingdom* the ECtHR examined whether there was *'an accessible and coherent mechanism'*, in that case, for the enforcement of the applicant's contact rights under an order. However, the approach is far more widely applicable.

(30) A well-known example of this is the right of parental participation in proceedings concerning their children to ensure adequate protection of their interests. The European Court will review whether the parents have been involved in the decision-making process as a whole, to a degree sufficient to provide them with the requisite protection of their interests.[31] This is an essential ingredient which, if absent, will result in a breach of Art 8 and probably also Art 6. If this is an essential ingredient to provide parents with the requisite protection of their interests, should not the same ingredient be independently required in order to provide the necessary protection of children's interests?

(31) Applying the same approach to children, as to parents, children should be involved in the decision-making process to a degree sufficient to provide them with the requisite protection of their interests. None of the Strasbourg cases, referred to below, looked specifically at the rights of the children and there are few European cases which have considered the separate rights of children under Art 8.[32] In a recent decision the ECtHR decided, by 4 votes to 3, not to award a child applicant damages for a breach of her Art 8 rights, in addition to the damages awarded to her father[33] for the breach of his rights. However, in my view, there is the potential for considerable development in this area, in particular because the message from all the Conventions referred to in this paper is clear.

(32) The consistent message is that children have rights of their own, including a right to maintain a relationship and contact with both parents. Under Art 8, the child's rights are *'the paramount consideration'.*[34] It is difficult to see why the positive obligations resulting from *these* rights should not, as per *Glaser*, be implemented through an accessible and coherent mechanism. If this is applied, there should be (as the UK Government itself relied on in *Glaser*) an effective and accessible framework available to children to protect and secure their right to respect for family life. This would include procedural requirements, implied in Art 8, to ensure effective respect for family life.

(33) The cases relied upon by the father in Re T,[35] which all concerned applicant fathers, were the following:

(a) *Elsholz v Germany*[36]
This was a Grand Chamber decision of 13 July 2000. The father complained that the German court's decision, dismissing his request for contact with his son, amounted to a breach of

---

[28]   *Sylvester v Austria* 20 April 2003, para 58.
[29]   *Glaser v UK* [2001] 1 FLR 153, para 63.
[30]   *Sylvester v Austria*, para 68.
[31]   *W v United Kingdom* (1987) 10 EHRR 29 and *Elsholz v Germany*, para. 52.
[32]   *Eriksson v Sweden* (1989) EHRR 183 considered the rights of the child very briefly in addition to those of the mother; in *Scozzari and Giunta v Italy*, a mother applied also on behalf of her children who were awarded separate damages.
[33]   *Sylvester v Austria* Chamber decision 24 April 2003; in contrast, for example, to *Scozzari and Giunta v Italy*.
[34]   *Yousef v Netherlands* [2003] 1 FLR 210 at para 73.
[35]   [2003] 1 FLR 531.
[36]   [2000] 2 FLR 486.

Art 8. In the course of two applications the District Court judge interviewed the six-year-old child three times. The child said that he did not want to see his father. The German Court refused to obtain a psychological expert opinion as recommended by the local Youth Office and as requested by the father. The Grand Chamber found (13 votes to 4) that there had been a violation of Art 8. The District Court's reason for refusing to order an expert's report, namely that the facts of the case were clearly established, was held to be insufficient. Further, the importance of the issues at stake meant that the court should have had expert evidence in order to be able to evaluate the child's statements. This, combined with the absence of a hearing before the Regional Court, revealed (in the ECtHR's opinion) an insufficient involvement of the father in the decision-making process. The Court also found a violation of Art 6.

(b) *Sahin v Germany*[37]

This was one of three Chamber decisions given on 11 October 2001. The father argued that the German court's decision, dismissing his request for contact with his daughter, amounted to a breach of Art 8. The Regional German Court had ordered a psychological expert opinion on the question of whether contact with the father was in the child's best interests. The expert did not directly ask the child about her father and at no stage in the proceedings had the child (aged 4/5) been heard in court. This was based on the expert's opinion that direct questioning of the child was not appropriate because of the risk the child might have the impression that, in the conflict between her parents, her statements would be decisive. This was insufficient for the ECtHR, which said that the domestic courts should not have been satisfied with the expert's vague statements about the risks in questioning the child. The ECtHR (Chamber) held: 'It is essential that the competent courts give careful consideration to what lies in the best interest of the child *after having had direct contact with the child*'[38] (emphasis added). Correct and complete information on the child's relationship to the applicant as the parent seeking contact to the child was 'an indispensable prerequisite for establishing a child's true wishes and thereby striking a fair balance between the interests at stake'.[39] The Court found that the German court's *failure to hear the child* revealed an insufficient involvement of the father in the contact proceedings and hence violated his Art 8 rights.[40]

(c)   *Sommerfeld v Germany* (11 October 2001)

The German District Court refused the applicant father's request for contact, having heard both the parents and the child, then aged 13, who said that she did not want to have any contact with her father. The ECtHR (Chamber) found that the District Court should not have been satisfied with hearing only the child as to her wishes, without having expert psychological evidence in order to evaluate the child's seemingly firm wishes. The ECtHR found that the German court's failure to order a psychological report on the possibilities of establishing contact between the child and the father revealed an insufficient involvement of the father in the decision making process.[41] The Court found a violation of the father's rights under Art 8.

(d) *Hoffmann v Germany* (11 October 2001)

The father was denied contact. The German courts had relied on statements made by the father and the mother, on a report from a Catholic welfare organisation, on the comments of the Youth Office, and 'in particular' on the statements made by the child (aged 7) who was questioned by the District Court. The ECtHR (Chamber) found that the father had been sufficiently involved in the decision-making process. The District Court had had regard to several reports on the question of contact, one of them being based on the experience of meetings between the father

---

[37]   [2002] 1 FLR 119.
[38]   *Sahin v Germany*, para 47.
[39]   *Sahin v Germany*, para 48.
[40]
[41]   *Sommerfeld v Germany*, para 43.

and the child in a child guidance centre. No violation of Art 8 was found.

(e) *Kutzner v Germany*

Two children were placed in care. This was a complex case in which reports had been obtained from a number of experts. One of the considerations referred to by the Chamber Court, when finding a breach of Art 8, was that the children had at no stage (between the ages of about four and nine) been heard by the judges.

(34) On a literal application of these decisions, it would appear that the only means of complying with Art 8 would be for the court to have '*direct contact*' with the child and to obtain a comprehensive expert psychological report. It might also have been thought that the Chamber decisions were following the precedent set by the Grand Chamber in *Elsholz*. However, even before 8 July 2003, this would be not have been the whole picture.

(35) In *Hoppe v Germany*,[42] the father alleged that the German courts' decisions reducing contact with his daughter and awarding parental authority to the mother breached Arts 6 and 8. The ECtHR found that the domestic courts had carefully considered the questions of contact and of awarding parental authority. The District Court had relied on expert reports (from a psychological expert, a therapeutic pedagogue and a social worker) and on the evidence given by the parents at hearings. The ECtHR decided that this put the domestic courts in a better position than the European judges to strike a fair balance between the competing interests involved. Reference was also made to the fact that the District Court's judgments had been upheld by the Court of Appeal. The ECtHR was satisfied that the national authorities acted within the discretionary margin afforded to them. There was no reference in this decision to the fact that there had been no direct contact between the child (aged 4/5) and the domestic courts. The decision in *Hoppe* was unanimous; two of the judges had also been in the *Sahin* etc cases. Could the distinction have been simply because *Hoppe* dealt with a restriction of contact rights, rather than a complete dismissal of such rights?

(36) On 8 July 2003 the ECtHR (Grand Chamber) published its judgments in the cases of *Sahin* and *Sommerfeld*. The Chamber's decisions were reversed and there was found to have been no breach of Art 8 in either case. In *Sahin* the Grand Chamber decided that it was going too far to say that domestic courts were always required to hear a child in court on a contact dispute.[43] In reaching this decision it is clear that the Grand Chamber relied heavily on the fact that the domestic court's decision not to hear the child was based on the advice given by the psychologist. The German Regional Court had said that this was an exceptional decision. In addition, the domestic courts had evidence from the Youth Office and a number of nurses from the day nursery attended by the child.

(37) In Sommerfeld the Grand Chamber also said that it was going too far to say that domestic courts were always required to involve a psychological expert on the issue of parental contact.[44] The fact that the District Court had heard the child meant that it was 'well placed' to evaluate her statements and establish whether or not she was able to make up her own mind (aged 13). On that basis the District Court could reasonably reach the conclusion that forcing the child to see her father was not justified.

(38) In both cases the Grand Chamber said that the decision, on whether to hear a child in court and whether to involve an expert, would depend on the circumstances of the case, having due regard to the age and maturity of the child concerned.

---

[42]   [2003] 1 FLR 384; Application no 28422/95, 5 December 2002.
[43]   *Sahin v Germany*, para 73.
[44]   *Sommerfeld v Germany*, para 71.

(39) It might appear that there is something of a tussle taking place in the ECtHR. This may be partly based on a concern that the court has, in some respects, been acting like a further factual court of appeal. However, all these cases need to be seen in context. They all involved Germany, a jurisdiction in which it is usual for the judges to interview the child directly. This is an important distinction. In both *Sahin* and *Sommerfeld*, the Grand Chamber reiterated that, as a general rule, it is for the national courts to assess the evidence before them, including the means of ascertaining the relevant facts. If the means of ascertaining the relevant facts is usually to see the child directly, then there would need to be proper justification for departing from this approach. If judges are used to seeing children, then the decision whether they need assistance in evaluating their statements is also a matter for the domestic courts, again provided the decision is properly justified.

(40) Further, the Grand Chamber decisions in both cases were in part based on the ECtHR being satisfied that the German courts' procedural approach was reasonable in the circumstances. The mechanisms adopted by the German courts had provided them in each case with sufficient material to reach a reasoned decision. Accordingly, the procedural requirements implicit in Art 8 were satisfied.

(41) Finally, it is worth noting that Art 12(2) of the UNCRC states that a child shall be provided with the opportunity of being heard, 'either directly, or through a representative or an appropriate body, in a manner consistent with the procedural rules of national law'. In contrast to the European Court Chamber decision in *Sahin*, there is no requirement that a child be heard directly. As the Grand Chamber, in both *Sahin* and *Sommerfeld*, has stated that the UNCRC sets the rights and standards to which all governments must aspire, it must be unlikely that the ECHR would be found to conflict with the UNCRC. Furthermore, Art 6(b) of the ECECR expressly permits the court to consult the child 'through other persons or bodies'.

Summary

(42) What is required of our domestic family justice system when looking at the participation of children?
(a)   Children have the right to maintain a relationship and contact with both parents;
(b)   The State is under an obligation to have in place an accessible and coherent mechanism to enable the ties between parents and their children to be maintained;[45]
(c)   This will include procedural requirements, to ensure that the decision-making process is fair and to ensure due respect for the child's interests (safeguarded, for example, by Art 8[46]); it may also require pro-active steps by the State;
(d)   Children have the right, which the state is under an obligation to take steps to assure, to be heard. Again, the mechanism through which this is effected must be accessible and coherent. This will entail the right:
   (i) to receive all relevant information;
        the right to information is a key prerequisite for children's participation to be relevant and meaningful. According, for example, to the UNCRC, it is essential that children are provided with the necessary information, including about options that exist and the consequences of such options, so that they can make informed and free decisions;
   (ii) to be consulted, in a manner and form appropriate to the child;
   (iii) to express his or her views, by means of a meaningful opportunity;
   (iv) to a representative acting on behalf of the child, including representation at the hearing.

---

[45]   Eg *Kutzner v Germany* Application No 46544/99, 26 February 2002, para 65.
[46]   Eg *Hoppe v Germany*, para 52.

(e) The views of children must be given due weight in *all* matters affecting them.
The way in which these rights are effected will depend on the circumstances of the case, including the age and maturity of the child. As a general rule, it is for national courts to assess the evidence before them, *including* the means to ascertain the relevant facts. However, both the procedure adopted and the material relied upon must be sufficient to provide children with effective participation.

(43) In general terms, therefore, we must have a procedural approach which effectively provides for the authentic participation of children. This will inevitably include guidelines, for example, as to what and how information is to be provided and as to the circumstances in which a child is to be separately represented. Additionally, in each case the actual decision made must be supported by sufficient material about the child's views, which may involve expert assistance.

(44) **Domestic Provisions**

In 2002 there were 111,562 private law children applications and 103,191 s 8 orders made. There were 171,054 divorce petitions and 160,943 decrees nisi. Whilst there is, plainly, recognition that children should be separately represented more frequently in private law proceedings than they are at present, and this includes the Government, there is no clear structure through which children are to participate more generally in decisions which are taken consequent on their parents' separation. In moving beyond asking whether, to asking how, the participation of children should be effectively implemented, we need to consider the appropriate structures. Participation involves more than just representation.

(44) In the course of preparing for this paper, I found that much of the research provided a consistent view – that children are not at present considered to be effectively included in the process.

- The Children's Legal Centre conducted a survey,[47] through its contact dispute line, for which they interviewed in depth 200 parents involved in contact disputes. Of those parents who had been to court for a contact order, 66% said that the court had not been made aware of the children's wishes. Of those cases in which the children's views were made known to the court, 43% had been through a court welfare officer. 71% of the parents interviewed in these cases did not believe that the child's wishes had been accurately portrayed. 80% of the parents interviewed thought that children should have representation in court.
- The Scottish report, the 'Voice of the Child' under the Children (Scotland) Act 1995, contains a number of interesting findings. For example: 'none of the child informants felt that sufficient information was available to children'.[48] The lack of sufficient information, in a form and at a time when they needed it, was strongly felt by virtually all informants (para 4.6.1). Children, who had not been legally represented, did not feel that their views were elicited, let alone considered. Most of the children interviewed felt that much more could be done to improve their access to legal matters.
- In the NSPCC audit of the Children Act 1989, less than half of the children said that they thought they had been listened to and their rights had been respected.
- The NCH website[49] states: 'Years of experience of working with both children and parents have taught NCH that when parents split up it's usually the children who have the least access to information and support – at a time when they want and need it the most'.
- Research conducted into the Family Court Welfare Service[50] found that one of the key

---

[47]   By Maggie French and Carolyn Hamilton, Children's Legal Centre; *www2.essex.ac.uk/clc/hi/childright.*
[48]   *www.scotland.gov.uk/cru/kd01*; para 4.1.2.
[49]   *www.nch.org.uk.news3.*
[50]   *Families in Conflict: Perspectives of children and parents on the Family Court Welfare Service* November 2001

themes in the children's interviews they conducted was their wish to have greater involvement in the decisions affecting them. They also wanted to have someone 'just for them' involved in the decision-making process.

- There is evidence that the delay in appointing Child and Family Reporters is such that judges are declining to order reports. How is the voice of the child heard in this situation?

(46) The question of how we should involve children in our domestic family justice system is not part of this paper. There are interesting models in other countries which potentially provide children with greater rights such as the Russian Federation.[51] Closer to home:

- What is the Scottish experience of the requirement that the court gives notice *to* any child in respect of whom it is considering the equivalent of a s 8 order, unless the court decides to dispense with notice?
- The Adoption (Scotland) Act 1978 requires that children aged 12 and over must consent to the proposed adoption.
- There is a statutory obligation that a person reaching any major decision involving the exercise of a parental right must have regard to the views of the child: s 6 of the Children (Scotland) Act 1995.

(47) In their article for Family Law,[52] DJJs Clifford Bellamy and Geoff Lord analysed those cases in Leeds in which an FPR r 9 (5) appointment (separate representation of children) had been made in the year to 30 April 2002. They concluded that the presence of one or more of the following factors could form the basis of a useful guide to those cases in which such an appointment would be appropriate: intractable cases; significant foreign element; significant ethnic/cultural element; significant health problems; violence and/or sexual abuse; complex family relationships.

(48) There is sometimes said to be a tension between a rights-based approach and a welfare-based approach. I do not see that. The right of children to participate and to be heard is part of the mechanism by which a decision is made in their best interests. There may be a practical tension in how this is to be effected in individual cases but, in any matters affecting them, children have the right to full participation.

---

by Ann Buchanan, Joan Hunt, Harriet Bretherton, Victoria Bream.

[51] *A Child's right to veto in England and Wales – another welfare ploy?* by Christine Piper and Artem Miakishev, CFLQ Vol 15, No 1, 57: under the Russian Family Code 1996 certain steps can be taken only if the child consents (including change of name and adoption from the age of 10); children have the right to express their opinion and be heard.

[52] Reflections on Family Proceedings Rule 9.5 [April] 2003 pp 265–269.

REPRESENTING CHILDREN

Mark Powell
Association of Lawyers for Children

Summary of paper

Mark Powell said that he started his talk from the perspective of someone who has been representing children for some years. He went on to explain how, at a family conference two years ago in Llandrindod Wells, a group of young people gave a presentation which gave a striking indication of how we as professionals approach young people: sometimes they do not understand a word we say to them. Communication involves more than talking, it means talking in a language which both children and adults understand.

Mr Powell set out different categories of representation and pointed out that there are so many different tests which have to be applied and so many ways of representing children. There are public and private law proceedings, Adoption Act proceedings and other family proceedings, including, for example, children's roles in injunction proceedings.

He referred to the old bugbear of 'demonisation', in other words, the way in which children in criminal proceedings are treated, compared to the way they are treated in family proceedings. Mr Powell argued that we may concentrate too heavily on family proceedings, and that the issue of children in criminal proceedings is a huge area of difficulty that perhaps we are not grasping.

He emphasised that different situations call for different approaches: Children Act proceedings may need different advice, and different levels of information. He said that in the end we are all human and inevitably our practice reflects the way we conduct our private lives and our own personal value systems have a bearing on our professional lives. Mr Powell's message was that along the spectrum from criminal proceedings to family welfare, our approach must be flexible, no one size fits all.

Mr Powell shared with the conference some of the difficulties he has encountered in representing children:

- *The difficulties of the personal undertaking. His feeling was that it is honoured more in breach than the observance.*
- *Matching solicitor with the child. He gave the example of the difficulty faced by a teenage girl victim of sexual abuse who is told that her future is to be placed in hands of an unknown male solicitor. He said that in his area of practice, South Wales, the cab rank rule operates, and argued that that system is highly unsatisfactory and must be changed.*
- *The tandem model, with the guardian and solicitor working hand in hand. Mr Powell was against the abolition of the tandem model and felt that there was a danger of throwing the baby out with the bath water. He pointed out the recent experience of getting rid of a system which was peripherally flawed but sound in its core, and replacing it with some thing endemically flawed, ie the guardian system.*
- *Cosy relationships. The idea that the same guardian appoints the same solicitor and because the relationship is too comfortable there is no challenge between the two. There is the perception that some solicitors get more work than others. There is also the danger of the court clerk having a cosy relationship. Mr Powell felt that most of this is an error of perception but that there is a need for caution. He argued that the key to avoiding this problem is rigorous self-examination and mutual examination of practice.*
- *The representation of children must involve seeing the child. This inevitably involves establishing a relationship with the child. There has to be preparatory work, some sort of assessment of how to*

establish the relationship, and solicitors have to prepare an explanation of what their role is; what child can expect from the solicitor and what the solicitor can expect from the child. Children give instructions in many different ways and different places. Children will respond better to the informal approach. Mr Powell emphasised that all of this involves time which is unlikely to be available, and funding which is just as unlikely to be available.

Mr Powell highlighted a further danger – that of playing the amateur psychologist or social worker. He also spoke of the dangers of paternalism which are hard to ignore, his view was that it is difficult to do the job without being paternalist.

He asked whether there was a conflict between the guardian and the child. He highlighted the difficulty of the kind of situation where a child understands that there is a guardian acting on their behalf and who is then told that the guardian does not accept what they say and is going to be represented by a different solicitor. He told the conference that he tries to ensure that that kind of conflict situation is a last resort.

Confidentiality is another difficulty. It can be a minefield for solicitors as well as medical practitioners and a major problem for the way in which childcare practice is conducted.

Disclosure of documents can be a problem, particularly if the solicitor is acting for one competent child and one non-competent one, and documents are therefore disclosed to one child and not to the other. The non-competent child may receive confusing messages about the contents of the documents from the competent child.

Another area for consideration is the question of taking the child to court. Is it enough to enable the child to meet the judge and see the court room enough? Mr Powell thought not.

The 'vanishing trick' was Mr Powell's final issue for consideration. The solicitor forms a relationship with a child before and during proceedings, goes to see the child afterwards and then the solicitor and the guardian disappear from child's life forever. Mr Powell argued that the recent decision of House of Lords not to permit further involvement by the solicitor was a grave error.

1. A cautionary tale; the Llandrindod Wells experience

2. Different categories of representation

(a) Public Law (Children Act).
(b) Private Law (Children Act).
(c) Adoption Act Proceedings – Note Variations in Party Status.
(d) Other Family Proceedings – eg Injunctions under the Family Law Act 1996.
NB: Compare the Court's attitude to the child litigant in Family Proceedings with the child defendant in Criminal Proceedings.

3. Do different situations call for different approaches?

(a) An Applicant or Respondent in Family Litigation.
(b) Different types of Family Law Applications; eg the approach to Secure Accommodation Applications under S 25 of the Children Act 1989.

4. Some difficulties often encountered

(a) The personal undertaking given by the Children Panel Solicitor to the Law Society – SEE ANNEX A.
(b) Matching the solicitor with the child.
(c) The tandem model of the solicitor and children's Guardian – problems caused by delay of appointment and limitations on the solicitor's role.
(d) Cosy relationships'.
(e) Seeing the child and the solicitor's relationship with the child.

   (i) Preparatory work.
   (ii) Establishing a relationship.
   (iii) Fact finding.
   (iv) An explanation.
   (v) The child's instructions.

NB. The danger of playing amateur social worker or psychologist.

5. Assessing the competence of the child

(a) The solicitor's role.
(b) Help from experts.

   'In these cases involving intelligent, articulate but disturbed children it is necessary for the Court to apply Rules 11 and 12 realistically to ensure that not only is the professional voice of the Guardian ad Litem heard through an Advocate's presentation but that also the wishes and feelings of the children, however limited the horizon, should be similarly presented. If there is any real question as to whether the child's emotional disturbance is so intense as to destroy the capacity to give coherent and consistent instructions, then I think that question should be the subject of specific Expert opinion from the Expert or Experts who are already involved in the case.' (Re H (a minor) (Care Proceedings: Child's Wishes) [1993] 1 FLR 440.)

'Doubts about the child's capacity should be resolved by a swift pragmatic enquiry conducted in a manner which involved the minimum of delay and the least possible distress to the child concerned. It would be very unsatisfactory if such issues themselves became the subject of detailed medical or other professional investigation.... The Solicitors judgement is to be respected and to be given great weight. But it is not conclusive.' (Re: CT (a minor) (Wardship: Representation [1993] 2 FLR 278.)

6. How paternalist should the approach be?

7. Is there truly a conflict between guardian and child?

8. Confidentiality and legal professional privilege

THE LAW SOCIETY'S GUIDANCE

(a) Circumstances which override confidentiality

(i) A Solicitor may reveal confidential information to the extent that he or she believes necessary to prevent the client or a third party committing a criminal act that the Solicitor believes on reasonable grounds is likely to result in serious bodily harm.

(ii) There may be exceptional circumstances involving children where a Solicitor should consider revealing confidential information to an appropriate authority. This may be where the child is the client and the child reveals information which indicates continuing sexual or other physical abuse but refuses to allow disclosure of such information. Similarly, there may be situations where an adult discloses abuse either by himself or herself or by another adult against a child but refuses to allow any disclosure. The Solicitor must consider whether the threat to the child's life or health, both mental and physical, is sufficiently serious to justify a breach of the duty of confidentiality.

(iii) In proceedings under the Children Act 1989 Solicitors are under a duty to reveal Expert's Reports commissioned for the purposes of proceedings, as these Reports are not privileged. The Position in relation to voluntary disclosure of other documents or Solicitor/Client communications is uncertain. Clearly Advocates are under a duty not to mislead the Court. Therefore, if an Advocate has certain knowledge which he or she realises is adverse to the client's case, the Solicitor may be extremely limited in what can be stated in the client's favour.

9. The disclosure of documents; particularly if acting for both a competent and incompetent child.

10. The child in court; the pros and cons

11. Performing the vanishing trick; how to you prepare the child?

12. The Teletubbies – a cautionary tale

Suggested further reading

King, P and Young I. 1992. *The Child as Client: A Handbook for Solicitors who represent Children*, Bristol: Family Law.

Solicitors Family Law Association. 2002. *Guide to Good Practice for Solicitors Acting for Children*, Keston, SFLA.

Mark Powell
Hugh James
Merthyr Tydfil

Annex A

The Law Society

Children Panel Undertaking

I undertake that, when representing a party in proceedings covered by the Children Act 1989:

1. Subject to paragraph 2, I will not normally delegate the preparation, supervision, conduct or presentation of the case, but will deal with it personally;
2. In each case I will consider whether it is in the best interests of my client to instruct another advocate in relation to the presentation or preparation of the case;
3. If it is in the best interests of my client, or necessary, to instruct another advocate:
    3.1 I will consider and advise my client or the guardian ad litem (if applicable) who should be instructed in the best interest of my client;
    3.2 I agree that, save in exceptional circumstances, any advocate that is instructed will either be;
    (a) another Children Panel member (approved as a Children Representative if my client is a child); or
    (b) a member of the Bar on my Practice's approved Counsel list;
    3.3 I will obtain an undertaking from that advocate to :
    (a)   attend and conduct the matter personally unless an unavoidable professional engagement arises;
    (b)   take all reasonable steps to ensure that so far as reasonably practicable a conflicting professional engagement does not arise.

Signed .... Date ....

Name in Blocks ....

Note: To be signed by applicants in Private Practice only

CHILDREN'S REPRESENTATION IN PRIVATE LAW PROCEEDINGS

Charles Prest
Director of Legal Services and Special Casework, CAFCASS

Summary of paper

Charles Prest made it clear to the conference that his paper comprised his personal thoughts. He emphasised that it was not CAFCASS policy, but an essay which was intended to provoke discussion. His aim was to address the issue of the representation of children in the court process and specifically, the question of representation in private law proceedings.

He attempted to identify the underpinning principles that might help define the principles about how to decide when children should be participating in proceedings:

- *the need for someone to orchestrate an investigation on behalf of the child;*
- *the need to ensure an argument is put which otherwise might not be put;*
- *some sort of recognition that at some point it just 'is right' for an older child to be allowed to participate.*

The origins of the system we have at present proceed from the basis that child is not party and there are a number of exceptions to that presumption. However, Mr Prest recognised that organisations like the Association of Lawyers for Children might want to press further and argue that the logical extension of the human rights argument is to say that all children should be party to all proceedings about them and then consider questions about the way in which that party status is to be managed.

Mr Prest explained that his paper wrestles with uncomfortable questions about resources and realities. He explained that he has his own wish list for the family justice system and for CAFCASS. He accepted that CAFCASS has not been good about hearing the voice of the child and would like it to become a truly child-centred organisation. He would like to see CAFCASS making children's guardians available from the outset, and providing a before and after service. He would particularly like to see officers spending more time ascertaining the wishes and feelings of the child in private law cases and that he had been struck by comments in the papers by June Thoburn and Penny Lancaster that even babies have a story to tell. He would also like to see more widespread representation of children in private law cases, where appropriate.

Mr Prest's paper compares the changes in the family justice system to the Copernican revolution which was initially accepted by a minority but took a long time to establish itself as the accepted orthodoxy. He called for the family justice system to be seen as being part of a wider system for the improvement of social justice in England and Wales. He said that he was impressed by Gillian Schofield's comment that enabling the child to participate in proceedings can be developmentally beneficial for the child.

Mr Prest emphasised the breadth of issues faced by the different agencies involved in working with children and the uncomfortable question of prioritising which must be faced. He asked the conference to suppose that there were more money to spend on children and asked where the family justice system would come in the list of deserving causes. Didn't the papers of, for example, Al Aynsley-Green and Guinevere Tufnell, suggest areas of greater priority?

Mr Prest felt that the question of whether CAFCASS is doing enough to make the case for more and better resources to enable it to do a better job for children and families was a legitimate one. But he also felt that it was legitimate for him to ask, 'What should CAFCASS do if there is no more money?'.

In relation to the question of the tandem model, Mr Prest emphasised that he considers it works well for children and that he is not part of any campaign to abolish it. He said that he would like to see it remain but explained that the challenge is how to make it work within the existing constraints. He argued that if it is to succeed, change is needed from all parties involved in making it work.

After the presentation of his paper Mr Prest was asked by Judge Donald Hamilton where the power for a CAFCASS manager to appoint a solicitor was. He replied that CAFCASS has no such power. It is clear in the statute that it is the responsibility of the court, but there has been practice in some areas for the court effectively to delegate it to CAFCASS. Mr Prest informed the conference that a forthcoming statement of good practice from a subgroup of the Lord Chancellor's protocol committee who have been working on that issue will explicitly confirm that the responsibility lies with the court.

Introduction

Where are we and how did we get here

Before CAFCASS was created, most children in private law proceedings that were not resolved before a report to the court became necessary were represented[1] by a court welfare officer from the probation service. Only a very small number of children were legally represented, which was done in one of three ways: by a local solicitor, acting on the child's direct instructions, pursuant to r 9.2 A Family Proceedings Rules (FPR) 1991; by the Official Solicitor pursuant to r 9.5 FPR 1991; or by a local solicitor who had himself been appointed the child's guardian ad litem pursuant to r 9.5 (who usually himself then sought leave to instruct an expert who almost invariably happened to be a self-employed guardian ad litem from the local GALRO panel) or, as a variation upon this theme, by a local solicitor instructed by some other person who had been appointed as the child's guardian ad litem pursuant to rule 9.5 (who again was almost invariably a self-employed guardian ad litem from the local GALRO panel).

I am not certain how the third of these came about[2] but I venture it was something like this. Originally private law cases in which children required legal representation were so rare they were invariably or almost invariably heard in the High Court and the representation was provided by the Official Solicitor. Several things then combined to change that including a gradual increase in the number of such cases, circuit judges sitting as High Court judges pursuant to s 9 of the Supreme Court Act 1981, the end of widespread wardship with the implementation of the Children Act 1989, the development of the tandem model in public law, the creation of the Law Society Children Panel, and the availability of self-employed contractors who had acted as guardians ad litem in public law proceedings. The result – I daresay spontaneously in a number of different areas – was the first appointments of local solicitors to act as a child's guardian ad litem, a step which was consistent with r 9.5 FPR 1991 even if it had perhaps not been intended. This development worked well for local judges, who might understandably prefer to have children represented by local lawyers and self-employed guardians ad litem with whom they were familiar rather than the Official Solicitor who was only an occasional visitor, and it certainly worked well for the local solicitors and guardians who were so appointed. There is no evidence I am aware of as to whether it worked well for the children but suffice it to say, based upon my own experience of acting in that role, I believe that in at least some cases it worked very well for them.

With time, the practice of a local appointment (which in some places might include the appointment of a member of organisations such as the National Youth Advocacy Service) grew, although whether the emergence of the practice and extent of its growth was known to, among

---

[1]   I set out different meanings of 'representation' below.
[2]   'Time immemorial' for me dates from 1986.

others, the Lord Chancellor's Department, the Official Solicitor and the senior judiciary, I rather doubt. In the meantime the Official Solicitor continued to be the preferred port of call of Family Division judges in the majority of their cases but also found himself with a growing number of cases from certain county courts (following the Official Solicitor's Practice Note[3]) to the point where they were equalling or even outnumbering the High Court cases for which he was responsible.

Throughout all this, a small body of case law emerged. Although there was no systematic guidance for identifying those cases in which a r 9.5 appointment should be made, in the last reported case before CAFCASS was created Hale LJ said:

> 'The evidence is now quite clear that children whose parents are separating, and especially if their parents are in conflict with one another, need a voice, someone who is able to listen to anything they wish to say and tell them what they need to know. Sometimes they need more than this and that is someone who is able to orchestrate an investigation of the case on their behalf. This does not always mean that they need separate legal representation. Often their needs can be met by the parents themselves; often they can be met by the court welfare service but the court welfare service cannot always make a thorough investigation of what needs to be done. As I said in *Re N* (unreported) 1 February 2000, anyone with experience of trying private family disputes encounters cases from time to time where separate representation of a child or children is necessary or highly desirable. As I also pointed out in that case, it is not in every such case practicable to involve the Official Solicitor, especially at first instance in a county court...'[4]

That was the position when CAFCASS came into being on 1 April 2001 and, broadly speaking, has remained the position since. The CAFCASS Practice Note[5] that I issued aspired to be 'helpful guidance' based upon the existing case law as to those cases in which a r 9.5 appointment might be appropriate as well as being a restatement of the existing process updated to reflect the transfer of the children's divisions of the Official Solicitor into CAFCASS; and in two cases during the autumn of 2001 the Court of Appeal upheld the approach set out in the Practice Note.[6]

But the truth is neither the existing situation nor the CAFCASS Practice Note is satisfactory. The Practice Note was based upon the belief that as at 31 March 2001 all r 9.5 cases should have been referred to the Official Solicitor and that the great majority of such cases were being handled by him. Rightly or wrongly, neither of these was true.[7] Further, the Practice Note does not address the provisions within r 9.5 (amended in several important respects with effect from 1 April 2001) that allow the court to appoint 'some other proper person to be the guardian ad litem of the child' if that person consents to the appointment. Add the fact that the number of such cases had come to exceed the capacity of the Official Solicitor and now CAFCASS Legal, confusion over the concept of CAFCASS Legal 'declining to act' (the Official Solicitor always could, CAFCASS plainly cannot[8]), the growth of human and children's rights' thinking, the growth (if I may be forgiven for saying so) of the industry in the representation of children, the piecemeal case law that sits uncomfortably with the simple and apparently broad words: 'If ... it appears to the court that it is in the best interest of any child to be made a party to the

---

[3]   The most recent of which was at [1999] 1 FLR 310.

[4]   *Re A (Contact: Separate Representation)* [2001] 1 FLR 715 at 721.

[5]   [2001] 2 FLR 151.

[6]   *Re D* [2001] EWCA Civ 1775 but otherwise unreported, and *Re W* [2003] 1 FLR 681.

[7]   A self-reporting survey conducted within CAFCASS, excluding referrals made directly to CAFCASS Legal, identified that between April 2001 and March 2002 four regions (East, London, South-West and Wales) had received no r 9.5 appointments, two regions had only one such case (East Midlands and North-East), but three regions had received between five and ten cases (North-West, South-East and West Midlands) and that Yorkshire and Humberside had 97 such cases.

[8]   Rule 9.5 (1) FPR 1991, although I think it remains right that it should be CAFCASS that should make the final decision about whether to provide an officer of the Service from CAFCASS Legal or from a local office.

proceedings…' of r 9.5(1) – the overall uncertainty about in which cases r 9.5 should be used and how representation should be provided in those cases – and the time has clearly come for fresh guidance for everyone.

Where should we be going: Part 1 –'representation' and 'participation'

'Representation' is a slippery word. In this context it can mean at least four different things. It can mean the person who represents (tells) to the court what the child's wishes and feelings are ('the reporting sense'), the classic role of the children and family reporter[9] and a basic responsibility of CAFCASS officers in almost all family proceedings whatever particular role they are performing.[10] Secondly, representation can mean the person who legally stands in for a child (who as a matter of law lacks capacity) and who gives instructions to a lawyer ('the instructing sense').[11] Thirdly, representation can mean the person (lawyer) with legal conduct of the case on behalf of the child and his advocate in court ('the legal sense'). Finally, it can mean all three of these senses combined ('the broad sense').

In the course of preparing for judicial review proceedings recently brought against CAFCASS in respect of delays in appointing children's guardians in specified proceedings[12] I had to give some thought to the meaning of 'representation' in the CA 1989 and the FPR 1991. My conclusion was that it is overwhelmingly used in the third sense described above, ie the legal conduct of the case.[13] For this reason I think it would be helpful if we confined 'representation' to the function of the legal conduct of the case on behalf of the child who is a party to the proceedings or at least distinguished between different meanings of representation as I have just tried to do.[14]

Partly because of the lack of clarity surrounding the word 'representation' and partly because it connotes something broader, I prefer to approach this subject in terms of children's 'participation' in proceedings, a point well made by various commentators. I find particularly helpful the report by Lyon et al *Effective Support Services for Children and Young People for when Parental Relationships Break Down – A Child-Centred Approach*.[15] The study identifies three elements of children's participation. Children and young people whose parents are separating need an information service; they need a consultation service; and they need a representation service. One of the most ringing observations of the report is that the information and consultation services should be available whether or not court proceedings have been issued.[16]

---

9   Formerly 'court welfare officer'.

10   The rules are the piecemeal. The roles of children and family reporter, children's guardian (in proceedings under the CA 1989), guardian ad litem and parental order reporter ultimately all bring one back to r 4.11 FPR 1991 and the requirement to have regard 'to the principle set out in s 1(2) and the matters set out in s 1(3)(a) to (f)…' However when it comes to the rr 6 and 18 of the Adoption Rules 1984. It is irrelevant to the role of reporting officer, and it is unsurprising that it is not mentioned in the exceptional role (for a CAFCASS officer) of litigation friend which is governed by Part 21 of the Civil Procedure Rules 1998.

11   As a children's guardian does in specified proceedings pursuant to r 4.12(1)(a) FPR 1991.

12   *R v CAFCASS* [2003] 1 FLR 953.

13   This is at its clearest at s 41(3)–(5) CA 1989 and r 4.11A(1) FPR 1991. The only exceptions to this I have identified are (1) the heading and cross heading immediately preceding s 41 CA 1989, (2) r 4.11A(2) FPR 1991 which relates to the situation where the legal representation is also provided within CAFCASS pursuant to s 15 Criminal Justice and Court Services Act 2000 (both of which use the word in the broad sense) and (3) r 4.16(2)(b) FPR 1991 which, as well as being the only place I am aware of in which the legislation talks of a party as being 'represented' by a children's guardian also speaks of the child having 'an opportunity to make representations'.

14   At the risk of being overly dry, it is also why I dislike the phrase 'tandem model of representation' and dislike even more strongly the phrase 'tandem representation'. I think the phrase should be 'tandem model for the representation and safeguarding of the interests of children' which I would be happy to abbreviate to 'tandem model'!

15   Published by the Calouste Gulbenkian Foundation.

16   See, for example, paras 10.7 and 10.28 of the report. Contrast this with the continuing lack of clarity,

The report does not particularly analyse different kinds of 'representation' in different kinds of cases but concentrates upon the point that where separate legal representation is appropriate[17] it should be the same as is provided in public law proceedings – ie the tandem model.

Where should we be going: Part 2 – Some comments about the tandem model

As far as I am aware no other jurisdiction in the world applies an automatic tandem model as effectively happens in all specified proceedings in England and Wales. In particular while preparing for the judicial review proceedings brought against CAFCASS I received confirmation that this did not happen in Scotland, Ireland, Germany, Finland, Catalunya (Spain), South Africa, New Zealand, Victoria (Australia) and Indiana (USA). Perhaps the most significant of these is Germany because it has only recently revised its procedures in public law cases. Germany, apparently, expressly considered our tandem model but rejected it, among other reasons on the grounds of expense.[18] My own conclusion was that even in those cases in which children should be made a party and have legal representation, whether in public law or private law, a tandem model is not a necessity as a matter of human rights. In other words, the law of England and Wales provides for a system in public law cases that is more resourced not only than is required by the European Convention of Human Rights but also than is provided by any other family justice system in the world.

More importantly than my own conclusions, Charles J noted that although the functions of the court, the solicitor for the child and the children's guardian differ, nevertheless:

> '[t]here is an overlap between roles and expertise of the guardian, the solicitor and indeed the court in examining and testing the strength of the evidence and reasoning that the local authority advances to establish the threshold conditions and the risk of harm to the children.'[19]

and

> '... the overlap between the roles and expertise of the guardian, a solicitor and the court in respect of: (i) the important analysis of the grounds advanced by the local authority to satisfy the threshold conditions and risk that warrants the removal of a child; and (ii) the directions for further evidence and assessments that should be given...'[20]

Overlap, of course, does not mean that these roles are identical and that there is no value in one or other role but it does give some pause for thought.

There are, I think, two elephants in the room labelled 'the representation of children in family law proceedings' and one of them is the tandem model. I have to give some of my own testimony here. Between 1991 and 2001 most of my work involved acting in children's cases. I represented local authorities,[21] parents, other family members and from 1994, particularly children.[22] I regularly worked in tandem with guardians ad litem[23] in public law, adoption and,

---

both as a matter of law and as a matter of policy, about the functions of CAFCASS.

[17] As to which, see further below.

[18] See the article by Hilary Pogge von Strandmann, 'Representing Children' [2002] 80. It is also interesting to note her explicit reference to 'the situation for CAFCASS, where there are decisions to be faced about rationalising provision across the [public and private law] jurisdictions'.

[19] Paragraph 58 at [2003] 1 FLR 971.

[20] Paragraph 82 at [2003] 1 FLR 975.

[21] I must be one of few people ever to have applied for an education supervision order or to have lost an application for an emergency protection order!

[22] By way of some insight into this role let me simply note that I remember meeting and talking with children at their home, foster home, children's home, in secure accommodation, at my office and at court, as well as attending with them at other meetings such as case conferences. This would be normal for any Law Society Children Panel member.

[23] Now called children's guardians in specified proceedings but still called guardians ad litem in r 9.5 FPR 1991, a common confusion to judge by the many directions I see for 'a children's guardian

on several occasions, in private law cases pursuant to r 9.5 FPR 1991. I welcome the opportunity, based on that experience, to put firmly on the record my belief that the tandem model provides a most thoroughgoing and powerful way of representing children in family proceedings. I am quite willing to accept that it is the best way of doing so, but it is an altogether different question, for example, as to whether it provides best value for money or whether it is a proportionate use of resources. In the foreign language of public sector management I have begun to learn, the tandem model may be highly effective but not necessarily efficient. Why the tandem model is so effective and what its weaknesses and limitations might be I can barely touch upon here[24] but I sound the warning that the representation of children in family proceedings must be properly and equitably managed within the resources available and if we in the family justice system treat the tandem model as untouchable and/or as the only adequate way of safeguarding and representing the interests of children then I think others may ultimately call into question its existence altogether.[25] Put somewhat differently, and mixing my metaphors, the tandem model might prove to be the millstone that the prevents the family justice system from achieving all sorts of other things it thinks are highly desirable, such as modernising and investing in the way we deal with private law cases (including extending the legal representation of children) and CAFCASS delivering a support service not only during family proceedings but also before and after them.

Where should we be going: Part 3 – Legal obligations

Given that the UK has ratified the United Nations' Convention on the Rights of the Child, that the UNCRC itself obliges States Parties 'to make the principles and provisions of the Convention widely known, by appropriate and active means',[26] and given the emerging references to the UNCRC in the domestic law reports[27] it seems to me that any discussion of this issue must set out Article 12:

> '12.1.States Parties shall assure to the child who is capable of forming his or her own views the right to express those views freely in all matters affecting the child, the views of the child being given due weight in accordance with the age and maturity of the child.
>
> 12.2. For this purpose, the child shall in particular be provided the opportunity to be heard in any judicial and administrative proceedings affecting the child, either directly[28] through a representative or an appropriate body, in a manner consistent with the procedural rules of national law.'

---

pursuant to r 9.5'.

[24] Reasons for success range from the adage that two heads are better than one (especially when they come from different professions working together to a common aim), the embodiment of the child in the proceedings as a whole and the courtroom in particular, and the transforming effect it has for the child's solicitor to have met his client. Apart from the question of how else the same money might be spent to benefit children, weaknesses include the possible over-reliance of courts on those representing the child (I have seen tables showing judges disagreeing with guardians' recommendations in fewer than 1% of cases and clearly there is a strong concern that guardians are sometimes being asked to do work that should be done by local authority social workers). The key limitation is that the roles are confined to legal proceedings.

[25] Paragraph 4.5 of 'Support Services in Family Proceedings – future organisation of court welfare services' specifically raised the possibility that representation by a solicitor may not be essential in every public law case.

[26] Article 42 UNCRC.

[27] According to the index to the [2002] FLR, the UNCRC was referred to in five cases reported that year, including a reference to Article 12 in *Re L (Abduction: Child's objections to return)* [2002] 2 FLR 1042.

[28] Whether or not this includes the possibility of a Gillick-competent child conducting his/her own case, it surely raises the prospect of children telling judges their views directly, something that was recently expressly raised by Thorpe LJ in *Re T* [2003] 1 FLR 531 at para 25. Note also the provisions of rule 4.16 about the attendance of a child at directions' appointments and hearings (a rule routinely more honoured in the breach than the observance) and the responsibility of a children's guardian to advise the court about the wishes of the child concerning the child's attendance at court (r 4.11A(4)(b)).

However, a careful reading of Article 12 suggests it does not go as far as some would like to believe. The concluding words of Article 12.2 seem to me to suggest a significant 'margin of appreciation.'[29] In particular I do not see that the words 'the opportunity to be heard' can mean a right to 'party status' in all judicial and administrative proceedings affecting the child,[30] in which case the three alternatives that follow (being heard directly, through a representative or through an appropriate body) would seem to be met in all cases by the appointment of a CAFCASS officer who tells the court the views of the child (representation in 'the reporting sense'). However it also seems to me that proponents of children's rights in the UK will rightly argue that Article 12 sets out what should be regarded as minimum standards, that the UK should set its sights much higher and that as the fourth largest economy in the world it can afford to achieve something rather better. I agree, and in any event the family justice system must ensure it complies with the requirements of the ECHR and in particular, of course, Arts 6 and 8 thereof.[31]

Where should we be going: Part 4 – Suggested lists and evidence-based practice

The consultation paper 'Support Services in Court Proceedings – future organisation of court welfare services'[32] that preceded the establishing of CAFCASS, considered the representation of children in private law cases, saying:

> 'It is not envisaged that legal representation or enhanced input by the welfare caseworker would be needed in more than a small proportion of private law cases. It might be helpful to codify the criteria for identifying such cases, which might include, for example:
>
> • cases where implacably adversarial parents are creating high levels of conflict, in which the child's interests are being disregarded; or where there is a history of violence; or where contact is being wholly denied to a child with an absent parent who apparently presents no risk to the child; or where the child is unaware of his relationship with the absent parent;
> • those where the court accepts the need for medical/psychological reports on a child within the proceedings;
> • those where there are concerns about the welfare of a child within the family which fall short of implementation of child protection measures or a direction under s 37 of the Children Act; and
> • unusual, complex, or difficult cases such as those with a foreign element, immigration problems, permanent removal from the jurisdiction, sexual orientation or change of sex of a parent, or where one parent has killed the other.'[33]

In addition to these, Lyon et al suggest children should also be eligible for separate representation in the following situations:

• 'a clear conflict of interests between one or both parents of the child which may include conflicts arising in the future as a result of the child disagreeing with court approved arrangements made some years earlier when the child may have been very young;
• any child who has been the subject of earlier divorce proceedings and who is now going through divorce proceedings for the second or third time (of which there are believed to be some 25,000 to

---

[29] For professionals who are not lawyers, the 'margin of appreciation' entails a measure of discretion to states when taking action in the area of convention rights. Where a common practice is apparent between states then the margin of appreciation will be narrow but where a common approach is not widespread then the discretion of states will be wider.
[30] At least for the moment: conventions such as the UNCRC and the ECHR are dynamic/living documents.
[31] The decision in *Elsholz v Germany* [2000] 2 FLR 486, for example, provides a sharp reminder of this.
[32] Issued in July 1998 by the Department of Health, Home Office, Lord Chancellor's Department and Welsh Office.
[33] Paragraph 4.11 of the report.

30,000 children per year);

•   any situation where there has been an unreasonable denial of contact or immediate provision where a child's parent is to be committed for contempt of a court order issued to allow contact with another parent.'[34]

A third proposed list was set out by the Association of Lawyers for Children:

'In certain groups of cases consideration should be given to the child being legally represented, in particular those involving:

•   termination of contact;
•   the implacably hostile parent;
•   when a court directs medical/psychiatric reports on a child within the proceedings;
•   where there are concerns about the welfare of a child within the family which fall short of the need to implement child protection procedures;
•   where a parent is under a disability and represented through a guardian ad litem or next friend;
•   exclusion orders;
•   unusual, complex or difficult cases, for example, those with a foreign element, immigration problems, permanent removal from the jurisdiction.'[35]

There is clearly a good deal in common between these lists, and almost everyone seems to agree that legal representation should only occur in a small minority of private law cases. But how small a minority, and in exactly which cases? At what point, for example, does a case 'where there is a history of violence' become one in which the child should be legally represented?[36] My own thoughts are these. First, just because one of these situations has arisen does not mean the court should automatically make a rule 9.5 appointment. In particular it should consider:

(1)   whether the child's interests can properly be safeguarded by an enhanced role for the children and family reporter. It may simply be that the children and family reporter needs to be allowed more time to carry out certain work. In particular the court should consider whether or not to make directions to the children and family reporter pursuant to (the new) r 4.11(2) FPR 1991;

(2)   whether it should be requiring the local social services department to carry out an investigation and to report to the court, whether under s 7(1)(b) or s 37 CA 1989, since it is social services (not CAFCASS) that is the agency with the primary statutory responsibility for child protection and that has power to institute protective measures including proceedings under Parts IV and V CA 1989;

(3)   whether the issue should be dealt with under the provisions of r 9.2A FPR 1991. I suggest that this is normally the appropriate route with the mature, older child;

(4)   whether the further investigations, and the continued and closer involvement of the child in the proceedings entailed by a r 9.5 appointment, may themselves be contrary to the welfare of the child. I think this is one of the major issues we should all have to grapple with during the next decade.[37]

---

[34]   Para 10.36 of *Effective Support Services for Children and Young People for when Parental Relationship Breakdown – A Child-Centred Approach.*

[35]   'The Future of Representation for Children' [1998] Fam Law 403.

[36]   If it is to be all such cases then we are in trouble. In its response to 'Contact between Children and Violent Parents' the Association of Chief Officers of Probation stated 'information which ACOP has received from local FCWS suggests that domestic violence is present in almost fifty percent of cases where a s 7 report is ordered'.

[37]   Including the question of proportionality between the resources used and the prospects of achieving anything positive. I suggest this question is one in a family of triplets, the others being (2) 'in what circumstances would contact be contrary to the interests of the child?'– that contact is normally in the

Secondly, I suggest that underlying these lists are three general principles: the need for someone to orchestrate an investigation on behalf of the child[38] the need to ensure an argument is put that might not otherwise be put, and (rather less clearly defined) some sort of recognition that at some point it is 'right' for an older child to be allowed to participate in the proceedings in this way. Whilst any one of these principles may be sufficient to warrant the making of a rule 9.5 appointment I suspect that in most cases where such an appointment is made a combination of these principles is at play although the particular matrix may not have been clearly expressed.

Finally, I need to make a simple point that is nevertheless often overlooked in discussions about the representation of children. For all our experience tells us that the arrangements we make have been helpful in ensuring the voice of the child in the proceedings and in enabling the court to reach its decisions, and for all that both of these are important aims, nevertheless we have little evidence about the extent to which those arrangements really help the child through the proceedings[39] or (at any rate in private law) about the medium and long term outcomes for the children and their families.[40] The phrase in the social work world is 'evidence-based practice' and it is a good and proper concern that lawyers and 'scientists' alike should be able to meet around.

Where should we be going: Part 5 – Resources and management

The first resource is people. More than half of CAFCASS' 1940 employed staff are over 50 years old.[41] CAFCASS is now recruiting case officers exclusively from among social workers, two previous sources of officer – probation officers and civil servants – having effectively been closed off. And you hardly need me to tell you that there are difficulties in the recruitment and retention of social workers and that these difficulties are at their most acute in relation to social workers to work with children and families.[42] While we are about it, let me add that if there aren't enough social workers to go around it seems to me that there is a forceful argument that children and families would derive greater benefit from having those there are working in the frontline (with local authorities and as children and family reporters in private law proceedings) rather than acting as children's guardians in public law cases.

---

best interests of a child seems to me to be a truism and is something that is achieved by many families without recourse to the family justice system, but whether it is appropriate to apply the mantra to situations of high conflict I gravely doubt; and (3) 'in what circumstances is it in the interests of the child to take steps to enforce a contact order and what methods of enforcement should be available to achieve this?'. The *Sturge/Glaser* report, published as 'Contact and Domestic Violence – the Experts' Court Report' at [2000] Fam Law 615 provides an excellent starting point for considering these questions and repays repeated rereading.

[38]　Per Hale LJ in *Re A* quoted above.

[39]　Indeed such evidence as we have suggests we may have been complacent about this. Listening to a presentation by Maria Ruegger about research she had conducted into the practice of guardians ad litem before CAFCASS was created I identified what I considered to be six – apparently relatively common – potential breaches of children's ECHR rights by those acting in tandem to represent and safeguard their interests.

[40]　I am aware of some, for example conducted by members of the Centre for Research of Family Kinship and Childhood at the University of Leeds, but taken as a whole I think we know a lot less then we need to. We also have difficulty integrating good research into common practice.

[41]　CAFCASS doesn't have the same information about its 457 self-employed contractors but I can think of no reason to believe the proportion is any less – indeed if anything I would expect it to be somewhat greater.

[42]　The Social Services Workforce Survey 2001, published in September 2002 by the Social Health Care Workforce Group indicates that 48% of local authorities were experiencing severe difficulties in recruiting field social workers to do children and family work, and over 30% were experiencing particular difficulties in retaining field social workers to work with this group. In both cases the percentages were the highest found among the eleven categories of social work employee identified within the survey. Whether current recruitment initiatives, such as *www.socialworkcareers.co.uk*, will bring about any significant improvement remains to be seen.

The second resource is money. I shall return to the wider economic issues towards the end of this paper but suffice it for now to make two basic observations. First, just as no-one would set out to buy a house or car without regard to what they could afford,[43] so no-one should set about operating a family justice system without regard to the money available to fund it. Putting it slightly differently, unless you have regard to the money available to fund the system you cannot expect that system to work well. Secondly, it is essential to be aware of the financial difficulties inherited by the Department for Constitutional Affairs from LCD. As far as I am aware no final figures are yet available for LCD for 2002–03 but it is no secret that these are likely to show a significant deficit. There has been particular concern about the ever-increasing cost of the Legal Services Commission and the legal representation it funds.[44] In those circumstances there is reason to be grateful that CAFCASS' funding has increased from £72m in 2001–02 to £95m in 2003–04.[45]

The third part of the equation is workload, and again there are two parts to this. First, there are more cases then there used to be. The year-on-year figures show an overall increase in private law applications (108,201 in 1993, down to 90,381 in 1999 but back up to 112,012 in 2001) and a more or less remorseless increase in public law cases (16,754 in 1993 up to 24,134 in 2001). The only area in which there has been a decrease is in adoption (6,751 in 1993 but only 4,452 in 2001).[46] What can we reasonably expect? Even more care cases, at any rate in the short term, as anxious local authorities respond to the Laming report, and a substantial increase in adoption applications as a result of stated government policy. Secondly, there seems to be common consent that cases have often become more difficult or at least require more work. This has certainly been demonstrated in care cases, the most time consuming of all. At the time of *R v Cornwall CC ex parte G*[47] guardians in care cases in Cornwall were averaging 92 hours per case, but this was amongst the highest in the country and in Dorset, for example, the figure was only 44 hours. Noone seems to have argued that it should not have been possible to complete most cases within the proposed benchmark of 65 hours. Yet by 1998–99 the average in England and Wales had risen to 124 hours per case while in Inner London (handling nearly four times as many cases as any other panel[48]) it was 160 hours per case.[49]

---

[43] See, for example, any of the plethora of television programmes about moving and living abroad, going and living in the country, changing your car, redecorating your house or rearranging your garden; or see Luke 14:28–30.

[44] Hence the recent announcement of initiatives to cut the costs of legal aid, particularly in immigration and crime. But note the press coverage on 6 June 2003 when, for all the xenophobic agitating, it was *The Daily Mail* and *The Sun* who alone made the two key points: *The Mail* with its headline 'Five years ago Lord Irvine vowed to slash the £1.5bn legal aid bill now it's almost £2bn' and *The Sun* with its comparison of what the £174.2m spent on legal advice for immigrants and asylum seekers would otherwise buy – 'That would be enough to pay the wages of 11,500 nurses or 6,000 new doctors for a year. It would also cover 17,500 heart ops, 35,000 hip replacements or building two hospitals. And it is enough to put 10,000 bobbies on the beat, build 39 secondary schools or equip the army with 35 Challenger tanks'.

[45] It is probably more realistic to treat the figure of £81m as the baseline for 2001–02 as this is what it actually cost to run CAFCASS during that year even on the most cheeseparing basis. It remains to be seen what effect, if any, there will be as a result of the transfer of responsibility for CAFCASS from LCD to the Minister for Children within the Department for Education and Skills, but the pressure on the Court Service and Legal Services Commission will presumably remain.

[46] Judicial Statistics reported annually by Family Law, the most recent figures being at [2002] Fam Law 856–858

[47] [1992] 1 FLR 270 .

[48] If one removes the figures for Inner London from the statistics the national average reduces to 117 hours. Inner London's average of 160 hours per case was equalled in Oxfordshire and exceeded in Avon, Devon and Surrey.

[49] 'Understanding variation in the hours guardians ad litem take to complete care cases' by Joan Hunt and Nancy Drucker on behalf of the Department of Health. They concluded that the factor that most strongly correlated to the hours spent by a guardian was the duration of the proceedings themselves – a subsidiary reason for supporting the objective of the Protocol for Judicial Case Management in Public Law Children Act Cases for the completion of all care cases within an overall timetable not more than

I don't think this adds up. You can't have fewer people spending more and more time on more and more cases. I think the family justice system, so far as it is concerned with children cases, was heading for breakdown (or spiralling costs or both) long before CAFCASS was created. It also seems to me that unless there is a significant change in recruitment to social work generally (out of CAFCASS' hands), a reduction in children's cases (unlikely) and/or a significant change in the way in which the family justice system deals with its work then the foreseeable future is worse not better.

That is the world into which CAFCASS was born. It was badly set up and caused damage to itself and to the family justice system by its mishandling of the real and difficult problem it inherited over contracts for self-employed children's guardians. However, it is not merely 'not helpful' but positively unhelpful, both for individuals and for the family justice system as a whole, for people to continue to dwell on the past and on might-have-beens, or to nurse hurts and angers. The hard realities I have just set out have to be faced. The real problems were there anyway.

CAFCASS clearly has a responsibility to operate within its budget, a budget that is fixed[50] irrespective of the number of cases issued in the year (over which, of course, it has no control). Unpopular though it may be, I think CAFCASS has an inescapable responsibility to manage the total number of available officer hours across the overall current caseload, however great or small that caseload may be, to ensure that those hours are divided up equitably between all the children and families who need them. Quite simply, unless CAFCASS does this, and unless it is allowed to do this by the courts and this is accepted by CAFCASS officers, both employed and self-employed, I think there is little chance, for example, of properly resolving the delays in the appointment of children's guardians in specified proceedings that are occurring in parts of England and Wales.[51] And unless and until CAFCASS is able to do this I cannot recommend – as I would like to do – any significant development in the representation (in the broad sense) of children in private law proceedings. In simple terms, every extra hour the family justice system wants CAFCASS officers to spend on a private law case is an hour that must be taken away from public law proceedings or adoption.[52]

The next step, and perhaps the one after that

The next step is clear. In February 2003, at the conference 'Making Contact Work', the President announced that she intended to issue a Practice Direction about the representation of children in private law proceedings. Work on drafting such a Practice Direction is underway. It is obviously not for me to pre-empt what the Practice Direction might contain. Suffice it to say that a clear statement, uniformly applied throughout England and Wales, about the circumstances in which a r 9.5 appointment should be considered and, where such an appointment is made, the way in which such representation is to be achieved, is highly desirable for everyone.

The step after that is for the Government. A late amendment saw the inclusion of what is now s 122 Adoption and Children Act 2002 that paves the way for the extension of the definition of 'specified proceedings' to private law cases. At the time, the Minister, Rosie Winterton, said in Parliament:

---

forty weeks save in exceptional or unforeseen circumstances.

[50] Unlike the budgets of the GALRO panels which, in many cases, were frequently topped up during the year.

[51] All else being equal, there would be little or no backlog in the allocation of children's guardians in London if the average hours per case there were the same as it is for the rest of England and Wales.

[52] 'It is envisaged that one of the advantages of an integrated court welfare service would be greater flexibility and management control, not only in the deployment of individual case workers but also in the overall allocation of resources as between public and private law cases' (para 4.1 of the Consultation paper 'Support Services in Family Proceedings – future organisation of court welfare services').

'The courts can already order that a child be made a party and separately represented in any family proceedings. However, we have listened to and respected the views of the House and the other place, and we agree that those powers should be explicitly referred to in primary legislation. The Government … seek to address three key concerns that have been raised … First, there is too stark a distinction between public law cases in which the state intervenes in a family's life – for example care proceedings – and private law disputes between individuals. Secondly, the power to provide for the separate representation of children is not referred to explicitly in primary legislation. Thirdly, children should have access to separate representation more frequently than they do at present.'[53]

But there is a history of family law legislation not being brought into force[54] and the latest information I have is that ministers have yet to agree plans for implementation. Presumably this will now be a matter for the Minister for Children, Margaret Hodge, as well as the Lord Chancellor, Lord Falconer. I think they will have to consider the sort of issues I have outlined so far in this paper but I also think they will have to consider the wider economic issues.

The starting point should be to know who is spending what on the welfare and protection of children in the circumstances that lead to their being involved in family proceedings. What is the overall expenditure of social services (their social workers, Part III Children Act 1989 provision, foster carers, their lawyers), the Court Service (judges and court staff), the Legal Services Commission (its own staff and the cost of the lawyers it funds to represent parents and children and the cost of attendant experts) and CAFCASS (its staff and the separate representation of its officers) plus their respective costs of premises, running costs and pensions, national insurance, training and so on? Only when this has been done will we all have a clear overview of the present allocation of money. There then needs to be a co-ordinated review of whether the present arrangements, and with them the present apportionment of money, represent the best value for money to achieve the common aims of the protection and welfare of children. This presumably requires decisions about desired outcomes, how they can be measured, and the research and information-gathering necessary to establish this. But in the end we need to know, for example, not only how a solicitor or CAFCASS officer can better enable a child to participate in family proceedings but also whether the child would have benefited more from a decent holiday with his foster carers than from extra visits by his lawyer and/or CAFCASS officer.[55]

Let me become more specific while remaining with the question 'Is the best use being made of the money that is available?'. It seems to me that there is a real danger in allowing the family justice system, which is a system within a wider system for the welfare and protection of children, to be designed wholly or largely by lawyers. Lawyers are surely likely to tend towards legal solutions (more applications, more representation, more evidence, more subtleties of process and argument) to what are, at the very least, socio-legal issues.[56] Although family lawyers are becoming much better versed in the wisdom of other professions, this is not their basic professional training nor, I suggest, their basic professional instinct and it is surely the case that most of us have little direct experience of the consequences of the legal process through which we put children and families. It seems to me that the family justice system has only just begun what amounts to a Copernican revolution in which the centre of the solar system is indeed to be understood to be the outcomes lived by children and families and not the legal process itself.

---

[53] Hansard, col 108, 4 November 2002.

[54] Including, of course, s 64 Family Law Act 1996, a forerunner to s 122 ACA 2002. The reality, I think, is that some legislation is now being passed provisionally, on the basis that further work will be done to decide whether or not to implement it – an interesting constitutional shift.

[55] If in fact these things have already been done I doubt I am alone in thinking that the information hasn't 'reached' the great majority of people who need to know about it.

[56] Let us leave aside, for the time being, important arguments about whether some of these issues are suitable for judicial determination: see, for example, the articles by Mr Eekelaar and Dr Cretney at [2002] Fam Law 271 and 900 respectively.

I said earlier that I thought there were two elephants in the room labelled 'the representation of children in family law proceedings' and that one of them was the tandem model. The second is that of in-house legal representation for children.[57] Some such representation has always been provided in-house, first by the Official Solicitor and now by CAFCASS Legal. The question will become 'What would provide the best value for public money?' Simply cutting out the direct costs of the Legal Services Commission in administering the scheme, of the courts in assessing bills, and of solicitors in having bills drawn, applying for public funding and maintaining a franchise, provide powerful reasons for going in this direction. There would also be a substantial attraction to Government of operating a fixed rather than an open-ended annual spend for legal representation just as has been achieved for the social work element by the abolition of the GALRO panels and the creation of CAFCASS.[58]

Should there be more money for the welfare and protection of children in these circumstances? The answer to that is, I think, almost certainly 'yes' but that is not to say it should be spent on more representation (in any of the senses I have defined) of children in family proceedings. It might, for example, be much better spent in preventing such proceedings ever happening or in care and support after they have taken place.

It seems to me there are a number of problems here. There is the problem that we may all too often only talk among ourselves when it is easy to agree we all need more money. But how successful are we at talking with those who, in a democratic society, are responsible for making the decisions about how much money we are to have? Or to those, such as the media, who might influence those who have to take such decisions? Related to this is the problem that we tend not to see beyond the needs of the family justice system to the much wider (and deeper) socio-legal needs of children and families. Then there is the problem that, in our enthusiasm and exasperation, we use or seem to be using an argument that sounds something like 'as it's all about vulnerable children, money shouldn't come into it'. That just won't do when it comes to tough decisions about public spending when every additional social worker is one fewer nurse or increased taxes. Which brings me to what I call the Cabinet problem. Who, sitting around the Cabinet table, is going to vote for more money for lawyers?[59]

Finally, and most fundamentally, there is the problem of what aims our Government is to pursue. There is some evidence that discontent with our way of life is growing despite generally increasing prosperity. This shows itself not only in 'levels of happiness' surveys but also in trends such as people choosing or wishing to live abroad or to downshift their lives. Successive Governments have essentially used Gross Domestic Product as a proxy for well-being but somewhere along the way our material needs may have been sufficiently met and GDP may no longer be the right yardstick.[60] Free time ('the new money') is of no value if well-

---

[57] The point is touched upon at paras 4.4 and 4.15 of '*Support Services in Family Proceedings – future organisation of court welfare services'*. The statutory power for this to be done through CAFCASS already exists: see ss 12(1)(c) and 15 CJCSA 2000.

[58] At a recent garden party, three out of the five specialist children's lawyers I spoke to for any length of time asked me whether or when this would happen. One of them twice described it as being 'inevitable' that this 'milch cow' for solicitors in private practice would be ended.

[59] Leaving aside the influential if inaccurate view that all lawyers are fat cats (contrast the average earnings of legal aid lawyers with the projected average of £82,000 per annum for GPs by 2005) there are few votes in more money for the legal system. In any event there are much harder reasons for the Cabinet to reject any such proposals. The report on the future of publicly funded legal work published by the Law Society in February 2003, which explicitly addressed the issue 'within the context of a cash limited legal aid budget', has as its final appendix a comparison of spend between different EU states. In England and Wales the spend was 2600m euros. The next highest expenditures were Germany (358m euros), France (235m euros) and Scotland (207m euros). When the figures are converted to per capita expenditure England and Wales came first (49 euros) followed by Scotland (40 euros). Further down the list one finds, for example, Norway (16.8 euros), Ireland (10 euros), Germany (6 euros), France (3.9 euros), Italy (2.6 euros) and Sweden (2.1 euros).

[60] The problem was apparently foreseen by John Maynard Keynes in 1930 in his essay 'Economic possibilities for our grandchildren' but I am dependent upon a secondary source, namely the essay

being is measured by GDP – indeed increasing GDP may well be at the expense of our free time. If there is to be a fundamental reassessment of the aims Government should be pursuing on our behalf then that is the moment to press the case 'that childhood is entitled to special care and assistance'[61] and that our individual and collective welfare would be improved by greater investment in children and in family life in all its diverse[62] forms.

'How to be happy' by Richard Tompkins in the Financial Times of 8/9 March 2003!
[61]   United Nations' Universal Declaration of Human Rights, recalled in the Preamble to the UNCRC.
[62]   As to which s 144(4) Adoption and Children Act 2002 is surely welcome.

PLENARY EIGHT

'PROTECTING CHILDREN FROM HARM' – REFLECTIONS ON THE GREEN PAPER

Jane Held
Director of Social Services, Camden, ADSS Children & Families Committee
Andrew Cozens
Director of Social Services, Leicester, Senior Vice President, ADSS

Andrew Cozens presented Jane Held's paper on her behalf and provided an analysis of the Green Paper published earlier that week. He said that the ADSS had wanted to see a number of key principles espoused in the Green Paper. These were locally collaborate universal services which children should be at the heart of; a national framework; and shared responsibility and clarity about responsibility. In his view those principle were in the Green Paper, albeit in varying degrees.

Mr Cozens stated that the establishment of a Minister for Children was a major change and to be welcomed. However, he pointed out that it is not a cabinet level post and said that there are concerns about the areas which will remain outside her remit.

He identified the four main themes of the Green Paper:

- *Supporting parents and carers;*
- *Early intervention;*
- *Accountability; and*
- *Issues in respect of the workforce.*

Supporting parents and carers

The Green Paper sets out aspirations to provide a wider range of support for parents and carers. However there are concerns about the connections between this programme and the National Service Framework, and about the Department of Health's commitment to continuing to drive forward those connections. The key question is what priority will children's services have?

There are plans to expand training and support for foster carers, including better financial support, and there is a range of suggestions about recruitment and retention of foster carers, including leave to bring payment in line with maternity pay. Mr Cozens said that he welcomed that initiative, but remained concerned about funding. He said that there were real issues about mainstream funding.

Early intervention

Mr Cozens identified information sharing between agencies as being a key element of the strategy of early intervention. The government is planning to move towards a common assessment framework and there are plans to integrate staff and to expand children's centres.

Accountability and integration

Mr Cozens suggested that the key to improvement in this area was the creation of a Minister for Children, Young People and Families. He also highlighted the requirement that all local authorities appoint a Director of Children's Services, replacing the requirement for Directors of Education and Directors of Social Services. However, he felt that it was significant that the Green Paper does not address the issue of engagement of other partners. It must be clear nationally and locally where the buck stops. Mr Cozens was concerned about whether this post might be managerial, rather than genuinely strategic.

Mr Cozens said that the creation of the Children's Trust was a welcome initiative but stressed that it would be important to ensure that there would be discretion and flexibility for the local authority.

One of the key issues for looked after children is access to education, and Mr Cozens felt that the Green Paper should have addressed the questions of school funding and admissions. He welcomed the proposal to create a lead council member for children.

Mr Cozens welcomed the establishment of Local Safeguarding Children Boards, but said that clear practice standards relating to each agency would be required. He also welcomed the rationalisation of performance targets and performance indicators.

He highlighted the intention to create an integrated inspection framework across children's services which Ofsted is to take the lead in developing. He also mentioned the improvement and intervention function which is intended to drive up performance everywhere.

Another initiative mentioned was the creation of a Children's Commissioner for England. However, Mr Cozens felt that this position had been somewhat watered down, and said it appeared to be intended to be a strategic post, not bogged down with individual cases.

Workforce

Mr Cozens said that the government's intention to create its own children's workforce unit was controversial. He welcomed the general intention to improve the status of those working with children in terms of pay and profile in the community and the incentives to encourage people to work in children's services.

Introduction

This paper was prepared before the Government's publication of the Green Paper on Children's Services, *Every Child Matters*. Indeed at the point of writing, it was not clear that it will be published by the Conference date. As a consequence the actual content may not be that which is expected so perhaps the more accurate title should be reflections on what the Green Paper might contain. Given this, we crave the Conference's indulgence if we depart from the pre-issued text.

What does the Green Paper say?
A focus on four main areas: • supporting parents and carers: through universal services, targeted and specialist support, compulsory action (*Parenting Orders*); • early intervention and effective protection: improving information sharing, developing a common assessment framework, introducing a lead professional, developing on the spot service delivery; • accountability and integration: locally, regionally and nationally; Director of Children's Services, a lead council member for children, children's trusts, local safeguarding children boards, new Minister, Children's Commissioner; and • workforce reform: workforce unit and sector skills council.

How does this compare with what ADSS wanted to see in the Green Paper and crucially, will it ensure that it will create a climate where the many organisations involved in working with and providing services to children can genuinely 'listen to the voice of the child'. That is the theme of this conference and that is the devastatingly simple message at the heart of the Laming Report. Lord Laming concluded that Victoria Climbié died because no one listened to her voice.

The Green Paper is the Government's response to the Laming Inquiry and as such, one of the litmus tests has got to be the extent to which it has addressed not just the central finding, and whether in fact it does improve on the efforts we all, together with many others, make day in day out, to safeguard and protect children at risk from harm. But we know that it will be much more than that. Indeed, it is being widely hailed as the most radical shake up of the way in which Britain provides services to children across the board.

In fact whether it would be a Green Paper on services to all children or whether it addresses the needs of just children at risk has itself been the subject of debate and speculation. The genesis of the Green Paper is understood to have originally arisen from work being undertaken in the Home Office on early intervention to prevent offending and anti-social behaviour. The Government put together a cross Cabinet Committee and team of officials, based in the Cabinet Office, led by the then Children's Minister, John Denham in the Home Office, chaired by a Treasury Minister, Paul Boateng, and supported by Ministers from each Government Department.

We, (and by we I mean the Association of Directors of Social Services) believe, together with many colleagues, (the Association of Chief Education Officers, Barnardos, NSPCC, NCH, The Children's Society, National Children's Bureau, the Confederation of Education Officers, the NHS Confederation, the Local Government Association, Society of Chief Education Officers, Metropolitan Police, National Council for Voluntary Child Care organisations, and the Connaught Group) that the Green Paper offers a unique opportunity to look ahead, reflect, and move forward to how we would like Children's Services to be in five or more years from now, to help ensure that every child in England has an equal chance in life, and to help put children at the heart of our society.

The views expressed in this paper are those of both the Association, and the other organisations listed. For the first time, over the last 18 months we have been meeting as an inter agency group, working firstly to prepare our contribution to and response to the Laming Inquiry, and then trying to contribute to and influence the work of the Green Paper Team. That is itself symbolic. The consensus between us is itself unique and demonstrates the foundations of what we believe will protect children – that to do so is everyone's business, everyone's responsibility, and has to be done by everyone working together.

Protecting and safeguarding children is not, in our view, the task of specialists alone, whether they are social workers, health visitors, psychiatrists, paediatricians, or the judiciary. In fact we believe it is quite the reverse, that the only way to do so is to ensure that Britain has strong and effective universal services, which protect vulnerable children as well as enhanced the lives of all children.

It is vital that we all seize the opportunity the Green Paper gives us to reconsider what we do and how we do it. We expect that the Green Paper's publication will mark the beginning of an important national debate about how we can work together more effectively across all professions and sectors to improve children's lives and children's services.

We know that the Government shares our aim of wanting to find effective ways to work together to do this and indeed they too (like the Children's InterAgency Group) have come together to do so, a change which gives us great optimism for the future.

So we are pleased that the Green Paper is not just a paper on safeguarding vulnerable children, but a Green Paper for all children. It is only through improving all services, that real change, change that genuinely safeguards the vulnerable will be achieved. Children are not, in Britain, seen as central to society; key to government policy-making; or cherished as Britain of the future. In fact much of society is 'child invisible', without any consciousness of how the adult world shapes and impinges on the way in which children grow up. It is a fundamental change to society that is needed, as much as a set of government changes to how some people do their job.

Can a Green Paper have that effect? It is inevitable that in thinking about what is to come, we think about the last radical changes to children's legislation. The Children Act 1989 was hailed as, and we believe genuinely was, the most radical legislation ever for children. Those heady days of the late 1980s and early 1990s, when we saw a completely new approach are now long gone, and it is easy to forget those key 'new principles' in the familiarity of the every day. And yet those principles are now absolutely central to our society and our thinking.

The Children Act was indeed radical, creating a single unifying piece of legislation (rationalising the complex legislative frameworks that had 'grown like topsy' over the previous 20 years) and a set of basic principles for society as regards the care of children. It is easy to forget the impact of those key principles, especially the welfare principle – the need to make children's welfare paramount. It is also easy to lose sight of the principle that reference to court should be the last resort, and that protection of children should be achieved through the provision of family support.

We believe that those key principles still hold good, and we see no reason to change them. We believe strongly that the Children Act is fundamentally excellent legislation, and we do not want to see, in the Green Paper, (nor can I see at first reading) any proposals to change that legislation. It has proved its worth. It provides a sound legislative base, containing those strong principles, and has a focus on the best interests of children.

Indeed, it is very easy to make a false assumption that the system is not working. We, as specialists are, after all immersed in those situations where families are, for one reason or another struggling, or indeed failing, to put the welfare of their children first. We know that we see the worst, most complex, most distressing things. We need to ensure we do not lose sight of the realities of how well most families do, and indeed, of how well we are serving some vulnerable children.

Focusing on the awful extreme failures of the whole system, the failure of any one case, and creating legislation based solely on those failures is not the way forward. Bad cases make for bad law. Focussing on failure creates bad practice, defensive practice. And focusing on failure presents a false image in the mind of the public about what we do, in particular what social workers do. The realities of the Climbié case are that it was a devastating whole system failure, by Local Authorities as a whole, Social Services, the Health Service and the Police. However if you asked the ubiquitous person in the street who failed Victoria, we would lay a bet the answer is Social Services or social workers.

We hoped the Green Paper would set a clear framework that makes it clear that universal services are child protective services, and that everyone has a duty to safeguard the children they see and serve, and equally that it reinforces and asserts the distinctive and continuing contribution of social work and social care to children's services. Indeed we hope that the Green Paper would reverse the recent tendency to 'air brush' social work out of the picture. Social Work is a crucial piece of the total jigsaw. Some of what social workers do can be, and is, done equally well by others, but the task and process of assessing, analysing, and deciding how best to protect and enhance the lives of children at risk is one that takes specific professional skills.

Indeed, I understand, one of the themes of the last conference was the issue of how to enhance and improve the role of social workers, and reduce the reliance on experts through recognising the expertise of professional social workers, and valuing their contribution. We hope the Green Paper recognises the unique contribution of social work, and indeed the unique contributions of every profession, as part of the 'whole system' that has to be in place if we are to achieve our aspirations and respond to the findings not just of the Laming Inquiry, but of the Joint Chief Inspectors' Report on Arrangements to Safeguard Children.

That report contained some strong, important, not to mention disturbing, messages about the uneven priorities that children have been given across agencies. It shows how everyone 'relies' on Social Services, many overlooking as organisations and individuals, their own critical responsibilities, and role.

There is much to be quietly pleased about in the 12th Annual Report of the Chief Inspector of Social Services about the steady improvements in Children's Social Services. But that improvement can only have an impact if it runs alongside and in part of improvement by all. We hoped that the Green Paper would not be based on a defensive approach to what has gone wrong, or on prejudice or opinions that are outdated and erroneous. But instead built on the basis of good evidence of what works for children; of the way in which children develop; and of how confident professionals can create real sustained change for children. To do this they need effective management structures and strong professional leadership, working in an integrated framework, focusing on children's needs, and contributing individually to outcomes for children which collectively create a sum greater than the parts. ADSS can only echo the Chief Inspector's words, 'Social Services alone cannot serve children'.

No one is denying that change is not needed. Lord Laming's findings and conclusions demonstrate powerfully the case for change. We want the Green Paper to provide the platform for that change, and whilst holding onto the Children Act, make amends for those elements of the Act that time, evidence, and, sadly, some failures show are not working.

Strong universal services are the key, but in focusing on that it is crucial that those universal services are actually protective, supportive of all families but targeting those who are in most need of family support, and founded on the concept of shared responsibility and shared accountability. Section 17 of the Children Act was designed to improve and enhance the 'whole systems' focus on prevention and avoidance of statutory actions. Its principles are sound, but services for children in need have increasingly been seen as a 'proxy' for what social services does, allowing everyone to define a child as in, or not in, need, and then behaving differently depending on that 'threshold'. That in turn allows others to 'pass the parcel', to deny their role and responsibility, not just for universal services or community based prevention, but for individual children and families.

Both Lord Laming and the Safeguards Inspection Report arrive at the conclusion that this threshold is having the reverse effect to that intended. It rations out and allows for denial of responsibility. This is undoubtedly partly because s 17 was never properly funded. However, that is no longer actually the case. This Government is spending more on prevention, through Sure Start, Connexions, and the Children's Fund than ever before. That spend though is fragmented and incoherent, focuses on groups not individuals and reflects a wider trend which is steadily diluting the principle of 'Children in Need', and fragmenting the principles of the Children Act overall. Asylum legislation, Criminal Justice legislation (particularly for Young People), Housing legislation, Health and Education legislation have all in their way created tensions, diluted the concepts of the Act, and indeed in the case of Youth Justice reintroduced some of the concepts of 'mad, bad, sad and sick' that the Children Act was meant to remove.

We want the Green Paper to address this. We want it to reinforce the responsibilities of all organisations to accept their role in, and accountability for, providing family support services, to individuals and their families, not just to groups. We believe that together we hold the solution, and the Green Paper needs to reinforce that and make children a priority across the board. We also wanted the Green Paper to bring in some Central Government 'children proofing' that requires all Ministries to assess the impact of new policies and legislation on the lives of children and families before they arrive on the statute book, and ensure what is done protects and enhances the lives of the most vulnerable children, not increase their vulnerability.

Even terminology shows what has happened. The universal concept of children in need is currently translated into children at risk, children in need, children in need of protection, vulnerable children, children at risk of offending, and so it goes on. We wanted the Green Paper to recognise the continuum of children's needs and simplify the way in which children who need more than just universal services are described and recognised. All children need services, some children need more services than others, some children need services specifically designed to protect them from harm.

There are encouraging signs. The establishment of the new Children's Minister is a very positive indication that Government recognises the fragmentation that undermines the way children are supported and are pulling together everyone with a role to play. That they recognise the crucial, pivotal role of family law is reflected in the fact that it is part of that Minister's portfolio, and of the new Department in the DFES, as is the Family Policy Team from the Home Office.

It is unfortunate that youth justice and child health are not part of Margaret Hodge's portfolio in our view. A whole system includes crucially child health, particularly when it comes to protecting and safeguarding children at risk of serious harm. We are concerned that child health will, far from becoming a priority in the Department of Health, become a low priority marginalised activity that is the preserve of a small band of paediatricians and child and adolescent psychiatrists, and that the focus on access to treatment, waiting lists, and discharge, obscures the need for a focus on children. We are confident that the will is there to improve the life chances and health of children through the Children's National Service Framework and hoped the Green Paper would reflect and integrate that NSF.

Equally we are concerned that increasingly populist and simplistic approaches to youth justice, based on concepts of dangerousness, and risk indicators, on the need to intervene forcibly in the lives of families, and to enforce particular forms of parenting and compulsory care. We remember (our ages give us away!) the evidence that accumulated about the failures of those forms of intervention in young people's lives prior to the Children Act. Indeed those very failures were a major part of the impetus for the Act.

We wanted the Green Paper to address the needs of children and young people holistically, and to contain imperatives to require the youth justice system (multi-agency though it is, it is inward looking and 'set apart') to be an integrated part of the whole system for children.

Integration at national government level is crucial. We believe it is equally crucial at the local level. However, we also believe that exactly how that is achieved locally should be locally determined. We want to ensure locally that there are good, strong, accessible universal services, such as schools, children's centres, and primary health care settings which are the core means of supporting and protecting children. The development and co-ordinated funding of more services geared towards prevention, and early intervention will ensure that these universal services are most effectively deployed to deliver positive outcomes for children.

We also hoped that it recognised that there will always also be a need for specific services for the most vulnerable children who will require intervention, protection and alternative care – the children all we at this conference, spend our working lives with. We want recognition of the need to co-locate those services alongside universal services, and to ensure they do not become the preserve of the isolated specialist, but a common part of everyone's responsibilities.

To achieve this successfully, we need to ensure there is a framework that effectively co-ordinates those services within a dynamic 'whole system' approach, focusing on the needs of the child and their family at any point in time, and to focus on the outcomes achieved by that system for individual children, their families, communities and society.

Lord Laming made a series of recommendations about how to achieve effective local co-ordination. We agree fully with his view that Victoria was failed by the system and that children's services should and must be effectively and properly co-ordinated. However, we would argue for a simpler framework and hope that the Green Paper introduces a locally based, locally driven collaborative multi-agency approach to this through the establishment of a local multi-agency strategy. *Serving Children Well*, published jointly by the ADSS, LGA, and the NHS Confederation sets out some proposals for such an approach.

Similarly, Children's Trusts are a very welcome new initiative and one that we believe heralded strongly some of the Governments intentions within the Green Paper. The large number of Pathfinder Children's Trusts that have been announced recently shows the eagerness locally of partners to work together differently in a local whole system way.

However, we do not want to see the baby thrown out with the bath water. It is crucially important that a local partnership is given the powers concurrent with the responsibilities it will hold, and is in a position to compel all agencies to co-operate, and ensure they both give children priority and take their responsibilities seriously, and to be able to hold the partners to account. We hope the Green Paper's follow up legislation will propose changes to statute to ensure local partnerships can exercise their responsibilities and authorities together.

We believe strongly that it local authorities are best placed to act as the accountable body locally. With this accountability should go the necessary authority to ensure the consistent engagement and active participation of other public, voluntary and community organisations.

That responsibility should be about securing effective leadership, strong co-ordinated service planning, and the best methods for service delivery. It should be geared to ensure services are provided in the best way locally, often through the voluntary sector, who are in our view best placed to take on a leading role in developing service provision and not see itself as necessarily a service provider but as a commissioner of services.

We agree with Lord Laming that it needs to be clear in such an approach, who is accountable all the way to the top. We wholly agree that a partnership can be collectively accountable and responsible but that some one has to carry the can. We wanted the Green Paper to require local partnerships to identify a locally accountable elected member, and to appoint a shared officer on behalf of the partnership who holds the day-to-day accountability. The Green Paper goes beyond that with its proposal for a Director of Children's Services.

We would also expect the partnership to ensure it has a specific sub-committee, focusing on and ensuring that the processes of protecting and safeguarding children are properly managed, integrated, and delivered well and that the whole system can and does effectively listen to the voice of the child – a strong statutory ACPC or its equivalent. We are pleased to see this included.

Councils and their partners are best placed to develop responses that suit local needs and conditions. The Government should give them the flexibility to do so and not try to prescribe this centrally. The Government's role should be to set national standards for all children's services, and to monitor progress against them. We believe that achieving this strategic balance will be crucial to improving children's services and outcomes for children across the country. We hope, therefore, that the Green Paper will not be unduly preoccupied with proposals for reorganisation and structural change. Indeed, as the Chief Inspector notes, reorganisation has become a constant for the NHS and that structural change has had a negative impact. Indeed Councils have provided an organisational stability lacking elsewhere. Reorganisation creates upheaval and disruption, and disrupts staff – and vulnerable children are more at risk when staff are distracted. We hope therefore that the Green Paper combines in its ambitions to create real radical innovative change for children, that ambition with a sensible, pragmatic, and continuous approach to implementation on the ground

That accountability should be clearly set within a framework. We agree with Lord Laming about the excessive bureaucratic processes and systems that exist, the overload of guidance and requirements, detailed and prescriptive. The fragmentation of current systems means a child can be subject to four different assessments at once. Research has recently shown that it takes a social worker 26 hours to conduct a core assessment at a cost of £700 plus. That is one of many. The system is too complex.

We hoped therefore the Paper would focus on the principle that Government sets national frameworks and national standards, which will provide boundaries within which the local children's partnership, the partnership's local commissioners, and local providers can decide how they can most effectively deliver services that meet children's needs, according to local conditions. Any changes to existing ways of working should, in our view, demonstrably enhance integration and accountability. They should be designed with sufficient flexibility to promote this across the diversity of local areas. A balance is needed between national prescription and local discretion.

Similarly, the role of the person appointed as the 'accountable' officer, a director of children's services on behalf of the local partnership should be to hold all the partners to account for the services they provide to children collectively and separately. They can do this through agreed, explicit, statements of accountability, clear systems of governance and locally agreed standards and performance measures. We had hoped the Green Paper would avoid too prescriptive a definition of such a role.

The balance between accountability, good governance, effective management and professional leadership is a subtle one requiring local approaches if it is to successfully bring a diverse workforce and diverse organisational arrangements together in each area.

Similarly we hope that nationally there will be a framework for inspection, and that locally, the Partnership can set its own framework of inspection, governance and audit.

We are still hope that simplistic quick fixes and structural solutions such as requiring local authorities to amalgamate Social Services for Children and Education are not seen as the only solution to a far more complex whole system.

It is crucial that locally, the distinctive importance of each professional discipline contributing to the work of safeguarding children is recognised and enhanced, and that good professional leadership is given priority over simplistic managerialist solutions. It is after all the frontline that protects children. It is our staff, nurses, GPs, teachers, nursery nurses, play workers, social workers, psychiatrists, health visitors, paediatricians, and police officers who deliver the goods. The process of doing that requires confidence and the exercise of skilled professional judgement in very complex structures. We must avoid increasing rules and procedures, and indeed ensure that it simplifies processes. A common assessment tool, simple protocols, and shared case recording systems will help, not increasing the rules in the face of disaster. Interestingly, forensic processes did not protect Victoria, they over-burdened people. They need simplifying not made more complex.

To help, we are pleased the Green Paper will build on the work being developed through the Information, Referral and Tracking pilots ongoing in various parts of the country. Not with-standing the challenges of Data Protection Legislation and indeed the Caldicott requirements, it is crucial information is shared. Poor communication is increasing and more effective information sharing mechanisms must be developed, in partnership with children and their families. To do that does not just mean technical solutions – it means real professional and cultural change too but it is crucial if children are not in our increasingly mobile, transient, and complex, not to mention technology dependent society, slip through the net.

And professional respect, as well as professional change is crucial to this, as it is to improving standards. Our workforce must be properly developed, trained, and respected. Children's voices will not be heard if there is no one to listen, or those listening are too burdened and overwhelmed. It is critically important to the success of the Green Paper, and we wanted it to cover thoroughly and exhaustively the whole area of workforce development, recruitment and retention. Without social workers, health visitors, guardians, and other professionals currently at critically low levels within the system nothing will change. Staff need to be well trained, professionally developed and supported, given opportunity for research and reflective study, guided not criticised, valued not rubbished.

For social work there are some crucially important developments – a three year degree, requirements to undertake post qualifying training and continuous professional development, a registration requirement through the General Social Care Council (GCSC), an academic and research body, the Social Care Institute for Excellence (SCIE) and the development of ongoing vocational opportunities. But we need social work students to benefit from these developments, and we need to plan ahead. If the Green Paper makes the work of protecting children as valued as running a commercial company, we will really be making progress.

Finally, it is crucial that the Green Paper is ambitious in its vision for children and ambitious for the services that exist to help them. Families, communities, children and young people themselves are all key participants in the process of change.

They must always be recognised and involved as key stakeholders in the process of planning, developing, and co-ordinating services, as well as in the design and delivery of evaluation.

We welcome an Independent Commissioner for Children, who can ensure children's real participation in society, in services and in planning for their own futures. Someone to hold us all to account, judiciary not excluded, for the way we as adults care for our children. To protect, to improve society and to ensure our future we must listen (and respond) to the voices of children.

References

SWRDU/University of York. 2003. *Costs and Effectiveness of Services for Children in Need*, London: HMSO.

Modern Social Services – A Commitment to the Future. The 12th Annual Report of the Chief Inspector of Social Services 2002–03, London: HMSO.

LGA, ADSS, ACEO, NHS Confederation. 2002. *Serving Children Well*.

2003. *The Victoria Climbié Inquiry*, London: HMSO.

ISSUES RAISED BY THE GREEN PAPER: PRELIMINARY VIEWS

Professor June Thoburn said, in relation to workforce reform, there is a striking chart deficit of social workers. She also spoke of the confusion between pre-professional, professional and post-professional training. She said that it would be important not to destabilise professional training.

Andrew Cozens said that he has worked very hard to make sure that social work has not been airbrushed out. He welcomed the introduction of the three-year social work degree.

Carolyn Hamilton asked for more information about the Children's Trusts.

Andrew Cozens said that they are a unit in the Department of Health which is overseeing them. The core idea is that of flexibility and the ability to work more collaboratively. He said that there are 30 pilots. They share the intention to co-locate staff, and to create a family of children's services that cross boundaries. He said that the idea that they might be forced as an intervention on failing authorities is worrying.

The President asked Bruce Clark about the uncertainty in respect of the relationship between the Department of Health and the new organisations coming under Children's Trusts. She was particularly concerned about CAMHS. She said that her experience was that it is badly overloaded.

Bruce Clark said that the policy responsibility for Children's Trusts is to transfer in full to the DFES. That will be happening any time from 13 June 2003 onwards. In relation to CAMHS, responsibility for the delivery of child and adolescent mental health services will remain within health, but there will be substantial contributions from children's social services, responsibility for the delivery of public service targets is vested in the NHS and local government. It is proposed that intervention mechanisms will be implemented through pilot Children's Trust arrangements.

Mr Justice Hedley said that he felt it was important not to forget those young people who become involved in the criminal justice system. If we are arguing that the family needs to be viewed in round, it is important we do that in relation to children who are in prison.

Mr Cozens said that the Green Paper is good on mad and sad children, but not on bad children. He said that they have managed to secure CAMHS workers offering fast track services to those children who fall foul of the criminal justice system

The President asked to what extent YOTS is likely to fall in line with what comes into the Green Paper. She asked whether it will wither into the general work of the directorate in charge.

Mr Clark said that the Green Paper gave clear signals about the 'includability' of the Connexions Service and Youth Offending Teams within Children's Trusts.

Elaine Laken asked about the inter-relation between youth justice and family justice. She said that if we do have welfare concerns within criminal proceedings then a cross-over should be available to drive it into the family court. She also said that the under 10s should be in a family court and not in a youth court. She said that there should be a response to the Green Paper in those areas, in particular about trying to make the link between offenders and children in need.

Liz Goldthorpe said that there are statutory obstacles to information sharing and to inter-agency working. She stated that we have had s 27 of Children Act long in force, there have also been a number of excuses on the part of those agencies who do not want to join in or to fund participation. She asked whether there will be a review by the government in respect of the blocks to inter-agency working. She also criticised the proposal that funding for legal advice to refugee children should be cut to five hours.

Amanda Finlay said that there have been a number of responses to the legal aid for refugee children proposals, the Lord Chancellor is considering them and considering the question of what is the best way forward in order to meet the needs of the most vulnerable. As far as information sharing is concerned, she agreed that there are a whole series of statutory obstacles, she said that we need to look at what the blocks are and make changes where necessary.

The President said that statutory changes would involve the DCA but suggested that it should also involve the judiciary and legal profession. She said that it may need to involve the issue of medical confidentiality. She said that it was an issue which had to be tackled. She stated that she is in favour of sharing information, but said that there were serious obstacles. A working party that includes lawyers, judges and medics is needed to look at the statutory blockages and long established confidentiality issues.

Ms Finlay commented that it was important to distinguish between blockages which should be removed and safeguards which must be protected.

Ms Goldthorpe said that with s 27, the difficulty, even more than with s 47, is that the caveats and qualifications mean that children have been left under supported in an interagency mode. This issue was addressed in relation to homelessness, and she said that we want to use that experience to beef up the duty of cooperation.

Dr Neela Shabde said that information sharing and confidentiality is a crucial issue if we are going to safeguard children. She said that the Royal College of Psychiatrists (RCP) has set up a working party to investigate this issue, and that in a couple of months there would be guidance about confidentiality.

Dr David Jones echoed the interest in information sharing and the implications of that. He expressed concern about the many different groups that are looking at the issue of confidentiality separately.

The President said that there should be some judicial and legal presence on the RCP working party because there are areas that courts have to deal with.

Judge Isobel Plumstead commented that at p 42 of the Green Paper there was a bullet point for 'family mediation services' without a proposal. She said that there is no mention of supporting contact between children and families. She said that the concept of family group conferencing ought to be much wider if it was to have any meaning at all.

Christina Blacklaws said that another omission was the issue of children in domestic violence.

Peggy Ray commented on the section on tackling child poverty. She said that the benefits agency does not seem to have been referred to at all.

Ms Finlay responded that it was inevitable that some things get left out of a paper like this, but emphasised that that does not mean that they are not regarded as important. She said that she would continue to argue for the importance of domestic violence. The DWP is big delivery agency which is outside ministerial responsibility, but she said that she will be working with them in the future. She said that there is real desire from the Minister, not just to be responsible, but to be a powerful customer.

Mr Cozens said he thought that what has been brought together in the Green Paper is a good analysis of policy and said that it does include references to benefits and domestic violence. He emphasised that the Bill intended to be as quick as possible and that the Green Paper discusses a series of achievable things woven into the bigger picture. His view was that we have to press hard for the remit of Children's Commissioner, and he said that he personally will be lobbying hard for a Children's Commissioner with sharp teeth and sharp elbows.

ISSUES RAISED IN SMALL GROUPS AND DISCUSSIONS

Information

The President said that her group had discussed the importance of giving information to children right across the board, including upon separation and post divorce, across to public law cases. Her group was keen that there should be information available for different age groups, which could be given to parents, schools, nursery schools, and perhaps GPs' surgeries so that children would have access to information. In public law cases, simple information should be provided by the social worker.

Need for adults to handle children's complications, rather than oversimplify

Professor June Thoburn said that her group had talked about the fact that children want adults to be able to handle muddle rather than pretend it does not exist. We try to tidy complicated situations up for them, but in fact, what they want is for us to find arrangements that handle their complications

Need for consistency and flexibility

Beverley Prevatt-Goldstein said that her group had felt that one of the critical issues was the mixture of the need for consistency and flexibility. Consistency is needed in terms of training; common standards of competency; guidelines; participation and representation. In terms of flexibility there is a need to bear in mind the idea of mixed and changing feelings and ensure that gateways are left open so that children can change their minds, for example about whether or not to withdraw from proceedings, or to join in. She said that another theme that came up often in her group was the need for time to hear the voice of child.

Dichotomy between needs and resources

Mr Justice Hedley said his group considered that the demands that are made, in particular the demands for time and space to hear children stood in stark contrast to professional diaries and court lists. His group felt that it was important to acknowledge that there will be a gap between what we would like to deliver and what we can deliver.

Guardian system and independent advocates for children

John Kemmis said that the issue of representation for children was a general one. He said that a clear theme had emerged that it is important that children can get their voices heard throughout the process, and the court process must be seen in the context of all the other processes. He said that it is crucial for the child that they have someone to help them through the complex processes. The guardian is the key person in the court process for the child and the guardian system has to be made to work. Mr Kemmis also commented on the issue of independent advocacy for children and said that the current proposals did not go far enough in establishing a right to independent advocacy outside the control of social services.

Carolyn Hamilton said that it was essential that advocacy systems are supported, and that an independent advocacy service should be available to all looked after children, not just to those who want to complain.

Separate representation for children in private law proceedings

Judge Isobel Plumstead said that the discussions amongst her group were concerned more with private law disputes than with public law disputes. She said that a high percentage of private law cases are brokered to a solution acceptable to the parents without the child's voice being considered at all. Her group considered how barriers to children getting their view heard might be lowered. She suggested that children's solicitors might be more accessible and the President might consider revisiting her predecessor's Practice Direction on children's access and a child having to go to the High Court to seek permission to have representation.

The President said that she is interested in the issue of children's access to courts, however, she said that during her period as President there had not been a single case of children asking for leave. She said that she did not see why there needs to be a barrier. It was put in place because it was thought that there would be a flood of teenagers coming to court, but in fact there have been very few cases. She said that if there is a ground swell of opinion that the requirement for leave should be withdrawn she would consider it carefully.

Judge Iain Hamilton said that he believes in allowing children to have separate representation in private law proceedings where necessary and appropriate. But one of the real issues is that there is no guidance as to what the role of guardian should be. He said that there needs to be a review of the rules and additional guidance from CAFCASS in relation to private law proceedings under s 9.5.

The President said that she and Charles Prest were in the process of trying to put together a set of criteria that might be of help as to the sort of cases that might come up under r 9.5. The intention is that the CAFCASS reporter will become the guardian, so that a totally new person is not brought into the frame after the first report.

Katherine Gieve emphasised that it is important that there be training for those CAFCASS reporters who also act as guardians. She pointed out that it is a different task and it needs different knowledge and experience.

Parents' role in listening to their children

Katherine Gieve raised a general point in respect of private law cases. She said that the conference had not been discussing the issue of the voice of the child within the family and how children relate to their parents. We need to think about the impact of intervention from outside on the way that a family functions. We have to respect that parents are listening to the voices of their children and they should be encouraged to. That is the first source of a child's voice and we should not be too enthusiastic about thinking we can elicit the voice of a child without thinking about the impact of that within the family. We need to consider how a family will feel about an invasion of professionals.

Cost effectiveness – looking at prevention

Professor June Thoburn spoke about the challenge of cost effectiveness and said that one area which should be looked at is the question of risk aversion, ie playing it safe and taking a case to court without considering the other options. She said that we need to ask whether more can be done to accommodate some children without bringing them to care proceedings and consider avoiding using the courts unless we have to.

Liz Goldthorpe said that there is some interesting work going on in Nottingham looking at how and why you intervene, and the effect of intervention on cooperation. The majority of cases go through a child in need conference rather than child protection unless it is obvious. The child in need conference looks at how intervention can be supported, giving reality to both parts of s 17, and making sure that in the process the welfare of the child is safeguarded. If it is not you move to the child protection arena. She considered this to be an interesting way of avoiding the problem that you only get the services you need by going through the child protection services or the court.

Bruce Clark agreed with the view that ways of helping the child more preventatively must be looked at.

Dr David Jones felt that unless we have effective services at the point of prevention then the social worker taking principal responsibility is a mere broker at worst and little in the way of actual intervention is available to plug into. It is therefore not surprising that little happens at that stage. Unless we have a whole system perspective right from beginning through to the end we will have blocks in the system.

Inter-agency cooperation

Dr Jonathan Green expressed his sense that we are participating in a cultural change and an acceleration of the way the idea of a child centred focus is incorporated into practice. He said that we need to consider how developments in the legal, psychological, and cultural sense can be put together into a practice that goes across different agencies. Many of the questions about children's contact with courts apply to children's contact with hospitals. He suggested that there ought to be a mechanism by which we are able to share in the experience of different agencies and avoid unnecessary duplication.

CONSOLIDATION AND SUMMARY OF SMALL GROUP DISCUSSIONS

Skills and training

It was a generally held view that the court system as presently structured means that too many people are trying to communicate with children within the process, and that some of them are unskilled and untrained.

There should be a greater focus on skills and training, particularly amongst the legal profession. Lawyers are not taught how to communicate with children they are just expected to know how to communicate. A family lawyer needs all sorts of skills that traditional legal training does not provide. However, other groups, such as foster carers, may also benefit from training, for example in how to cope with an insecurely attached child.

In-house training of the judiciary, the Bar, and solicitor advocates, on how to question children was suggested. Criminal lawyers were identified as particularly in need of training. The issue of training for the judiciary is a vital one if the English courts are to accept the inevitability that more children will wish to take an active role in the proceedings and communicate directly with the judiciary.

It was emphasised that this kind of training must be interactive, and include practical exercises such as role play. Learning theory is not sufficient; skills must be practiced.

CAFCASS reporters must receive adequate training. Interviewing children is a highly skilled task which requires specific expertise. It would be important to ensure that the CAFCASS training module includes expert instruction in how to interview children for reports.

Early intervention

It has been recognised that the earlier a child gets substitute care, the better. Situations that drag on for too long are counter-productive. The groups discussed the difficult issue of how to resolve the question of rehabilitation with the need to ensure substitute care is put in place as soon as possible.

Attachment

There was much discussion about the different concepts and terminology around bonding, attachment, relationship etc which served only to prove to those non-experts in the field that a little knowledge may be a dangerous thing when using concepts and terms such as 'attachment'.

The groups discussed the difficulties for children in care of building relationships with foster carers and then moving on to different carers and having to build new relationships, and perhaps never seeing their previous foster carers again. It was felt that that kind of situation is counter-productive and there is evidence to suggest that it can affect psychological development. Attachments can be developed with a number of different people, at multiple levels. It is not the case that where there is no contact there is no attachment.

Sibling relationship can be supportive. However, where children come from abusive homes or where they have suffered maltreatment the relationships between siblings may reflect parental maltreatment and the relationships can be abusive.

Information banks

One group discussed the idea of setting up information banks for children who have lost contact completely with their biological parents and/or siblings through adoption, foster care, or for some other reason. These banks would contain specific personal information which children could have access to at a stage in their lives when they are ready and want to find out more about their heritage. Children who use this kind of information bank would need to have thorough before-and after-care.

Children's evidence

The groups expressed concern that in criminal trials, children sometimes do not see the video of their evidence-in-chief before they are cross-examined. It was felt strongly that all children should be able to see their video before giving evidence.

Interviews with children

It was felt that we have laboured for too long in the Family Justice System with a Memorandum Interview system designed to deal with the criminal justice system – *Achieving Best Evidence* should be seen as a tool for the Family Justice System.

Extracting information from children is different to obtaining information about their wishes and feelings and explaining the court process to them. A child's wishes and feeling may not be inchoate – it is important that we do not automatically expect them to be.

There must be a message that we do not ignore what the child says when the information has been given. It will stop the child from saying anything if they are consistently ignored.

Guidance is important on preparing statements for the child. The child's language should be used, but it is often the case that the language of the author of the statement appears.

One group suggested that where an interview with a child is being recorded in writing, because video or audio recording is not possible or appropriate, the following technique might be helpful: the page should be split into two columns, the child's verbal responses should be recorded on one side, and the interviewer's observations of non-verbal responses should be recorded on the other side, with both columns linked temporally. There should be a general convention as to what information should be recorded in the second column, and as to how it should be recorded. The group recognised the distinction between observation and inference and suggested that there should be third space for recording the inferences drawn from the observations, if the interviewer is trained to draw inferences.

It was felt that consideration should be given to the use of audio-taping interviews and supplementing the tape with a written note recording the interviewer's observations of non-verbal communication, this would be an easier method of reporting on non-verbal communication than an interview recorded entirely in writing. However, in some situations this would not be appropriate as it would be inhibiting and uncomfortable for the child.

There was a plea from the experts that there should be more interdisciplinary planning of assessments at an early stage to avoid if at all possible duplication of interviews and questions.

In the quest for the authentic voice of the child, one group thought that three matters needed clearly to be borne in mind:

a)   that the purpose of an interview with a child should be clear (ie was it therapeutic or forensic or simply seeking views and wishes?) as it significantly affected the required style of interview;

b) that interviewers should regularly check that they and the child understood one another and that the same words meant the same thing (eg the word 'fence' which has at least three distinctive meanings), particularly where the child had English as a second language or used a distinctive dialect like 'scouse';

c) that interviewers needed to be patient over time and needed to remember that a child may have different conceptions of speed, time and distance.

Three general problems were underlined:

a) that the first interview was crucial and often significantly affected the succeeding ones, yet; it was often carried out by the least experienced professionals particularly in relation to child protection issues;

b) that damaged children often had distorted relationships with and perceptions of adults and the consequences of that had to be allowed for in the assessment process;

c) that a child's body language and non-verbal communication was often at least as important as what he says which gives rise to two related problems –
i) the interpretation of that communication; and
ii) the need to convey to the court both that communication and its interpretation.

Confidentiality

There is concern about information sharing and whether and how the child's consent is obtained. Experts are placed in a dilemma when asking children questions, because they cannot guarantee to the child what they will do with the information obtained. The difficulties of explaining confidentiality (at the outset) to a young child were highlighted.

Interactive court model

It was felt that all children, even very young children, might benefit from having a better idea and understanding of the court and of how it works. Many children are very interested in the role of the judge. They understand that the judge is the person making the decisions, and see him or her as a 'wise owl' figure who will take over the burden of decision making. One group suggested the development of an interactive court model which could be accessed via the internet and could show children of all ages what a court looks like and explain the roles of all the different people in the court.

Expert evidence

There is a vital need for expert evidence in important areas such as complex care planning exercises.

Complexity

The experts reminded the groups that children often actually like complexity. In our legal system we are actually striving constantly to make things simple whereas children are quite happy to deal with the complexity that is their lives. Children expect adults not to unravel that complexity, but to deal with it and to make it work.

It was also recognised by all that whilst the principle of empowering children and giving them a voice may not automatically mean that all children would wish to exercise it.

Voices of children outside the court arena

It is important to ensure that the voice of those children outside the court arena, whether in voluntary care or post care orders in Local Authority care were not lost. It is important that there is some coherent system of accountability to call into question systems, processes and decisions made in relation to those children where the court is no longer 'watching over' their rights. This may well be an important area for the new Children's Commissioner.

Private law proceedings

The groups discussed the difficult area of giving children a voice within private law proceedings. Whilst generally recognised as a necessary progression of children's rights and our recognition of them, some delegates cautioned against riding roughshod over the pre-existing family dynamics particularly where children were inevitably remaining within the care of the family. It is important to recognise the danger of taking children and providing them with a voice from outside the family. It is necessary to recognise the importance of parental rights also and to ensure that empowerment does not cause damage to the family for the future.

Almost all the multi-disciplinary input relates to public law cases. However, very similar issues often arise in private law cases where as a rule children are not separately represented and where both time and resources available seriously compromise some of the methodology described by the speakers at the conference. In particular, delegates were aware of the dangers of superficial evaluations of the wishes and feelings of children: both in terms of simply reporting what they say without necessarily examining why they are saying it; and in the dangers of a superficial assessment of non-verbal communication.

Role of parents

Ascertaining the voice of the child is to be seen as an integral part of the assessment process whether professionally undertaken or as part of the court hearing process. Parents can play a valuable role in this and therefore the patient hearing of evidence-in-chief from parents can provide the court with valuable information.

Multidisciplinary input

Where, as usually will be the case, there is a multi-disciplinary input into this process, two things are essential:

a) that there is mutual respect and trust, as well as good communication, between all professionals involved; and

b) that experts are clear (and the court has made it so) as to exactly what is expected of them in the case.

CONCLUDING COMMENTS

The Rt Hon Dame Elizabeth Butler-Sloss
The President of the Family Division

The President began by congratulating the speakers. She said that their papers were excellent, and were papers to take away and reflect upon. She expressed her view that the conference had been held at a particularly well-timed moment in the shadow of the Children at Risk Green Paper. She felt that the effect of the Green Paper had been to put an extra edge on delegates' discussions but that it was an exciting moment which provided an opportunity to have some input into a crucial moment in the history of child legislation. She pointed out that we are fifteen years on from the Children Act and that we now have a real opportunity to express our views; to contribute to the next stage; and to help to mould the future arrangements for children. She called upon delegates not to lose the opportunity to make individual contributions.

In relation to the establishment of the Family Justice Council, she said that she was optimistic that this would start to be put into place in 2004. She assumed that the Council would take over this conference. She explained that the President of the day will be chairman of the Council and there will be a judge as vice chairman. She expressed her ambition for a designated family judge to take on leadership of the groups of family based organisations at a local level, but pointed out that this needs support from all professionals. She called for a revolution at local level and emphasised how important it would be for senior people of all relevant disciplines to take the trouble to attend and support local forums.

She thanked the Department of Health and LCD, now DCA, for funding the conference; the sub-committee; the conference organisers; and all who had given their time to attend.